5.29.79 R

DATE DUE

OCT 3 1 1983			
DEC. - 5.1937			
APR 1 9 1991			
APR 1 9 1991			
MAY 0 6 1991			
NOV 2 3 1993			
MAR 2 4 1999			
AUG 2 3 1999			
GAYLORD			PRINTED IN U.S.A.

KEATS

KEATS

by

JOHN
MIDDLETON MURRY

OCTAGON BOOKS

A division of Farrar, Straus and Giroux

New York   1975

First edition entitled *Studies in Keats,* 1930
Second edition entitled *Studies in Keats, New and Old,* 1939
Third edition entitled *The Mystery of Keats,* 1949
Fourth edition entitled *Keats,* Revised and Enlarged, 1955

Reprinted 1975

OCTAGON BOOKS

A DIVISION OF FARRAR, STRAUS & GIROUX, INC.

19 Union Square West

New York, N.Y. 10003

Library of Congress Cataloging in Publication Data

Murry, John Middleton, 1889-1957.
    Keats.

        First ed. published in 1930 under title: Studies in Keats.
        Reprint of the 4th ed. published by Noonday Press, New York.
        1. Keats, John, 1795-1821—Criticism and interpretation.
[PR4837.M8   1975]   821'.7   75-15580
ISBN 0-374-96027-5

Manufactured by Braun-Brumfield, Inc.
Ann Arbor, Michigan

Printed in the United States of America

CONTENTS

PREFACE TO THE FOURTH EDITION

THIS book is intended to be a companion volume to my *Keats and Shakespeare*. This is the third occasion on which it has been enlarged and drastically revised. The additions on this occasion consist of two short essays: *Keats and Friendship*, and *Keats and Claret*, and a much longer one, *Keats and Isabella Jones*, which is a rigorous examination and, I hope, a convincing refutation of the sensational theses concerning Keats's relations with this enigmatic lady put forward by Mr. Robert Gittings in his recent volume: *John Keats: The Living Year* (1954).

Mr. Gittings's book is perhaps the most important book on Keats, with the exception of Mr. Rollins's *The Keats Circle*, published in recent years; and I regret that my essay upon it is, perforce, confined to a critical attack on some of its major theses, and the methods on which they are based. There is much of permanent value in the book which I should like to have had the opportunity of praising.

THELNETHAM,
March 19th, 1954.

FROM THE PREFACE TO THE
THIRD EDITION

THIS book incorporates much of the matter which originally appeared in *Studies in Keats: New and Old*, but this matter has been drastically revised and rearranged. In particular, I have seized the opportunity of considering anew the character of Fanny Brawne and the nature of her influence on Keats in the light of all the new evidence which has been made public since *Keats and Shakespeare* was written, twenty-five years ago. I have had the deep satisfaction of being able completely to recant the harsh judgment I then passed upon her.

The chief value of this book, in my own eyes, consists in its effort to reveal a little more of what I have called — following Keats himself — the *prophetic* element in his work and life: the continual presence in himself of the power whose workings he discerned in Shakespeare, when he said 'Shakespeare led a life of Allegory: his works are the comment on it'. He discerned a kindred power at work in Milton, as Blake also did.

Whether Keats was right in this or not, I do not know for certain. I believe he was. But I am convinced that the working of such a power is visible in Keats himself. We know far more about Keats than we do about Shakespeare or Milton. The brief five years of his poetic life are astonishingly vivid. Considering how complete a failure he appeared to have been when he died, and how low was his repute for twenty years afterwards, it seems almost a miracle that so many of his letters were preserved. This was because his circle of acquaintance though small, contained men and women who were either convinced of his genius, or truly loved him, or both together: and they jealously preserved all they possessed of his writings. What Woodhouse did for his poems, the two Fannies and his brother George did for his letters.

While his close friends were holding on to the reality of Keats — often discordantly, for the reality had many facets — a legend about him was created. This was pathetic and poignant and sentimental — and false. If there is one thing which the reality of Keats repels, it is sentimentality. George Keats's outburst to Dilke, four years after his death: 'John was the very soul of courage and manliness, and as much like the Holy Ghost as Johnny Keats', applies almost as truly to the picture of him given in *Adonais* as to that put out in *Blackwood*, against which it was spoken.

Yet there *is* the stuff of legend in Keats's life and work. There is something extraordinary about it. The more it is studied, the more marvellous it is. But it is the legend of reality. It is as though we were privileged to behold the mystery of Life with the veil momentarily withdrawn, or as though forces and powers whose workings are otherwise diffused and dimly traceable or not traceable at all, were concentrated here for a special revelation of the universal in the particular. Of no poetic genius is the particularity so fully displayed to us as of Keats. Distinctness is the poet's luxury, he said. His life exemplifies it to a singular degree. His uniqueness is such that he can be adequately interpreted only by himself.

The phenomenon is at once bewildering and entirely satisfying. One has the sensation that the unknown power is making of the life of this gifted and short-lived genius a perfect work of art, a drama so human, so moving and so profound that one is baffled by the thought, which is nevertheless inescapable, that Keats himself is endowed throughout with a kind of foreknowledge of what is to come: that he collaborated with Destiny, and but for his collaboration the pattern could not have been revealed. He knows, and yet he does not know, how he will be consumed. By his capacity for living above and below the levels of normal human awareness, he is enabled to be responsive to what is mysteriously required of him. From these heights and depths he fetches a power of utterance and obedience which is wonderful to contemplate.

I know of no life which gives me so directly the sense of revelation, of a mystery being uttered through it. Yet equally it makes on me the impression of a life of singular simplicity, completely devoid and indeed impatient of complexity. And these two qualities are not in conflict. On the contrary each appears to be the condition of the other. The simplicity is, I feel, the effect of spontaneity: of a spontaneity that must itself have been the consequence of some unshakable instinct for fulness of life. There seems never to have been a moment at which Keats was less than the whole of himself, or acted or wrote from less. And this, I surmise, was the condition without which the revelation would have been impossible or incomplete.

I am certain of one thing: that our appreciation of the significance of Keats, which has so greatly grown in the hundred years since Monckton Milnes first published the *Life and Letters*, has still far to go before it is commensurate with what he really was.

THELNETHAM,
February 18th, 1949.

KEATS

CHAPTER I

FANNY BRAWNE

IT is not easy to shake one's heart free of the impression of the agonizing letters Keats wrote to Fanny Brawne in the summer of 1820.

If you could really what is call'd enjoy yourself at a Party — if you can smile in people's faces, and wish them to admire you *now*, you never have nor ever will love me. I see *life* in nothing but the certainty of your Love — convince me of it my sweetest. If I am not somehow convinc'd I shall die of agony . . . I do not pretend to say I have more feeling than my fellows — but I wish you seriously to look over my letters kind and unkind and consider whether the Person who wrote them can be able to endure much longer the agonies and uncertainties which you are so peculiarly made to create — My recovery of bodily health will be of no benefit to me if you are not all mine when I am well. For God's sake save me — or tell me my passion is of too awful a nature for you. Again God bless you.
No — my sweet Fanny — I am wrong. I do not want you to be unhappy — and yet I do, I must while there is so sweet a Beauty — my loveliest, my darling! Goodbye! I Kiss you — O the torments!   (*Letter 216*)

Again:

I am tormented day and night. They talk of my going to Italy. 'Tis certain I shall never recover if I am to be so long separate from you: yet with all this devotion to you, I cannot persuade myself into any confidence of you. Past experience connected with the fact of my long separation from you gives me agonies which are scarcely to be talked of . . .

You do not feel as I do — you do not know what it is to love — one day you may — your time is not come. Ask yourself how many unhappy hours Keats has caused you in Loneliness. For myself I have been a Martyr the whole time, and for this reason I speak; the confession is forc'd from me by the torture. I appeal to you by the blood of that Christ you believe in: Do not write to me if you have done anything this month which it would have pained me to have seen. You may have altered — if you have not — if you still behave in dancing rooms and other societies as I have seen you — I do not want to live — if you have done so I wish this coming night may be my last. I cannot live without you, and not only you but *chaste you; virtuous you.* The Sun rises and sets, the day passes, and you follow the bent of your inclination to a certain extent — you have no conception of the quantity of miserable feeling that passes through me in a day. — Be serious! Love is not a plaything — and again do not write unless you can do it with a crystal conscience. I would sooner die for want of you than ——   (*Letter 220*)

They are terrible letters, written in the blood of the spirit. At the first impact one cannot (it seems) escape the compulsion of their veracity. And yet one must.

There are only three letters of this kind. They are the last letters which Keats actually wrote to his love, for the period of peculiar torment during which they were written was brought to an end by Mrs. Brawne and Fanny taking him into their house and nursing him until he left England for Italy. From Italy he never dared to write to Fanny, nor to read the letters she wrote to him.

The letters he wrote from Italy or on his journey thither are not to Fanny; but all of them are about her. Although they are equally, indeed even more, painful to read for the depth of suffering they reveal, the suffering is of a different kind. Keats had passed beyond the condition in which he was tortured by 'jealousy' — if that is the word for it — he was no longer torn by the suspicion that Fanny did not love him as he loved her. He had entered upon his 'posthumous existence'. He was racked with misery, but not the misery of thinking of her in her bright reality. He could not, because he dared not, do that. He did not, and could not, think of her as she was, the girl of living flesh and blood. She was almost a spirit — the spirit of life and salvation, a possibility of happiness which he had once touched — from which he was being borne away by a destiny into darkness. 'The sense of darkness coming over me — I eternally see her figure eternally vanishing.'

And this does not conflict with his own declaration. 'My imagination is horribly vivid about her — I see her — I hear her. There is nothing in the world of sufficient interest to divert me from her for a moment.' For the figure of his imagination is a figure in an irrevocable past, to whom appeal, if it were necessary, is impossible. Nothing that Fanny now could do or leave undone could alter the edict of destiny. He is now finally separated from her and he will die.

At this moment, notably, Keats's words contain no hint of any fickleness or levity in Fanny. The cause of his agony is not at all mistrust of her. 'You think she has many faults,' he writes to Brown, 'but for my sake, think she has not one.' He himself, assuredly, was now in the condition of thinking she had not one. She was simply *his* woman — to be with whom was life, and to be parted from her, death.

Now in November 1820 he looks back to the time, a few months before, when he wrote to her the three agonized letters from which I have quoted. 'I cannot recollect, without shuddering, the time that I was a prisoner at Hunt's, and used to keep my eyes fixed on Hampstead all day. Then there was a good hope of seeing her again—Now!—O that I could be buried near where she lives?' (*Letter 240*) Why did the particular recollection make him shudder? I think partly because of the harshness to her which the torture of separation had forced from him.

The tragedy of Keats's love is the tragedy of his separation from Fanny Brawne. It was that in his own eyes, and it comes to be so in ours. 'I should have had her when I was in health, and I should have remained well,' he cried to Brown at the last. That was probably in part an illusion, for there is little doubt that even before he first met Fanny the latent seeds of the disease had been nourished into evil life by the hardships of his walking-tour in Scotland. But his life might have been prolonged a few years and made far happier if it had been possible for them to marry early in 1819; or if, at any rate, Keats had not ceased to be Fanny's neighbour at the end of June 1819.

That first separation at the end of June 1819, after a period in which they had come closer and closer together, was the real beginning of Keats's torments. It is important to realize this, for it has a direct bearing on our understanding of Keats both as man and poet.

Keats himself made this clear in two letters which he wrote shortly after the haemorrhage of February 3rd, 1820. That was the beginning of his final swift decline. Then, for the first time, Keats really had to face not merely the possibility but the probability of his own early death. Whether or not he actually spoke the words which Brown told Monckton Milnes: 'I know the colour of that blood — it is arterial blood — I cannot be deceived in that colour; that drop is my death-warrant. I must die,' he certainly feared that death might come soon, even immediately. 'On the night I was taken ill,' he wrote to Fanny, 'when so violent a rush of blood came to my lungs that I felt nearly suffocated — I assure you I felt it possible I might not survive, and at that moment thought of nothing but you. When I said to Brown "This is unfortunate" I thought of you.' (*Letter 176*) Whether he was softening his words for Fanny's sake or not, death had come very near. In the clarity that supervened he wrote to Rice on February 14th, 1820.

I have not been so worn with lengthen'd illnesses as you have therefore cannot answer you on your own ground with respect to those haunting and deformed thoughts and feelings you speak of. When I have been or supposed myself in health I have had my share of them, especially within this last year. I may say that for 6 Months before I was taken ill I had not passed a tranquil day. Either that gloom overspread me or I was suffering under some passionate feeling, or if I turn'd to versify that acerbated the poison of either sensation.

Six months backward from the haemorrhage takes us to July 1819. Keats parted from Fanny to go to the Isle of Wight on June 28th. In one of his notes to Fanny at about the same time as his letter to Rice, he says:

> My sweet creature when I look back upon the pains and torments I have suffer'd for you from the day I left you to go to the Isle of Wight, the extasies in which I have pass'd some days and the miseries in their turn, I wonder the more at the Beauty which has kept up the spell so fervently.
>
> (*Letter 186*)

The accounts of his feelings which he gives to Rice and to Fanny correspond exactly. What he describes as his 'ecstasies' to Fanny are what he calls 'suffering under some passionate feeling' when writing to Rice; but not even from Fanny does he conceal that his 'ecstasies' were of the order of 'pains and torments'. There was poison in both 'sensations' — his ecstasy and his misery. And we must remember that in the language of Keats 'sensation' is a most positive word, meaning an experience in which the whole being was involved.

What happened is clear. It was when he had to part from Fanny at the end of June 1819 that 'the hateful siege of contraries' began in Keats's being. That was the beginning of the spiritual torment that racked him continually till he found rest in death. Keats is explicit on this matter. He alone knew the truth, and he told it. The parting from Fanny on June 28th, 1819, was the beginning of his misery.

It cannot have been an accident that the writing of the *Odes*

occurred in the brief period between this parting and the day
when Fanny first became Keats's next door neighbour. The
Brawnes moved into Wentworth Place very soon after April 3rd,
1819, when the Dilkes left it for Westminster. April, May and
early June 1819, was the time when Keats came nearest to happiness in his love, when Fanny was living almost in the same
house. It was also the period when his poetic genius touched the
greatest heights.

Whatever else may be said about Fanny Brawne, two things
stand firm. First, she was the woman, or the girl, to be with
whom was life for Keats, and to be parted from whom was
death. Medical science might give a different report of the
matter; but that is how Keats as a man experienced Fanny Brawne.
Secondly, with due allowance for the difference between imagination and experience, that is how he experienced her as a poet.
The brief period during which he was coming nearer and nearer
to her, and she to him — I speak of simple physical proximity —
was the period in which his poetry touched its greatest splendour.
In order to describe the poetry of this period — the last canto of
Hyperion, The Eve of St. Agnes, The Eve of St. Mark, the sonnet
Bright Star!, the sonnet *To Sleep*, the Andromeda sonnet, *La
Belle Dame*, the Odes in their succession (with the one exception
of the *Ode to Autumn*) — one turns instinctively to the words
written shortly afterwards to Fanny Brawne.

> I cannot conceive any beginning of such love as I have for
> you but Beauty. There may be a sort of love for which, with-
> out the least sneer at it, I have the highest respect and can
> admire it in others: but it has not the richness, the bloom, the
> full form, the enchantment of love after my own heart.

Substitute 'poetry' for 'love' in that sentence and we have a
faithful characterization of Keats's poetry from April to June
1819. As distinct from another kind of poetry, at its best perhaps
equally great, the poems we have listed 'have the richness, the
bloom, the full form, the enchantment'. And they have this
quality, too, as distinct from Keats's poetry before and after-

wards. That before is tending towards this easy mastery and opulent perfection; that which comes afterwards — with the single exception of the *Ode to Autumn* — in comparison has its beauty marred by a sense of strain, as *The Fall of Hyperion,* or as *Lamia,* by a touch of sophistication and too deliberate 'making'. Nearly all Keats's great poetry which came, or seems to us to have come, in a pre-eminent sense 'naturally, as the leaves to a tree' was written in the brief twelve weeks when Fanny Brawne and he first lived under one roof at Wentworth Place. This is her surpassing title to our gratitude and our reverence. I regret that it was not as vividly present to my mind as it ought to have been when I wrote *Keats and Shakespeare.* It is present to me now; and under its influence I will try to tell the story of their love more truly than before.

It begins . . . where does it begin? No doubt in Keats's childhood, into which we can probe little further than Keats himself permits, when he wrote, in a letter to Bailey of June 10th, 1818:

> I have two Brothers one is driven by the 'burden of Society' to America the other, with an exquisite love of Life, is in a lingering state. My Love for my Brothers from the early loss of our parents and even for [from] earlier Misfortunes has grown into an affection 'passing the Love of Women' — I have been ill-temper'd with them, I have vex'd them — but the thought of them has always stifled the impression that any woman might otherwise have made upon me.

To speculate on what the 'earlier misfortunes' may have been is futile. It is sufficient that his father died of a fall from a horse when he was thirty-five and Keats was eight years old, that almost immediately his mother married again and unhappily, and died of consumption when he was fourteen, and that he was passionately devoted to her. We may begin with the situation as he depicted it to Bailey in June 1818.

His brother Tom, already marked for death, grown 'pale and

spectre-thin', had five months more to live. His brother George was on the point of departing for America. He was virtually cut off from his sister Fanny, now aged fourteen, because of her guardian's disapproval of his throwing up a respectable career as an apothecary and taking to poetry. He was on the point of setting off on a walking tour in Scotland with Charles Brown: in order 'to identify finer scenery' than he had experienced, that is, to absorb the unique 'countenance' of mountains, lakes and lochs, but also (I think) to escape for a while from the 'pressure of Tom's identity' upon him, to seek relief from the burden of Tom's now hopeless disease. It is sad to think of the lonely Tom, suddenly bereft of both his brothers; but Bentley the postman and his wife, with whom the brothers lodged in Well Walk, Hampstead, were devoted to them. George and John rode together on the coach as far as Liverpool, where George took ship.

The privations and exertions of the Scottish tour, the poor and unpalatable food, and the exhausting efforts required, were too much for Keats. He fell visibly ill by the time he reached Inverness, and had to return to London by sea from Cromarty, worn out. He reached Hampstead on August 18th. Thenceforward he lived in close company with Tom until Tom's death, on December 1st.

His letters of this period show him obsessed by the thought of a woman's love. More exactly three 'sensations' were contending within him; the pain of his love for Tom, the desire and dream of a loving and beautiful woman, as a refuge from his pain, and the 'abstract images' of *Hyperion*, as a refuge from both.

Keats had a wonderfully attractive face, witness the drawing by Haydon which stands at the beginning of this volume: of his personality there is no need to speak; but he was acutely conscious of his own diminutive stature — he was only a shade over five feet high. 'My dear love,' he was to write to Fanny Brawne, 'I cannot believe that there ever was or ever could be anything to admire in me especially so far as sight goes — I cannot be admired, I am not a thing to be admired. I hold that place among Men which

snub-nos'd brunettes with meeting eyebrows do among women
—they are trash to me—unless I should find one among them with
a fire in her heart like the one that burns in mine'. (*Letter 139*)
I believe that Keats was absolutely sincere in this estimate of his
attractiveness to women — or to women who looked for external
attractiveness in men. And he felt that his experience of women
had confirmed his view that this was indeed what most women
looked for. He thought the less of women for it, indeed, for he
knew his own worth. He was disillusioned about them.

I am certain [he had written to Bailey on July 18th, 1818]
I have not a right feeling towards Women — at this moment
I am trying to be just to them but I cannot — Is it because
they fall so far beneath my boyish Imagination . . . Insult
may be inflicted in more ways than by Word or action —
one who is tender of being insulted does not like to think
an insult against another — I do not like to think insults in a
Lady's Company — I commit a Crime with her which
absence would have not known . . . When I am among
Women, I have evil thoughts, malice, spleen — I cannot
speak or be silent — I am full of Suspicions, and therefore
listen to nothing — I am in a hurry to be gone. You must
be charitable and put all this perversity to my being disappointed since Boyhood . . . I could say a good deal about
this but I will leave it in hopes of better and more worthy
dispositions — and also content that I am wronging no one,
for after all I do think better of Womankind than to suppose
they care whether Mister John Keats five feet high likes
them or not.

The irony of his last sentence is at once biting and scrupulously
fair.

But the hunger for the love of a woman was not to be killed by
irony. All through the weeks at Well Walk while he waited for
Tom to die, the undertone of his passionate longing is heard.
At the encounter with 'Charmian' the undertone becomes the
dominant.

I never was in love [he wrote then to Reynolds] yet the
voice and the shape of a Woman has haunted me these two
days — at such a time when the relief, the feverous relief of
Poetry seems a much less crime — This morning Poetry has
conquered — I have relapsed into those abstractions which
are my only life — I feel escaped from a new strange and
threatening sorrow—and I am thankful for it.—There is an
awful warmth about my heart like a load of Immortality.
Poor Tom — that woman — and Poetry were ringing
changes in my senses.—Now I am in comparison happy.

(*Letter 87*)

That is a powerful and haunting phrase — 'an awful warmth
about my heart like a load of immortality'. Only genius could
have coined it, and only an exceptionally passionate nature
provided the metal to be stamped. 'I never knew before,' he was
to write to Fanny Brawne shortly after their first separation,
'what such a love as you have made me feel was; my Fancy was
afraid of it, lest it should burn me up.' And we remember the
imaginary girl 'with a fire in her heart like the one that burns in
mine'. All these phrases produce the sensation of a smouldering
fire only waiting for the breath that will fan it into an intensity of
heat that will consume him.

Nothing more powerfully prepares a man's instinctive and
unconscious nature for passionate love than prolonged contact
with hopeless illness in a loved one. The deep unconscious being
reacts away from the menace of death and the pain of beholding
its approach. The consciousness may strive to suppress this
motion as callous and heartless, but the motion persists. The
instinctive being turns away from physical death and seeks to be
renewed by plunging into the instinctive life of which passionate
physical love is the consummation, and longs for this renewal
most desperately in the extremity of its own suffering for the
dying one. The inordinate demand of unavailing spiritual love
on the man's nature creates a void in the total being that craves
replenishment in love of a woman.

Everything was prepared for the conflagration in Mister Keats five feet high. But it required no ordinary woman to set it off. She had (I think) to be the right height. Fanny Brawne was. 'She is about my height' was the first thing Keats registered when he drew her detailed portrait for his brother and sister-in-law. She had, of course, to care whether Mister John Keats liked her or not. Fanny Brawne did. Had she to be beautiful? 'Love adds a precious seeing to the eye.' Although Keats insisted that her beauty was the cause of his love — 'why may I not speak of your beauty, since without that I could never have loved you? I cannot conceive any beginning of such a love as I have for you but beauty' — I am not sure that Fanny Brawne *was* beautiful in the ordinary meaning of the word. I do not see quite that in the familiar miniature. I see the long pale face, the hyper-sensitive nostrils, the lips ready to part in a smile which would be enchanting, and a pair of lovely wide-set blue eyes. But it is a face whose beauty needs to be discovered rather than proclaims itself — a face easy to be transfigured into Beauty incarnate by a sudden adoration, but without that alchemy more truly an interesting face than a beautiful one. But to Keats she became at once the nonpareil. 'If you should ever feel for man what I did for you at first sight, I am lost.'

What she indubitably had was genuine spontaneity — sometimes extravagant, 'flying out in all directions', as Keats described it — but springing from an authentic vitality. And she was quick in intelligence, quick to discern the quality of Keats, quick in the gaiety of repartee, quick to submit to a finer taste than her own in matters of which she had but a schoolgirl knowledge, quick, too, in extricating herself from an awkward situation. Not very long after Keats's death, when she had made friends with Fanny Keats, she preferred to be alone when she visited her at Walthamstow. Naturally, because she felt that she could only thus speak freely of Keats. But this meant that she had to give Mrs. Dilke the slip: for Mrs. Dilke was a much older friend of Fanny Keats, and Fanny Brawne had at first gone with her to see Fanny Keats. Moreover Mrs. Dilke was a very slow starter and always kept

Fanny Brawne waiting. All that preamble is necessary to set off this example of Fanny Brawne's quickness, unselfconsciously recorded in a letter to Fanny Keats.

> I dined with Mrs. Dilke a day or two after I saw you. She asked whether you were in town but luckily never inquired whether I had seen you yet so I equivocated (which you know is much the same as telling a story) at once and said I did not mean to call on you at present for fear the Abbeys should think I came too often — true enough.

That was quick-witted.

The picture of herself which she conveys in her letters is in pretty complete accord with the one Keats conveys in his. When we make allowance for the fact that in his descriptions of her to his brother, he is pretending much more detachment than he feels, and, even more important, that the two descriptions of her were probably written before he definitely knew that she was attracted to him, we read into Keats's words: 'But she is ignorant — monstrous in her behaviour, flying out in all directions, calling people such names that I was forced lately to make use of the term *Minx*' nothing more and nothing worse than she herself admitted to Fanny Keats. 'I never can make compliments, which is no merit but a great awkwardness and particularly foolish in me who am not at all bashful and hardly modest.' She was inclined to extravagance, she also admits. She ran through her allowance quickly and was generally too hard up 'a month or two after quarter-day' to ride, but had to walk — back to Hampstead even after the play. She was fond of dress, with a decided taste of her own, and a good deal of skill in designing what she wanted to wear. She went to an expensive dress-maker, and on Keats's own testimony, she took great and successful pains with her hair. 'Goodnight,' she writes to Fanny. 'I have got all my hair to curl, everybody is in bed and the fire is out.' She knew, and studied, how to make the best of herself.

There is a pleasant little interchange between the two Fannies which is illuminating in its quiet way. Fanny Brawne writes to

say that she has been at a quadrille party at the Davenports',
where she met the Lancasters. 'I think Miss Lancaster plain and
very common and ungenteel looking.' That evidently alarmed
Fanny Keats. If Miss Lancaster looked as bad as all that, how
would she herself appear at a quadrille party? Fanny Brawne
replies:

> Don't alarm yourself about Miss Lancaster's appearance,
> I trust you would cut a better figure than she did. You might
> feel shy at first (which is not that I know of her failing) but
> any person of sense who goes out a little can soon get over
> all that — dress, manner and carriage are just what she wants,
> a person must be a great beauty to look well without them,
> but they are certainly within the reach of anybody of
> understanding.

It was sensible advice: and Fanny Brawne herself followed it.
She took pains over her dress, her manner and her carriage,
certainly for their own sake, but also because she was aware that
she had not the kind of beauty which could afford to dispense
with them. The effect impressed Keats at first sight. The grace-
fulness of her movements is to the fore in both his descriptions of
her. The 'monstrousness' of her behaviour of which he pretended
to complain was in her conversation. He put it down to 'a pen-
chant for acting stylishly'. I do not believe it really offended him.
It was part of a 'strangeness' which intrigued him. We get a glimpse
of what it was at the end of one of her letters to Fanny Keats.

> How *very* delightful it would be to have you with me
> tonight, I am quite alone. I am always glad to get my
> '*family*' out (to provoke me they scarcely ever go) and then
> highly favoured indeed is the person I would wish for
> or even admit. There is one and only one person in the
> world besides yourself that I would admit tonight and her
> coming is about as possible as yours. So you see you *are*
> highly favoured — I was asked out to tea by some friends
> who thought I might feel 'lonely' — *for my part I think
> people are all mad.*

When Keats called her a 'minx' to her face, it was probably with a delighted appreciation of her vivacious unexpectedness. Traces of the self-repressed 'minx' are visible in her letters to Fanny Keats. Fanny Brawne had to tread warily, because she was not quite certain that a letter might not fall into the hands of the egregious Mrs. Abbey, and because she had a genuinely protective attitude to Fanny Keats, and toned down her 'shockingness' accordingly. But when she wrote that she 'had all but sworn' at her greasy ink, or when she wrote 'I have no pity whatever for your nerves because I have no nerves', I think Fanny Keats gave a gasp of shocked delight at such an onslaught on Mrs. Abbey's and Miss Tuckey's conception of the lady-like. Or she discusses the inability of the pigeons which Fanny Keats had given her to sit quietly on their eggs. 'They generally set on the egg a few days before they have the misfortune to break it, which accident I really believe happens from their fondness for it, as both wish to hatch at once. It is people of this disposition that invariably spoil their children and bring them up such plagues as I no doubt was, and for what I know, may be still.'

From some points of view Fanny Brawne was a spoilt child, but she had been spoilt by a genuinely warm-hearted mother, and the effect seems to have been no worse than that she grew up more natural than most young ladies of her class and time. Of Mrs. Brawne's warm-heartedness there is no question. Most mothers, in the circumstances, would have insisted on Fanny Brawne breaking off her engagement to Keats. The utmost we hear of her doing is that she said she could not prevent it, and that her only hope was that it would go off: which sounds more like a defence against the criticisms of the worldly wise than her own attitude. No earthly mother could be expected to rejoice at the engagement. The evidence is that she did nothing to gainsay her daughter or increase Keats's unhappiness. The promptitude with which she took him into her own house in August 1820 after the wretched affair of the intercepted letter at Hunt's, the kindness and assiduity with which she nursed him, convince one that Fanny Brawne was speaking the simple truth when she told

Fanny Keats that John 'loved' her mother. 'I wish,' the unhappy
Severn wrote to Mrs. Brawne, when the truth had dawned on him
that Keats had been doomed to die before he left England, and
the voyage to Italy had been an utterly unnecessary increase of
his misery, 'I wish many, many times that he had never left you
... In your care he seems to me like an infant in its mother's
arms.'

I am, belatedly but entirely, convinced that Fanny Brawne
shared her mother's warmth of heart. She was forthright, quick,
witty, graceful, and strange: I almost believe a bit of a tomboy.
And she was very young.

Keats fell in love with her almost at sight. When precisely this
happened is uncertain. He may actually have seen her on several
occasions between September 1818 and Tom Keats's death on
December 1st. But, if he did, he did not allow the impression she
made to dwell in his consciousness while Tom was still alive. The
letter he wrote to her and tore up, I believe was written shortly
after Tom's death, when Keats had removed, at Brown's invita-
tion, to Wentworth Place. After the move things happened
swiftly. He was now under the same roof as his old friends the
Dilkes, to whom the Brawnes were frequent visitors. And in a
very short time he became close friends with the Brawnes.
Brown and the Dilkes were both away from Wentworth Place
for Christmas, and Keats spent Christmas Day with the Brawnes,
probably at Elm Cottage, 'round the corner' from Wentworth
Place, on Downshire Hill. Fanny Brawne described this Christmas Day to Fanny Keats, when writing to her just before Christmas 1821.

We dine with [the Dilkes] on Christmas day which is like
most people's Christmas days melancholy enough. What
must yours be? I ask that question in no exultation. I
cannot think it will be much worse than mine, for I have to
remember that three years ago was the happiest day I had
ever then spent, but I will not touch on such subjects for
there are much better times and ways to remember them.

From this it has been generally deduced that Fanny became engaged to Keats on Christmas Day, 1818. This is demonstrably mistaken. It is impossible to reconcile this supposition with what Fanny Brawne had previously written about George Keats. Fanny Keats had been influenced against George by the belief, at first generally held by Keats's friends after his death, that George had heartlessly denuded him of money. (Incidentally there could be no better evidence of Fanny Brawne's scrupulous honesty than her defence of George.)

> In a letter you sent me some time ago you mentioned your brother George in a manner that made me think you had been misled about him. He is no favorite of mine and he never liked me so that I am not likely to say too much in his favor from affection for him. But I must say I think he is more blamed than he should be. I think him extravagant and selfish, but people in their great zeal make him out much worse than that — Soon after your brother Tom died, my dear John wrote to him offering him any assistance or money in his power. At that time he was not engaged to me and having just lost one brother felt all his affection turned towards the one that remained — George I dare say had at first no thoughts of accepting his offers but when his affairs did not succeed and he had a wife and one child to support, with the prospect of another, I cannot wonder that he should consider them first and as he could not get what he wanted without coming to England he unfortunately came — By that time your brother wished to marry himself, but he could not refuse the money.

In the event, George cleared himself thoroughly, in the eyes of the most fairminded of Keats's friends, of the imputations against him. But that is not the issue here. The question is the date of Fanny Brawne's engagement to Keats. There are two points of time between which, by Fanny Brawne's clear statement, the engagement took place. The latter is fixed definitely. George Keats returned to England to collect money early in January

1820. Keats and Fanny Brawne were engaged by then. The former point is not so easy to fix. But it is easy to show that 'soon after' Tom's death, the point of time at which Fanny Brawne says Keats offered George all the help in his power, and after which the engagement took place, must at least be later than January 3rd, 1819. For we have Keats's letter to George in which he gives the news of Tom's death. It begins on December 16th, 1818, and ends on January 3rd. It contains no promise of help, nor any indication that Keats felt that help might be necessary. Since it is quite impossible that Keats could have written any other letter to George between Tom's death and January 3rd, 1819, it follows that Keats and Fanny Brawne were engaged at some time after the latter date.

When was it? Here we are reduced to probable conjecture. But I believe Fanny Brawne's account was, in all essentials, accurate. On or about July 6th, Keats had a letter from George asking him to urge Abbey to send him all his available capital and apparently setting out the posture of his affairs in such a way that Keats asked Abbey how much of his own capital he could afford to lend George. But it was not until September 10th, 1819, that Keats had news that George's straits for money were desperate, and on September 17th he promised George: 'Your wants shall be a fresh spur to me. I assure you that you shall more than share what I can get while I am still young — the time may come when age will make me more selfish.' Four days later in the same letter, on September 21st, he more definitely pledged himself. 'Rest in the confidence that I will not omit any exertion to benefit you by some means or other. If I cannot remit you hundreds, I will tens and if not that ones.' I believe that this is the promise to George to which Fanny Brawne refers, and that she and Keats were not finally and definitely engaged until after that. Probably it happened soon after October 10th, 1819, when after long striving to hold himself back from seeing her, he saw her and was overwhelmed.

Some months before this, in June, there was a provisional engagement between them. To this we will come, in due course.

For the moment all we have established is that Keats and Fanny probably did not become engaged until October 1819, and certainly not on Christmas Day, 1818. That was the happiest day in Fanny's life till then not because they became engaged, but for a reason equally valid. It was probably the day on which Keats declared his love for her and learned it was reciprocated. It was the moment in their love which Keats imaginatively celebrated three weeks later in *The Eve of St. Agnes*, which he wrote during his stay at Chichester and Bedhampton. In the same tide of new inspiration he wrote the fragment of *The Eve of St. Mark*, and (I believe) the third canto of *Hyperion*.

All that Keats told his brother, or apparently anyone else, is in the phrase to his brother 'Miss Brawne and I have every now and then a chat and a tiff'. He wrote that on February 14th, 1819, while he was working on *The Eve of St. Mark* (which was written from February 13th to 17th). The Brawnes were still living 'round the corner', and although the off-hand phrase was obviously meant to throw the curious off the scent, perhaps to the outward-looking eye their meetings looked as casual as that. But on April 3rd, it must have seemed the gods were on their side. For the Dilkes left their part of Wentworth Place on that day to live in Westminster and the Brawnes took it over from them. Now Keats and Fanny were under one roof, about as close as two lovers could be without being in the same house. They knocked on the wall to each other, they shared the same garden in the spring of the year, talked and walked together to their hearts' content. There was a sombre undercurrent to Keats's felicity, the perplexity of a vague doubt, fleeting premonitions of disaster to come; but we must believe that this was the happiest and richest period of his life. With his faculty for living in the moment, and his old conviction:

> But for the general award of love
> The little sweet doth kill great bitterness,

his happiness, like his poetry, must have touched the heights.

Then came the fatal separation. The physical separation itself was due to Brown's habit of letting his house furnished for the summer. It was a desirable country villa, easily accessible from London, and doubtless commanded a good rent for the summer months. The profit he made from it seems to have been an important part of Brown's modest income. To let it was no doubt a necessity; and it may well be that unless he had done so, he would not have been able to lend Keats the money on which he lived during this year. For Abbey, Keats's trustee, had stopped supplies.

Probably it appeared to Keats just as necessary as it did to Brown that they should leave Wentworth Place during the summer. But it turned out to be disastrous: to Keats the pain of separation proved almost too great to be borne. One cannot help dreaming of what might have been, if Keats could have gone on living through the summer where he was, and had not been compelled to add to the strain of the labours he had undertaken the strain of being far away from his beloved. Or if he could have had money enough to marry Fanny and go on writing poetry; if he had not suddenly, at the very moment of his falling in love, been confronted with the necessity of making a living; if he had not had to snatch desperately at the best chance of making a living that offered itself to him. But such dreams are idle. 'There was working in him,' as he said of Milton, 'that same sort of thing as operates in the great world to the end of a Prophecy's being accomplish'd.'

At the moment when Keats most needed money, what little he had was frozen. From the beginning to nearly the end of this year, he did not receive one penny from his guardian and trustee, because a Chancery suit had been filed against the estate. He lived on borrowed money all the year, while he attempted the impossible against time and circumstance — to write a successful play, and complete a successful book of poems.

The venture was desperate. Yet the choice Keats made was indubitably the right one. He must somehow, if he could, make enough money to be able to marry Fanny. Four possibilities presented themselves to him. First, to study at Edinburgh to become a physician. But that required money; and it involved a still longer separation from Fanny. Second, to become, with the qualification he already had, a surgeon on an Indiaman. That did not require money, but it involved endless separation from Fanny. Third, to try to make his living by journalism. Fourth, to try to write an acceptable play in collaboration with Brown, who had once made £300 by one, and at the same time to prepare a book of poems — adding to those already written one which might, in spite of *The Quarterly*, catch the public taste, a tale in poetry that would hold the average reader's attention. That was *Lamia*.

Of all these choices, if they may be so called, that which Keats actually made was the best. It offered him a slender chance, but the best he had, of achieving his one and only end — which was to reduce his separation from Fanny to a minimum, and to marry Fanny as soon as he could. For this purpose the practical choices were really only two; journalism or the one he chose. And the one he chose was much the more likely of the two.

Keats was desperately practical when he left Fanny at the end of June. He evidently discussed his plan with her before their parting. Probably, she did not understand the urgency of his desire to marry her, or the tenseness of his resolution either to make a financial success of his writing during the summer or not to return to her at all. It would have seemed to her harsh and unnecessary. She had no objection to a long engagement. She was ignorant of the precarious state of his health, and he himself had no certain knowledge of it; but he had doubts about it. The obstinate persistence of his 'sore throat' ever since his return from Scotland, his fits of exhaustion and lassitude, made him at times profoundly uneasy.

It was Keats himself who insisted at the moment of parting that any engagement between them must be provisional. On July 1st, 1819, immediately after reaching Shanklin, he wrote to her:

As I told you a day before I left Hampstead, I will never
return to London if my Fate does not turn up Pam or at
least a Court-card. Though I could centre my Happiness in
you, I cannot expect to engross your heart so entirely —
indeed, if I thought you felt as much for me as I do for you
at this moment I do not think I could restrain myself from
seeing you again tomorrow for the delight of one embrace.
But no — I must live upon hope and Chance.

Fanny did not then feel as much for Keats as he did for her.
It is no criticism of her, and I am sure Keats at this moment did
not mean it as such. He felt, partly because of his deeply and
rightly sensuous nature, partly because of his inner warning that
the time might be very short, a devouring physical hunger for
her, which she did not, or did not yet reciprocate. A long engagement would burn him up. Either he must get himself into a position where he could marry her soon, or he must renounce her.
And he deliberately made their full engagement provisional upon
his achieving enough financial success during the summer to
make their early marriage possible.

Fanny Brawne seems to have misunderstood his letter. He
quotes a sentence from her reply. 'You mention "horrid people",'
he writes, 'and ask me whether it depend on them whether I see
you again.' I interpreted this in *Keats and Shakespeare* in a sense
unfair to Fanny. I now think that the reference is to Keats's
phrase that he would not return to London unless his Fate turned
up Pam or at least a Court-card, and to their previous conversation on the matter; and that the 'horrid people' are those in whose
hands Keats's financial destiny lay — his Aunt who had filed the
Chancery suit, Abbey who would take no risks, and the public
whose favour he so desperately needed. Keats's reply to her is
none too clear, perhaps because he was trying particularly hard to
make himself understood.

Do understand me, my love, in this. I have so much of you
in my heart that I must turn Mentor when I see a chance of
harm befalling you. I would never see anything but

Pleasure in your eyes, love on your lips, and Happiness in your steps. I would wish to see you among those amusements suitable to your inclinations and spirits; so that our loves might be a delight in the midst of Pleasures agreeable enough, rather than a resource from vexations and cares. But I doubt much, in case of the worst, whether I shall be philosopher enough to follow my own Lessons: if I saw my resolution give you a pain I could not. (*Letter 136*)

The meaning of this needs pondering, but when pondered, it is fairly plain. The harm which Keats sees befalling Fanny is engagement and marriage to him so long as he has not means to support her without her having to endure vexations and cares, from which their love would in that case be only a refuge. Of that harm she is in danger if he were to return to London as penniless as he now is. To warn her against that, 'he turns Mentor'. But, 'in case of the worst', — that is, if his plans of financial success fail — he doubts whether he will have the strength to abide by his resolution. If the keeping of it gave her pain, he could not.

Keats was, as ever, speaking the truth about himself. With part of him, he is determined to keep away from Fanny, if he does not succeed. With another part he feels that he may not be able to abide by his determination. With yet another part he knows that if his keeping away from her gave her pain, he could not stick to it at all.

I have told in *Keats and Shakespeare* the detailed story of his heroic effort to abide by his determination during the summer months of 1819: it is unnecessary to tell it again. It was a twofold effort, first to work to achieve his purpose; and second, to keep away from Fanny by stifling his hunger for her in the very intensity of his labours. He was doing a kind of heroic violence to his own creative nature, by shutting out from it the 'sensational' experience by which it lived. But not even so could Keats really write for the market. Deliberate pot-boiling (which was confined to *Otho the Great*) was, and had to be, automatic and mechanical. Brown gave him the plot of the tragedy scene by scene and Keats tagged it out in blank verse. Thus it is unique among Keats's productions: it contains almost nothing of him, expresses almost nothing of his nature and genius. But apart from this mechanical effort, his genius was truly at work, though under the unnatural conditions he had been compelled to impose upon it. 'I have three or four stories half done,' he wrote to Fanny on July 15th, 1819, 'but as I cannot write for the mere sake of the press, I am obliged to let them progress or lie still as my fancy chooses.' What were they? *Lamia* was one, *Hyperion* another, *The Eve of St. Agnes* the third, and the fourth *The Eve of St. Mark*. That under these circumstances he made what he did of *Lamia* and the revision of *Hyperion* is marvellous. But in the effort of imaginative concentration he gradually worked himself into an attitude of pride and contempt for the public, whose favour he was trying to win, and almost of resentment against Fanny herself for kindling the passion which compelled him to the enforcement of his genius. 'I equally dislike the favour of the public with the love of a woman,' he wrote to Taylor after two months of the struggle. 'They are both a cloying treacle to the wings of independence.'

The torments had begun in grim reality. And the cause of them is simple and single: his separation from Fanny. If he could only be assured that it was as painful to her to be separated from him as it was for him to be separated from her, he felt his pains would have been eased. But then, if he had known it, he could not have kept away from her, even so long as he did. He dreaded coming to London to see her, because of the pain of parting from her again. He dreaded even the thought of trying to work as a journalist in London because, as he gently put it to her, 'I should not like to be so near you as London without being continually with you'.

We know Keats's side of the story. What of Fanny's? It seems clear to me now, having regard to the sequel, that the separation from Keats, though it may have lain rather lightly upon her at the beginning, became more and more grievous to her. She became aware of his deep unhappiness, and of the painful effort he was making to 'wean himself from her'. Probably she did not know how to deal with such a lover — at once so passionate and so tender, so stubborn and so generous — and she was out of her depth. It was surely not at first easy for her to conceive or to feel that she was the object of a love so devouring that Keats felt he dared not come near her. But as the weeks of separation dragged themselves along, Fanny's love for this strange, intense and simple being deepened immeasurably, until she was, I think, ardently longing for him to be near her again.

At the end of August when Keats was in Winchester, came the first thunderclap. Kean, on whose acting the tragedy depended for success, was going to America. 'That was the worst news I could have had.' The second followed on September 10th, when he heard that George's straits were really and truly desperate. He had lost all his money. Keats dashed to London to see Abbey, their guardian, on George's behalf, but he dared not see Fanny.

> I love you too much to venture to Hampstead, I feel it is not paying a visit, but venturing into a fire. Que ferai-je? as the french novel writers say in fun, and I in earnest: really what can I do? Knowing well that my life must be passed in fatigue and trouble, I have been endeavouring to wean myself from you: for to myself alone what can be much of a misery? As far as they regard myself I can despise all events: but I cannot cease to love you.   (*Letter 150*)

Really what could he do? Keats's resolution not to return to London if he were unsuccessful was growing, as he had feared, too hard to keep. On August 28th he wrote to his sister Fanny that Kean was going to America, and that for all he could guess he would remain at Winchester until the middle of October 'when Mr. Brown will return to his house at Hampstead, whither I shall return with him'. In other words, although success had become more doubtful still, he was going to return to Fanny Brawne. He wrote in the same sense to George on September 17th; but either that was a blind, or by that time Keats really did not know what he intended to do. For there is reason to believe that when he went to London on September 10th, in instant response to George's S.O.S., to see Abbey about their finances, and learned how desperate they were, he came suddenly to a new resolve — to try to make a living as a journalist, and to that end to take a cheap lodging in Westminster. That, of course, involved his parting company with Brown at Wentworth Place. And he seems to have written to Brown from London, to that effect, asking for a speedy reply. But no reply came, for the good reason that Brown was not where he had said he was going, namely, Chichester and Bedhampton, but in Ireland making an illegal marriage with Abigail Donohue.

Keats wrote again and yet again to Brown: still there was no reply. When at last he did get one, it was apparently to dissuade him from his plan, and to suggest he should continue to be Brown's lodger at Wentworth Place, borrowing the money from Brown. Keats was moved by Brown's objection to the extent of not sending a letter he had written to Dilke telling him of his plan, and asking him to find him a room in Westminster. He agreed to let his final decision wait till he had actually seen Brown. Meantime, he told Brown: 'If you live at Hampstead next winter — I like [Miss Brawne] and cannot help it. On that account I had better not live there.' When Brown returned to Winchester, Keats stuck to his guns. On October 1st he wrote to Dilke asking him to get him a room in Westminster, and thither Keats went some time in the following week.

It is very notable that Keats said not a word of his new plan of journalism, which fills his other letters of the time, in his letter to George (September 17th-24th). The reason for this striking omission is pretty plain. He did not want to distress George by the knowledge that the failure of his speculation in America had driven Keats to work of a kind which George knew to be un-congenial to him. The whole letter is an obvious effort to put the bravest face on a very grim situation. And I suspect that his telling George that 'the term of Brown's house will be up in the middle of next month when we shall return to Hampstead' was a deliberate blind. Certainly at the moment he wrote Keats had a quite different intention.

For he had learned from Abbey that, even if the Chancery suit were withdrawn, there was precious little money left. In fact George and John between them had used up all their own small capital — and all they now had was their share of what remained of Tom's. If George was to have the minimum of what he needed, he would have to take not merely his own but most of Keats's share of Tom's estate, which was what he eventually did in January 1820. To that Keats pledged himself in his reply to George, and in a mood of determination and confidence, which does his heart more credit than his head, he promised even more — to share with George anything that he actually earned. 'If I cannot remit you hundreds, I will tens and if not that ones.' Meanwhile he had caused to be sent to George £100 from Tom's estate.

George understood Keats's promises as Keats intended he should. All the available capital belonging to them both after Keats's debts were paid would be sent to him. Keats made this perfectly clear to George.

> What he [Abbey] can send you will not be a sufficient capital to ensure you any command in America. What he has of mine I nearly have anticipated by debts. So I would advise you not to sink it, but to live upon it in hopes of my being able to increase it. To this end I will devote whatever I may gain for a few years to come. (*Letter 156*)

How precisely Keats was not merely to make a living for himself but have a surplus to remit to George he does not make plain. He had made up his mind to attempt journalism; but he said not a word about that. He gave George to understand that there was still hope for his tragedy, and he quoted Reynolds's opinion that he expected more from Keats's new volume of poetry than Keats himself did.

Meanwhile Keats was making a desperate attempt 'to wean himself' from Fanny Brawne. It was indeed necessary, for by his

promise to George he had put the possibility of his having money
enough to marry her quite out of range. And there are indications
that he was trying his utmost to detach himself from her in imagination also. 'Nothing,' he wrote to George on September 17th,
'strikes me so forcibly with a sense of the ridiculous as a man in
love. Even when I know a poor fool to be really in pain about it,
I could burst out laughing in his face,' and he goes on to compose
the amusing verses on an imaginary tea-party of lovers.

> Pensive they sit and roll their languid eyes,
> Nibble their toasts and cool their tea with sighs . . .

On the next day he copied out from Burton's *Anatomy* an
onslaught on the illusions of lovers about their mistresses.

An even more interesting indication appears in his revision of
The Eve of St. Agnes. That poem was — in essence and inspiration — a celebration of their acknowledgment of their love for one
another. But just before he went to London on September 10th
he had been revising it in a sense which gave him a vicarious
fruition to his love. Keats read the revised poem to Woodhouse
in London on September 12th. Woodhouse promptly wrote to
Taylor:

As the poem was originally written, *we* innocent ones
(ladies and myself) might very well have supposed that
Porphyro, when acquainted with Madeleine's love for him,
and when he arose Ethereal flushed etc., etc. (turn to it) set
himself at once to persuade her to go off with him and went
over 'the Dartmoor black' (now changed for some other
place) to be married in right honest chaste and sober wise.
But, as it is now altered, as soon as M. has declared her
love, P. winds by degrees his arm round her, presses breast
to breast, and acts all the acts of a bona fide husband, while
she fancies she is only playing the part of a Wife in a dream.
This alteration is of about 3 stanzas; and tho' there are no
improper expressions and all is left to inference, and tho'
profanely speaking, the interest on the reader's imagination
is greatly heightened, yet I do apprehend it will render the

poem unfit for ladies and indeed scarcely to be mentioned to them among the 'things that are'. He says he does not want ladies to read his poetry: that he writes for men — and that if in the former poem there was an opening for a doubt what took place, it was his fault for not writing clearly and comprehensibly — that he should despise a man who would be such a eunuch in sentiment as to leave a maid, with that Character about her, in such a situation: and should despise himself to write about it etc., etc., etc. — and all this sort of Keats-like rhodomontade.

The turmoil in Keats's heart and mind at this time was desperate indeed. He was not actually engaged, as we have seen. The terms of the 'provisional' engagement into which he had entered shortly before parting from her in June could now not possibly be kept. There was nothing to do, Keats felt in that part of him which, 'however selfish he might feel, could not act selfishly', but break it off. And he dared not, while he was in London from September 10th to 15th, venture into the fire which would burn up his resolution. Yet it was well-nigh hopeless to venture into London at all. The only possible safe place for him was miles away from Fanny in the country. But there the journalism on which he had resolved was impossible. And, even if he had the money to keep himself there, writing poetry, the pain which he would give Fanny had to be considered. From the beginning he had known that, if a final parting from Fanny were to give her pain, parting would be impossible. It would be the proof that she loved him as he loved her — not with the same agony of frustrated physical passion, indeed, but with a love as true as his own: not of the same intensity but of the same kind.

Keats could not keep away from her any more. They met on October 10th and Fanny showed him plainly that to be parted from him had been pain to her. Her joy at seeing him again was so obvious and so sincere that it burned away in a flame of rapture all his doubts and all his resolutions. She was *his* woman, and he was *her* man. I can imagine that Keats went to Wentworth

Place on that day 'to see Brown' — as one part of him would tell himself — in order to take away the possessions and books which were stored in Brown's house: the rest of him went with a different purpose — to submit to the working of the prophecy. I believe that within a few days they were engaged. Anything else was inconceivable.

I am living [Keats wrote to her when he was back in his rooms at 25 College Street] today in yesterday: I was in a complete fascination all day. I feel myself at your mercy. Write me ever so few lines and tell me you will never for ever be less kind to me than yesterday—. You dazzled me. There is nothing in the world so bright and delicate . . . When shall we pass a day alone? I have had a thousand kisses, for which with my whole soul I thank love — but if you should deny me the thousand and first — 'twould put me to the proof how great a misery I could live through. If you should ever carry your threat yesterday into execution — believe me 'tis not my pride, my vanity or any petty passion would torment me — really 'twould hurt my heart — I could not bear it . . . Ah, hertè mine.   (*Letter 159*)

Two days later, he wrote to her:

The time is passed when I had power to advise and warn you against the unpromising morning of my Life. My love has made me selfish. I cannot exist without you. I am forgetful of everything but seeing you again — my Life seems to stop there — I see no further. You have absorb'd me. I have a sensation at the present moment as though I was dissolving — I should be exquisitely miserable without the hope of soon seeing you. I should be afraid to separate myself far from you. My sweet Fanny, will your heart never change? My love, will it? I have no limit now to my love. Your note came in just here — I cannot be happier away from you. 'Tis richer than an Argosy of Pearls. Do not threat me even in jest. I have been astonished that Men could die Martyrs for religion — I have shudder'd at it. I shudder no more — I could be martyr'd for my Religion — Love is my religion — I could die for that. I could die for you. My Creed is Love and you are its only tenet. You have ravish'd me away by a Power I cannot resist; and yet I could resist till I saw you; and even since I have seen you I have endeavoured often 'to reason against the reasons of my love.' I can do that no more — the pain would be too great. My love is selfish. I cannot breathe without you.   (*Letter 160*)

'My love has made me selfish. I cannot exist without you ...' 'My love is selfish. I cannot breathe without you.' The phrase, repeated, takes up the one he had used at the beginning of their separation. 'However selfish I may feel, I am sure I could never act selfishly ... I will never return to London unless ...' He could not keep his resolution, and now he abandoned it explicitly. He had proved on his pulses that in order to live he must be with Fanny.

On the 16th Keats went to stay with the Brawnes for three days. On the 19th he had given up his rooms in Westminster, for he wrote to Fanny from the Dilkes'.

On awakening from my three days dream ('I cry to dream again') I find one and another astonish'd at my idleness and thoughtlessness. I was miserable last night — the morning is always restorative. I must be busy or try to be so. I have several things to speak to you of tomorrow morning. Mrs. Dilke I should think will tell you that I purpose living at Hampstead. I must impose chains upon myself. I shall be able to do nothing. I should like to cast the die for Love or death. I have no Patience with anything else — if you ever intend to be cruel to me as you say in jest now but perhaps may sometimes be in earnest be so now, and I will — my mind is in a tremble, I cannot tell what I am writing.
                                                                        (*Letter 162*)

So Keats returned to London, to Wentworth Place, and to Fanny. It meant, of course, that the plan of journalism was given up, and that his only hope of making money was by his poetry. He was frequently sick and dispirited, though there were almost certainly the alternations of exaltation with despair to which the pthisic patient is subject. But he was happier than he could ever have been away from her. He bravely set to work on a poem in a new genre, *The Cap and Bells*, which, while not making the extreme demand on his creative energy, yet exercised it sufficiently to be an admirable poem of its kind. It is quite conceivable that had he been able to finish it it might have been a popular success. Not much is known of Keats's doings during the three or four months between his return to Wentworth Place and the haemorrhage in early February. But one has the sense that he was working as hard as he could. Besides continuing the revision of his poems, he wrote the eighty — on the whole admirable — stanzas of *The Cap and Bells*. It was a great deal for a sick man, racked by the torments of unsatisfied love. And in addition to these there were his love-poems: *The Day is Gone*, the *Lines to Fanny*, the *Ode to Fanny*, *I cry your mercy*. The haunting lines written in the MS. of *The Cap and Bells* which are generally printed as 'Supposed to have been written to Fanny Brawne' may or may not have been written to her. I do not now believe they were: they are rather the utterance of a despair of which no mortal being can be the cause, but at most the occasion.

> This living hand, now warm and capable
> Of earnest grasping, would, if it were cold
> And in the icy silence of the tomb,
> So haunt thy days and chill thy dreaming nights
> That thou wouldst wish thine own heart dry of blood
> So in my veins red life might stream again,
> And thou be conscience-calm'd — see here it is —
> I hold it towards you.

Personally, I cannot, save with an unnatural effort, imagine Keats even in the extremest of his torments, and even in imagination, thus addressing Fanny Brawne.

The other four poems to Fanny which (I believe) were all

KEATS

written between his return to Fanny and his haemorrhage convey
the gamut of his 'sensations'. Any closer placing of them is
entirely conjectural; but for what it is worth I give my guess that
The Day is Gone was written during his 'three days dream' in the
Brawnes' house. The longing to be Fanny's lover indeed, and
the regret that it should be denied him, though beautifully sub-
dued, is audible.

> Warm breath, tranced whisper, tender semitone
> Bright eyes, accomplish'd shape and lang'rous waist,
> Vanish'd unseasonably at shut of eve
> When the dusk holiday — or holinight
> Of fragrant-curtain'd love begins to weave
> The woof of darkness thick, for hid delight . . .

The *Lines to Fanny* may well have been written immediately
on his brief return to his lodgings in Westminster.

> What can I do to drive away
> Remembrance from my eyes? for they have seen,
> Aye, an hour ago, my brilliant Queen!
> Touch has a memory. O say, love, say,
> What can I do to kill it and be free
> In my old liberty?

He is perhaps but half-serious in praying to soar 'above the reach
of fluttering love'. At any rate a greater enemy to his peace of
mind is his thoughts

>   of that most hateful land,
> Dungeoner of my friends, that wicked strand
> Where they were wreck'd and live a wrecked life;
> That monstrous region, whose dull rivers pour
> Ever from their sordid urns unto the shore,
> Unown'd of any weedy-haired gods;
> Whose winds, all zephyrless, hold scourging rods,
> Iced in the great lakes, to afflict mankind.

It is North America where his brother and sister are banished.

The thought of them, and no doubt of all that their misfortunes involved for him and his love, is the hell from which he longs to be delivered.

> O, for some sunny spell
> To dissipate the shadows of this hell!
> Say they are gone — with the new dawning light
> Steps forth my lady bright!

Let this anguish of anxiety for his brother and sister be lifted, and he would be free to enjoy his love in happiness. At the thought he yields to the ecstasy of the memory of touch, which at first he had longed to drive away.

> Enough! Enough! it is enough for me
> To dream of thee!

It is a very impressive poem, which renders the complex and troubled emotion of his love with singular fidelity to his circumstance yet with rich and strange reverberations.

The lovely and touching *Ode to Fanny* is a simpler poem, except that the opening stanza seems to indicate a baffled desire to write a poem of another kind. It may itself be an example of the inability of his muse to regain her old freedom. His thoughts are now chained to his love. The poem was evidently written while Fanny was out at a dance, and some have been tempted to connect it with Keats's desire that Fanny Keats should 'teach him a few common dancing steps', in his letter of February 27th, 1819. A fortnight later he wrote to her. 'I went lately to the only dance I have been to these twelve months or shall go to for twelve months again. It was to our brother-in-law's cousin's.' But there is no reason to suppose that Fanny Brawne would have been invited to such a dance; moreover the whole point of the poem is that Fanny Brawne is at the dance and he is not. I feel certain it belongs to this later period of Keats's love. A cancelled passage in the autograph MS. connects it directly with the sonnet *I cry your mercy*, which to my mind indubitably belongs to the late months of 1819. Keats originally began the sixth stanza of the *Ode*:

> I know it. But sweet Fanny I would fain
>   Kneel for a mercy on my lonely hours . . .

Then he began again

> I know it. But sweet Fanny I would fain
>   Cry you soft mercy for a . . .

It was probably a day or two later, in deeper suffering, that Keats took up the abandoned phrase in the most moving of all his poems to Fanny.

> I cry your mercy — pity — love! — aye, love!
>   Merciful love that tantalizes not,
> One-thoughted, never-wandering, guileless love,
>   Unmask'd, and being seen — without a blot!
> O! let me have thee whole, — all — all — be mine!
>   That shape, that fairness, that sweet minor zest
> Of love, your kiss — those hands, those eyes divine,
>   That warm, white, lucent, million-pleasured breast, —
> Yourself — your soul — in pity give me all,
>   Withhold no atom's atom or I die,
> Or living on perhaps, your wretched thrall,
>   Forget, in the mist of idle misery,
> Life's purposes, — the palate of my mind
>   Losing its gust, and my ambition blind!

Nothing could have saved Keats save the physical consummation of his passion: and it is doubtful indeed whether that could have saved him. But it might have prolonged his life for a few years. At the very end of his life, when whatever bitterness he had ever felt against Fanny was completely purged away, he still believed that if he had been Fanny's lover, he would have been saved. 'I should have had her when I was in health and I should have remained well,' he wrote to Brown on November 1st, 1820. And in the very last days of all, just before the calm descended upon him on the near approach of death, Severn bears witness that 'he found many causes of illness in the exciting and thwarting of his passions, but I persuaded him to feel otherwise on this delicate point'. Severn was always sanguine. There is no reason to believe that Keats ever felt otherwise.

But he was assuredly mistaken in believing that he was in health when he first fell in love with Fanny. Tuberculosis had had some hold upon him well before that, even though he was ignorant of it, or at most dimly foreboding.* Nevertheless, the continuous pangs of frustrated desire counted for much in the weakening of his resistance. One has the sense that he was indeed burned up by his passion. But the fire was also a creative incandescence in the soul of one of the most richly gifted poetic natures the world has harboured.

The price Keats paid for being 'a miserable and mighty poet of the human heart' is fearful to contemplate. I dread the compulsion that drives me on to read and re-read the letters of his last years.

> Once again the fierce dispute
> Betwixt hell-torment and impassioned clay
> Must I burn through.

And I long that the consummation of his love should have been granted to him, and the consolation of the knowledge that Fanny had not withheld nor dreamed of withholding an atom's atom of herself.

But what fair-minded man can blame her for not feeling at the beginning of their love the same fire of passion as blazed up in Keats — an attraction so powerful that it would have swept away all the prudential arguments against their speedy marriage? Possibly Keats wondered why it was not so. That Fanny was only eighteen — in any case not so strong an argument in those days as today — can hardly have seemed a serious objection to Keats, seeing that Georgiana Wylie had married his brother George at sixteen. But George was at least going off to make his fortune, as he and Keats firmly believed; Keats was hamstrung by his vocation for poetry, and, whatever he may have felt in his heart, he seems chivalrously to have urged the prudential consideration more strongly than any-body, perhaps with a secret longing that Fanny herself would brush it aside. It is a pity that she did not. But I cannot blame her for not doing it. The fire in her heart was kindled too late. Keats's frustration was a destiny.

Between his return to London in October and Christmas 1819, he went to see his sister Fanny at Walthamstow only once. His familiar walk to Walthamstow was now too much for him, and even the journey by stage was too great a tax on his strength. Inspired by an unfortunate theory that it would clear his brain, he had 'left off animal food', at a time when he needed all the nourish-ment he could get. He wrote to his sister on December 20th.

> When I saw you last you ask'd me whether you should see me again before Christmas. You would have seen me if I had been quite well. I have not, though not unwell enough to have prevented me — not indeed at all — but fearful lest the weather should affect my throat which on exertion or cold continually threatens me. By the advice of my Doctor I have had a warm great Coat made and have ordered some thick shoes — so furnish'd I shall be with you if it holds a little fine before Christmas day.

Rather than alarm his sister, he laid himself open to the charge (which no brother ever deserved less) of neglecting her. Never-theless, two days later he has to write to her that his coming is unlikely, and to confess 'I am sorry to say I have been and continue rather unwell'.

At the beginning of January 1820 George arrived unexpectedly from America to get what money he could out of Abbey. Since he took back with him all of Tom's estate that belonged to both John and himself except £100, and since there is no doubt of the sincerity of his affection for his brother, it is plain that he had no idea that Keats was seriously ill. Moreover since the £100 was left avowedly to pay Keats's existing debts — his bills due the previous Christmas were still unpaid — it must be that Keats was keeping up the pretence of being able to earn his own living, and to honour his promise of September, although Abbey, quite rightly, protested against Keats's lending George his share of Tom's estate. Nor did Keats tell George that he was now engaged to Fanny Brawne. According to Fanny herself George, who now met her for the first time, did not like her. Had he known that John was deeply in love with her, he would (I think) have managed to conceal it even from her quick eyes.

Thus Keats was deliberately putting a brave, false face on his affairs while George was in England. He wrote a long, witty, and high-spirited letter to Georgiana for George to take back. Though in it he confessed to a weariness of society, he had been out to parties on three of the previous four days. It was probably an effort to keep George company. George left London for Liverpool on the way to America on Friday, January 28th. On the Thursday following, February 3rd, Keats was seized by the haemorrhage.

Since Brown was seriously alarmed, it is probable that Keats did use to him some such sombre words as Brown remembered. Fanny Brawne, who knew nothing of them, was deeply concerned by what she did know. For the first few days she was constantly with Keats until it was stupidly suggested — apparently by the doctor and Brown in concert — that her presence agitated him so much that it did him harm. And Keats seems to have been so weak that he acquiesced in the separation. He became very despondent. How could he make a living now?

> You know our situation [he wrote to Fanny] what hope is there if I should be recover'd ever so soon—my very health will not suffer me to make any great exertion. I am recommended not even to read poetry, much less write it. I wish I had even a little hope. I cannot say forget me — but I would mention that there are impossibilities in the world. No more of this. I am not strong enough to be weaned.
>
> (*Letter 180*)

Fanny did her best to encourage him by steadfastly refusing to break off the engagement, though Keats naturally could not help returning to the subject. But finally he put it aside.

> Then all we have to do is to be patient. Whatever violence I may sometimes do myself by hinting at what would appear to anyone but ourselves a matter of necessity, I do not think I could bear any approach of a thought of losing you. (*Letter 182*)

In one of his notes to her Keats wrote: 'I think you had better not make any long stay with me when Mr. Brown is at home.' This condition of Fanny's presence, which is mentioned in another note, is connected with the bitter denunciation of Brown in the letters of July and August.

> I cannot forget what has pass'd. What? nothing with a man of the world, but to me deathful. I will get rid of this as much as possible. When you were in the habit of flirting with Brown you would have left off, could your own heart have felt one half of one pang mine did. Brown is a good sort of Man — he did not know he was doing me to death by inches. I feel the effect of every one of those hours in my side now. (*Letter 220*)

And again,

> I am sickened at the brute world which you are smiling with. I hate men and women more. I see nothing but thorns for the future — wherever I may be next winter in Italy or nowhere Brown will be living near you with his indecencies — I see no prospect of any rest. (*Letter 224*)

Although there must have been some grain of fact that was exaggerated in Keats's tortured mind into these 'flirtations' between Fanny and Brown, it cannot have been more than a grain: for the plain fact is that, so far from breaking with Brown completely, as he said he would, Keats made him his sole confidant at the last. He bared his soul to Brown as to no one else. Probably what hurt Keats was something of the kind that happened at Keats's return to Fanny in October 1819. 'When Brown came out with that seemingly true story against me last night, I felt it would be death to me if you had ever believed it . . . Before I knew Brown could disprove it I was for the moment miserable.' That might well have been a story like the one Keats told against himself of his encounter with the major's wife at Winchester.

Brown was contemptuous of women; his intimate relations with them were certainly untinged with any idealism; and he had a broad sense of humour. So to be sure had Keats, though it was more delicate than Brown's. But Keats had, on his own confession, as well as the evidence of his poetry, an unshakable idealism, if not about women at large, about *the* woman. He had an intense faith in the possibility and significance of Love. He had believed, in spite of all disappointment, that he too one day would awake like Adam from his dream and find it truth. And there was a marked and lovely vein of chivalry towards women in Keats. It caused him pain 'to think insults' against a woman. It did not cause Brown any pain.

Keats, in fact, was very like Shakespeare in his attitude to women. There was, as in Shakespeare, a side of him which could meet and better Brown in bawdy humour; and there was a side of him with which Brown had no contact at all. I can well believe that Brown had no idea when he was giving offence to Keats by his manner with Fanny. But it seems to me, on reflection, in the highest degree unlikely that it was an understood thing between Keats and Fanny that she should not come to see Keats while Brown was at home, because of Brown's 'familiarities' with her. That would have meant not merely 'thinking insults' to Fanny, but expressing them. I cannot imagine a spirited girl like Fanny submitting quietly to such an imputation, any more than I can imagine Keats putting it upon her. Whatever the nature of Brown's offences in this matter — and I daresay they were trivial enough — at the time Keats gave no vent to the suffering they caused him. When, in the tortures of his separation, he flung at her the charge that she had been 'in the habit of flirting with Brown', she replied that he 'ill-treated her in thought, word and deed'.

I find no trace of any consciousness in Fanny that he thus ill-treated her while he was ill at Wentworth Place, and she visited him. Keats's notes to her contain no hint of it, as they surely would have done if things had come to such a pass that because of her behaviour with Brown Keats had to make it a condition that she should come to see him only when Brown was away.

It is conceivable that Keats did refer to it in notes which Fanny destroyed; but there is a much simpler explanation of the reason why it was an accepted thing between them that Brown's absence was the condition of Fanny's presence. Brown took the view that Fanny's visits did Keats harm. 'I think Mr. Brown is right in supposing you may stop too long with me, so very nervous as I am.' At that moment Keats acquiesced in Brown's view. At other moments he doubted it. 'According to all appearances I am to be separated from you as much as possible. How I shall be able to bear it, or whether it will not be worse than your presence now and then, I cannot tell.' Again: 'Believe too, my Love, that our friends think and speak for the best, and if their best is not our best, it is not their fault.'

It is probable that Brown with the best motives was doing what he could to keep Fanny and Keats apart, and I believe he was the chief and most influential of the friends 'who were plying me with discouragements with respect to you eternally'. He meant well, no doubt, according to his lights; but his mind inhabited another world than Keats's. The idea that a man could not live, could not exist, could not breathe, apart from his beloved woman, which was the simple truth about Keats, was romantic nonsense to Brown. And I have even wondered whether his behaviour with Fanny (which Keats in his anguish exaggerated and so bitterly resented) may not have been part of an uncouth strategy to discredit Fanny in Keats's eyes; and whether the same purpose may not help to explain the apparent callousness of Brown's subsequent action — when, in spite of Keats's illness, he persisted in letting his house for the summer. By so doing he drove Keats out into the misery of lodgings at Kentish Town and the agony of separation. Of all the cruel things

that were done to Keats in his last year on earth, that seems to me
the most cruel. Coming from a friend, it has appeared quite inexplicable: until the thought struck me that Brown may genuinely have believed, or half-believed, that he was doing Keats a
good turn by enforcing a physical separation from Fanny.

If this was Brown's attitude to the love of Keats and Fanny —
and the evidence points that way — what could be more natural,
or more inevitable, than that it was accepted between them that
Fanny should make a long stay with Keats only when Brown was
away? Only in his absence could they be unconstrained, could
they be close to one another, could his head be pillowed on his
dear love's ripening breast. That condition Fanny could understand, accept, and rejoice in: it was imposed by Love itself. The
other was one she must repudiate; it was an insult to her.

The impression made by Keats's notes to her while he was confined at Wentworth Place is that of a tender, often despairing,
lover whose moments of happiness came not only from being
alone with his beloved, but also from the knowledge that she was
always waiting as eagerly as he to seize the opportunity of being
alone with him.

> I have vex'd you too much [he writes]. But for Love! Can
> I help it? You are always new. The last of your kisses was
> ever the sweetest; the last smile the brightest; the last move-
> ment the gracefullest. When you pass'd my window home
> yesterday, I was filled with as much admiration as if I had
> then seen you for the first time. You uttered a half com-
> plaint once that I only lov'd your Beauty. Have I nothing
> else then to love in you but that? Do not I see a heart
> naturally furnish'd with wings imprison itself with me? No
> ill prospect has been able to turn your thoughts a moment
> from me. This perhaps should be as much a subject of sor-
> row as joy — but I will not talk of that.

And the note ends:

> Brown is gone out — but here is Mrs. Wylie — when she is
> gone I shall be awake for you.   (*Letter 197*)

And again:

> My dearest Fanny, whenever you know me to be alone, come, no matter what day. (*Letter 200*)

And yet again:

> You think I may be wearied at night you say: it is my best time; I am at my best about eight o'clock . . . How can you bear so long an imprisonment at Hampstead? I shall always remember it with all the gusto that a monopolizing carle should. I could build an Altar to you for it. (*Letter 202*)

The notes from Keats to Fanny ended some time in March 1820. Keats had recovered sufficiently by the middle of March to be able to make an occasional journey to town — he dined in town with Taylor on March 14th — but not enough to visit Fanny Keats at Walthamstow. We must imagine him resuming his walks with Fanny Brawne on the Heath, only slower than before, happy in her presence, trying to be confident, but a prey to the dark fear of coming separation. The approach of the moment when he would have to leave Wentworth Place must have been dreadful to him. And soon there loomed up before him the still more dreadful prospect of going to Italy.

Probably, by the time Keats actually went to Italy in September, his early death was certain. The agonies of his separation from Fanny during the three months from May to August, the memory of which made him shudder, must have had a disastrous effect upon him. Compared to them the previous three months of illness at Wentworth Place had been felicity itself. But the sending of him then to Italy was an unspeakable aggravation of his torment. Keats would have died happily in Fanny's arms. If he could have been nursed by the Brawnes, or even continued his existence at Wentworth Place, with Fanny next door, his life might have been sensibly prolonged — perhaps only a few months or a year — but his last year of life would have been utterly different from what it was. He would have come near to the ecstasy of which he had dreamed. 'I have two luxuries to brood over in my walks,' he had written to her on July 25th, 1819, 'your Loveliness and the hour of my death. O that I could have possession of them in the same moment!' Instead, he was torn from Fanny six months before his death; and death came to him as a merciful release from a terrible agony which ought not and need not have been inflicted upon him. It makes the contemplation of Keats's 'posthumous life' amost unendurable. There is nothing in the whole range of imaginative experience known to me which requires a sterner effort of soul to endure to the end.

The strange and terrible thing about the decision to send Keats to Italy was that he seems to have been left in ignorance of it for some months. It was, as it were, plotted behind his back. In a letter to Brown in June 1820, Keats wrote: 'My book is coming out with very low hopes, though not spirits, on my part. This shall be my last trial; not succeeding, I shall try what I can do in the apothecary line.' Certainly Keats was mistaken in thinking that his physical condition would have allowed him to do anything in the apothecary line: but that he was shortly to be sent to Italy had evidently not entered his head. Not till a letter to Fanny on July 5th did he make any mention of Italy. 'They talk of my going to Italy.' His reaction was instant. ''Tis certain I shall never recover if I am to be so long separate from you.' Yet he acquiesced. He was not strong enough to resist the plans of his well-meaning friends, partly because of his physical weakness, partly because he had no money and his friends were providing him with some for the specific purpose of going to Italy, but above all, surely, because to refuse involved telling them why it would be fatal for him to go. It meant a public confession to his friends of the nature of his love for Fanny.

It is public to us today: and it has been ever since 1878 when Harry Buxton Forman had the courage and conviction to publish Keats's letters to Fanny Brawne. It is not easy to remember how secret Keats and Fanny kept it. 'Your name never passes my lips,' Keats wrote to her, 'do not let mine pass yours.' Concealment like a worm in the bud devoured his power to resist being sent to

Italy, although he knew it was a sentence not only of death, which he could have borne, in pain but almost with equanimity with Fanny near, but of torture, with her far away.

Twice — to Shelley and to Taylor — he speaks of going to Italy as like 'marching up to a battery'. To Taylor, as the closer friend, he puts it more nakedly. 'This journey to Italy wakes me at daylight every morning and haunts me horribly. I shall endeavour to go though it be with the sensation of marching up against a Battery.' Sending consumptives to Italy was common form in those days. It was the stock advice of the physician. But long before the physician recommended it for Keats, Brown had proposed it in his letter to George telling of Keats's illness. The letter could hardly have been written before the middle of March, because George did not reply to it until June 18th, and it would not have been possible even for Brown's robust optimism to have written before then that Keats was in the condition he reported to George.

> Brown says you are really recovered, that you eat, drink, sleep and walk five miles without weariness, this is positive, and I believe you nearly recovered but your perfect recovery depends on the future . . . Since your health requires it to Italy you must and shall go.

I may be unjustly suspicious of Brown; but I feel that his sanguine account of Keats was intended as much to justify himself for what he was about to do — namely, turn Keats out of Wentworth Place — as to comfort George. I also feel that Brown started the Italian plan as much with the idea that it would separate Keats from Fanny as with the idea that the climate would benefit his health. Others of Keats's friends — as we might guess from his letter about the 'laughers' — made no secret of this collateral benefit of the exile to Italy. Miss Reynolds wrote to Mrs. Dilke:

> I hear that Keats is going to Rome, which must please all his friends on every account. I sincerely hope it will benefit his health. Poor fellow! His mind and spirits must be

bettered by it, and absence may probably weaken, if not break off, a connection that has been a most unhappy one for him.

Of those of Keats's close friends who knew her, apparently the only ones who sincerely liked Fanny were the Dilkes. The others regarded their separation as a blessing to him. In the misery of separation Keats denounced them bitterly to Fanny:

> Do you suppose it possible I could ever leave you? You know what I think of myself and what of you. You know that I should feel how much it was my loss and how little yours. My friends laugh at you! I know some of them — when I know them all I shall never think of them again as friends or even acquaintance. My friends have behaved well to me in every instance but one, and there they have become tattlers, and inquisitors into my conduct: spying upon a secret I would rather die than share it with anybody's confidence. *(Letter 223)*

In a mild mood, with Fanny near, Keats could say quietly of them: 'If their best is not our best, it is not their fault.' We may believe that to be as near the truth as the harsher judgment. But how little they understood of Keats! Perhaps we, had we been in their place, should have understood no more than they. We might have believed that it was 'the best thing that could happen' that he should be sent away to Italy; we might even have subscribed our penny to the good cause.

But now we know what they did not know — what Keats would have died rather than tell them — and we see as if we were God's spies, the suppressed pain that lay beneath Keats's words to Brown.

> Fact is, I have so many kindnesses done me by so many people, that I am cheveaux-de-frised with benefits which I must jump over or break down. *(Letter 218)*

He could do neither. Kindness sent him to Italy; kindness flayed him alive.

He postponed thinking about the journey to Italy as long as he could. He could not bear to add to his load of misery while he was in Kentish Town. Once Hunt took him for a drive to Hampstead, and they sat together on a bench in Well Walk — where in the Bentleys' house he had lived with his brothers, watched Tom die, and whence he had gone to his first meeting with Fanny. 'He suddenly turned on me, his eyes swimming with tears, and told me he was dying of a broken heart. He must have been wonderfully excited to make such a confession, for his spirit was lofty to a degree of pride.' So Hunt wrote in 1823. Keats's torment reached breaking-point when, at Hunt's house, a letter from Fanny was withheld from him by the spite of a dismissed servant. Perhaps it was her reply to the last of his known letters to her — that in which, in the midst of his despair, he wrote pathetically: 'I enclose a passage from one of your letters which I want you to alter a little — I want (if you will have it so) the matter expressed less coldly to me.' Whatever it was, the opening and withholding of one of Fanny's letters was a fearful shock to him. 'He wept for several hours, and resolved, notwithstanding Hunt's entreaties, to leave the house. He went to Hampstead that same evening,' says Mrs. Gisborne. He probably went straight to Fanny. Mrs. Brawne insisted on his remaining at her house. There she and Fanny nursed him for his last few weeks in England.

'He has many times talked over the few happy days at your house — the only time when his mind was at ease,' Severn wrote to Mrs. Brawne in January 1821 from Rome. Only in this security could Keats address himself to asking Taylor to make the arrangements for his journey. It was now mid-August, although the decision was taken in early July. He left Wentworth Place and Fanny on September 13th. 'O I would that my unfortunate friend had never left your happy Wentworth Place,' cried Severn. We echo the cry.

After the news of his death came to Fanny, she waited some weeks before she was calm enough to write to Fanny Keats.

You will forgive me, I am sure, my dear Fanny, that I did not write to you before. I could not for my own sake and I would not for yours, as it was better you should be prepared for what, even knowing as much as you did, you could not expect. I should like to hear that you, my dearest Sister, are well; for myself, I am patient, resigned, very resigned. I know my Keats is happy, happier a thousand times than he could have been here, for Fanny, you do not, you never can know how much he has suffered. So much that I do believe, were it in my power I would not bring him back. All that grieves me now is that I was not with him, and so near it as I was. Some day my dear girl I will tell you the reason and give you additional cause to hate those who should have been his friends, and yet it was a great deal through his kindness for me for he foresaw what would happen, he at least was never deceived about his complaint, though the Doctors were ignorant and unfeeling enough to send him to that wretched country to die, for it is now known that his recovery was impossible before he left us, and he might have died here with so many friends to soothe him and me *me* with him . . .

One hesitates to comment on that letter, so genuine is its grief. But it shows that Fanny believed that Keats's friends had forced them apart at the end. That does not affect the truth of her other statement that Keats acquiesced in being sent to Italy because he desired to spare her the witness of his actual death. I believe that: it is a characteristic gesture of the Keats we know — chivalrous and heroic. Yet I am sure that the longing to stay with her was dominant in him, and the longing to keep him was dominant in her. That his and her desire could not prevail was due, first, to the fact that well-meaning friends had taken control of his destiny — friends who were either completely ignorant of his passion for Fanny, or understood it only so much that there was mingled with their sincere belief that he might recover in Italy an equally sincere belief that it would be good for him if

Fanny and he were parted. The only way Keats could have resisted their good offices was by telling them the truth: that separation from Fanny would kill him. He could not do it. He clung to his secret, and went to his agony.

I wrote in *Keats and Shakespeare*: 'Fanny Brawne killed him. That is true; but it is a partial truth.' It is not even a partial truth, and it was a terrible thing to say, though I said it in good faith, ignorant of the very existence of the evidence that has made such a judgment for ever impossible. I recant it entirely. In the sense in which something other than pthisis may be said to have killed Keats, in the same sense in which it was meaningful to say 'Fanny Brawne killed Keats', the opposite is the truth. Separation from Fanny Brawne killed him.

But this radical change in my conception of Fanny Brawne does not invalidate any one of my interpretations of Keats's poems. For example, I believe, just as firmly as I did twenty-five years ago that Keats's love for Fanny is the underlying theme of *Lamia*. It must never be forgotten that Keats dreaded the onset of love for a woman in himself lest it would burn him up, or that, in imagining it, he felt 'an awful warmth about my heart — like a load of immortality'. Would his passion for Fanny be his salvation or his destruction? To say that Fanny was the *Lamia* of his imagination is surely not to be cruel to her, or unfair to him. Is not the Lamia lovely and kind? Does Lycius-Keats ever think otherwise of her than as his dream of beauty and the ministrant of life to him? Does he not, when her loveliness and love is taken from him, die immediately?

The working out of a theme, appropriated by his deepest experience, in the creative imagination of a poet such as Keats, is not a literal translation. I did not write *Keats and Shakespeare* for 'the shallow people who take everything literally', but for those who are prepared to believe, as Keats himself believed, that 'a man's life of any worth is a continual allegory'. I believe that my interpretation of the 'allegory' of Keats's life in *Keats and Shakespeare* is substantially true. The fact that Fanny Brawne was not, as I then supposed, an unworthy object of Keats's consuming passion, but a worthy one, is comforting in itself, but it makes little difference to the effect of the passion on Keats. If anything it makes my interpretation of *Lamia* more credible. The Lamia did not kill Lycius: but separation from her surely did.

One cannot insist too strongly, at least with those for whom such statements have meaning, on the significance for an understanding of Keats's life of his own statement about Milton which I have already quoted. 'There was working in him that same sort of thing which operates in the world to the end of a Prophecy's being accomplish'd.' Such a statement is either full of meaning or nonsense: there is no possibility of taking a middle line about it. One of the few things of which I am convinced is that 'that same sort of thing' was working in Keats. Keats said that the great prerogative of poetry was that its extraordinary beauties were better described in themselves than by a volume; so it is the great prerogative of a nature such as Keats's that, in the last resort, he is only to be explained by himself; he must be treated as he would have had us treat 'a page of full Poetry or distilled Prose', that is to say 'wander with it, and muse upon it, and reflect upon it and bring home to it, and prophesy upon it, and dream upon it, until it becomes stale — but when will it do so? Never'. That injunction must be deepened as befits when the object of our contemplation is the whole life and work of a young man of genius, who enjoyed greatly and suffered greatly and in a brief five years rose to such a height of poetry as has been reached by no one of like age. If the injunction is obeyed, then I am certain that the life and work of Keats will more and more appear a revelation of that mystery which he tried to express when he imagined the Grecian Urn as the friend of man, saying to him:

> Beauty is Truth, Truth Beauty — That is all
> Ye know on earth, and all ye need to know.

There is revealed in the life and work of Keats — I know not how — a strange and predestined identity of Truth and Beauty.

His life and work are a mysterious and simple whole: a spiritual universe in which we enter, where everything is itself and is more than itself, a continual Allegory, a Prophecy being accomplish'd, a figurative Scripture. These are Keats's own phrases for a quality he discerned in the life and works of the man of great genius. To understand or glimpse their meaning we must speculate on Keats himself. *He* is the key to his own meaning. There is no other. What, for instance, does he mean by saying 'One of the most mysterious of semi-speculations is, one would suppose, that of one Mind's imagining into another. Things may be described by a Man's self in parts so as to make a grand whole which that Man himself would scarcely inform to its excess'? The answer is to be found in his own life and work. The moment comes when we simply see that something greater than himself is uttering itself in all his perfect and his partial achievements, so that his partial achievements seem even bigger with meaning than his perfect ones. There is a terrible completeness about Keats. His frustrations are consummations. The imperfect is perfect.

It is a mystery, and it is simplicity itself. Life or God is speaking through this wonderful instrument of his purposes. At the end of his agony, when we listen once again to the words through the boiling phlegm: 'Severn — I — lift me up, for I am dying. I shall die easy. Don't be frightened! Thank God, it has come,' we can only cry: 'Servant of God, well done! Servant of Life, well done!'

'I am certain of nothing', Keats wrote three years before his death, 'but of the Holiness of the heart's affections and the truth of Imagination. What the Imagination seizes as Beauty must be Truth whether it existed before or not — for I have the same idea of all our Passions as of Love: they are all in their sublime creative of essential Beauty.' What did he mean? When we have followed his life to the end, we know — as perhaps Keats himself, when he wrote those words, did not know. The prophecy was accomplish'd in him.

There is one document with which a champion of Fanny

Brawne has to come to terms. It is the draft of a letter which she wrote to Charles Brown on December 26th, 1829. He was proposing to write and publish a biographical memoir of Keats, and he asked her permission to print a letter which Keats had written to him about her from Rome and also 'those poems addressed to you which you permitted me to copy'. He naturally promised that he would 'scrupulously avoid intimating who you are, or in what part of England you reside . . . Your name will be as secret to the world as before'. He indicates his own sense of the difficulty she will feel.

> We live among strange customs; for had you been husband and wife, though but for an hour, every one would have thought himself at liberty publicly to speak of, and all about you; but as you were only so in your hearts, it seems, as it were, improper.

Fanny's draft reply to this letter is a fascinating document. It is the most intimate revelation of herself we possess, with the possible exception of the letter in which she unbosomed her grief to Fanny Keats. But in that she was uttering herself to a younger girl of whose own grief and innocence she must be tender. In her letter to Brown, with all its corrections and deletions, we come as near as we are allowed to come to the secret emotions of Fanny's soul — to the mixture of deep emotion and self-control, of forthrightness and intense reserve in the living woman who took entire possession of Keats's heart. She is ten years older — a woman where she had been a girl, and a woman who has learned the necessity of protective armour. She is writing to Brown, and therefore on the defensive.

In any case she would have been disquieted and embarrassed by his request. But it came to her at a time when something almost as terrible as Keats's death had happened to her. Only four weeks before, her mother had been burned to death in the house at Wentworth Place where the Brawnes were still living. Brown, who was in Italy, did not know of Mrs. Brawne's horrible death, or he would not have written. Fanny, characteristically, does not breathe a word of the tragedy to him. Mrs. Brawne had been deeply implicated in her daughter's unhappy love. Keats had loved her too, and she and Fanny had nursed him tenderly during his last weeks in England. At the moment when she received Brown's letter Wentworth Place must have seemed to Fanny a house of doom, and Brown's letter must have opened the old wounds to the depth.

The letter thus calls for allowance and patience in interpretation; moreover it is manifestly the work of a woman of no ordinary intelligence, who will not wear her heart upon her sleeve for daws to peck at. Nevertheless, it gives us an authentic revelation of the same Fanny of whom we have brief and tantalizing glimpses towards the end of Keats's life and after his death. This is the Fanny whom her mother felt it was impossible to try to persuade to break off her engagement to Keats. 'The thing must take its course.' This is the Fanny who said to her mother 'I believe he must soon die, and when you hear of his death tell me immediately. I am not a fool'. This is the Fanny of whom Brown wrote to Severn: 'It is now five days since she heard it. I shall not speak of the first shock, nor of the following days — it is enough she is now pretty well — and thro'out she has shown a firmness of mind which I little expected from one so young and under such a load of grief'. Colvin also tells that Brown, in a mutilated letter of which I have no further knowledge, 'gave glimpses of moods in her, apparently hysterical, of alternate forced gaiety and frozen silence'.

Fanny Brawne's reply is remarkable for several qualities — its self-control, its extraordinary effort at honesty, and its subtlety in setting out what was a very complex reaction to Brown's request.

She begins by saying that she is answering Brown's letter on the day she received it. But, 'although I received it only this morning, in the hours that have intervened before I sit down to answer it my feelings have entirely changed on the subject of the request it contains'. Had she answered instantly 'I should have told you that I considered myself so entirely unconnected with

Mr. Keats except by my own feelings that nothing published respecting him could affect me; but I now see it differently'.

She explains her changed attitude. 'We have all our little world in which we figure and I cannot help expressing some disinclination at the idea that the few acquaintance I have should be able to obtain such a key to my sensations.' But that, she hastens to add, does not mean that she will refuse Brown's request. 'Perhaps when I assure you that though my opinion has changed my intention of complying in every respect with your wishes remains, you will think I am mentioning my objections to make a favour of my consent, but indeed, my dear Mr. Brown, if you do, you mistake me entirely.'

It is only to justify myself, I own, that I state all I think ... I assure you I should not have hinted your wishes were painful to me did I not feel the suffering myself to be even alluded to was a want of pride. So far am I from possessing overstrained delicacy that the circumstance of its being a mere love-story is the least of my concern. On the contrary, had I been his wife I should have felt my present reluctance would have been so much stronger that I think I must have made it my request that you would relinquish your intention.

We may pause at this point. Fanny's first impulse had been to say 'I consider myself so entirely unconnected with Mr. Keats except by my own feelings that nothing published concerning him can affect me'. It is worth remembering that that *is* what Fanny wanted to say. That is the spontaneous Fanny speaking — the forthright Fanny whom we glimpse at the very beginning of her relation to Keats. She says, or wanted to say: 'Provided my identity is entirely concealed, publish anything — letters about me, poems to me.'

Then came her second thoughts. The reason why she mentions them is 'to justify herself' against the imputation of want of proper pride in giving the permission, 'in suffering herself to be even alluded to'. She herself feels that she *is* lacking in what others would call proper pride, or womanly reserve. Yet she owes it to herself not to let it appear that this is so. There is an obvious conflict between the spontaneous Fanny and the reflecting one. Her inward sense that she is connected with Keats only by her own feelings is denied by the fact that she is connected with him in the minds of certain people who know that she is the woman about whom the letter was written and to whom the poems were addressed. Some of them are within her circle of present acquaintance, some are outside it. Both will impute to her want of pride in permitting them to be published. She will have enabled the former to obtain a key to her sensations which she is reluctant that they shall have. (Fanny has crossed out 'feelings' and replaced it by 'sensations': that characteristic word of Keats, which she uses as Keats used it.) We have only to think of the shock given to the proprieties of fifty years later by the publication of Keats's letters to Fanny to realize what she risked, in permitting the publication of the poems to herself, among those of her acquaintances who knew that she was the woman. To have been the willing object of so devouring and so sensuous a passion was almost to be damned.

She denies, very rightly, that she possesses 'overstrained delicacy', and directly contradicts Brown's argument that it was only because Keats and she were not married that the publication might be considered indecorous. It is the exact contrary as far as she is concerned. If she had been Keats's wife, she would have had to refuse the permission. The reasons were indeed obvious. She would have been connected with Keats quite otherwise than by her own feelings alone; she would have felt a quite different responsibility; and she would never have dreamed of giving to the wide world a key to her own sensations or her husband's. Brown's lack of sensitiveness deserved the rebuke. It is the fact that she was not married to Keats that makes it possible for her to give her permission. Except for a few their connection is unknown to the world. 'The only thing that saves me now is that so very few [of my acquaintance] can know I am in any way implicated and that of those few I may hope the greater number may never see the book in question. Do then entirely as you please. . . .'

She begins another train of thought.

'Be assured that I comply with your wishes rather because they are yours than with the expectation that any good can be done.' She does not believe that Brown's projected memoir will raise Keats's reputation. (One may add that Brown's memoir is extant, and is a lifeless and disappointing affair, warped by an obsession of revenge on the *Quarterly*, and at times unpleasantly disingenuous where Brown himself is concerned. Had it been published, it would have done nothing to raise Keats's reputation in the eyes of others than the few who already admired his poetry.) Then Fanny goes on to say something which has been often quoted to damn her.

I fear the kindest act would be to let him rest for ever in the obscurity to which unhappy circumstances have condemned him. Will the writings that remain of his rescue him from it? You can tell better than I, and are more impartial on the subject, for my wish has long been that his name, his very name could be forgotten by everyone but myself — that I have often wished most intensely.

Her next remark is deleted, but it belongs to the same train of thought

I was more generous ten years ago: I should not now like ['endure', is crossed out] the odium of being connected with one who was working up his way against poverty and every sort of abuse.

Since the sentence was crossed out, it would be wrong to hold it against Fanny. Since I do not hold it against her, I may stress its importance. The honesty of Fanny's mind is impressive. She admits, to herself at least, that ten years — it was almost exactly ten years from the Christmas Day of 1819 — have changed her. Then she was prepared actively to share in Keats's struggle against adverse circumstance; now, though she could endure, she would dislike the odium of being connected with one who was a failure, whose life was an unavailing struggle against adversity and his name 'writ in water'.

Again two Fannys are revealed: a private Fanny and a public Fanny. The first clings to and cherishes the memory of her love; the second is sensitive to and careful of her reputation. They are different persons, though they are one, and with different motives, they desire the same thing: that Keats should be forgotten.

The most necessary, and the most difficult, thing to do in order to judge fairly this attitude of Fanny's, is to get clean out of our minds the notion that Fanny was now, or ever had been, concerned with Keats as a poet. She was not. And the fact that she was not had been a great comfort and delight to Keats while he lived. One might almost say it was a necessary condition of Keats's falling in love with her. He wanted to be loved simply for himself as a man. He wrote to her on July 8th, 1819:

> I am at the diligent use of my faculties here, I do not pass a day without sprawling some blank verse or tagging some rhymes; and here I must confess that (since I am on that subject) I love you the more in that I believe you have liked me for my own sake and for nothing else. I have met with women whom I really think would like to be married to a Poem and given away by a Novel.

That counted for much with Keats. It may have caused some of his friends to shake their heads, just as it causes some of Fanny's champions to ignore it. But those who, in their zeal to defend her, maintain that she was a girl who had an admiration for Keats's poetry and cared deeply about it, are inventing an imaginary person. Her surpassing title to our affection is that she did love him simply for himself. Assuredly something of Keats's poetic genius irradiated him as a man, the more so because Keats's poetic genius was in a peculiar sense the emanation and expression of the whole man. But in Keats as a poet Fanny Brawne was not interested. To point the contrast crudely — Fanny Brawne was not, and never would have been, a Mary Shelley, or anything like her.

As she had not been in love with Keats's poetry or with Keats as a poet, so ten years later she was not vitally interested in any attempt to establish his poetic fame. If his character as a man could be vindicated — that was another matter. We may follow her letter to the end, before considering it further.

I entirely agree with you that if his life is to be published no part ought to be kept back, for all you can show is his character. His life was too short and too unfortunate for anything else. I have no doubt that his talents would have been great, not the less for their being developed rather late, which I believe was the case. All I fear is whether he has left enough to make people believe that. If I could think so, I should consider it right to make that sacrifice to his reputation that I now do to your kind motives. Not that even the establishment of his fame would give me the pleasure it ought. Without claiming too much constancy for myself I may truly say that he is well-remembered by me and that, satisfied with that, I could wish no one but myself knew he had ever existed; but, I confess, as he was so much calumniated and suffered so much from it, it is perhaps the duty of those who loved and valued him to vindicate him also, and if it can be done, all the friends that time has left him, and I above all, must be deeply indebted to you.

I am glad you feel that Mr. Hunt gives him a weakness of character that only belonged to his ill health. Mr. Hazlitt, if I remember rightly some remarks used five or six years ago, is still more positive in fixing it on him.

I should be glad if you could disprove I was a very poor judge of character ten years ago and probably overrated every good quality he had; but surely they go too far on the other side. After all, he was but four and twenty when his illness begun and he had gone through a great deal of vexation before . . .

There the draft letter ends.

One's first reaction is that Fanny is more concerned with her own reputation than we should like. The letter is an uncomfortable document for those who try to sentimentalize Fanny. Since neither Keats nor Fanny were sentimentalists themselves, that is a good thing. But at the same time it is not an easy document to interpret. For Fanny was a person with a great deal of self-control; she has uncommon honesty, and an unusual capacity for self-analysis. However much we might like her to pretend, she is not going to pretend. At the first reading we feel that there is only a trace in her letter of the woman who jealously cherishes, in a secrecy that it is sacrilege to disturb, the memory of her love; and that the preponderant Fanny is the woman who is now nearing thirty and concerned for her reputation, and perhaps for her prospects of marriage. She regards her connection with Keats as a secret — that pleases the sentimentalist in us — but also as a disreputable secret: which is disconcerting to him. It is a disreputable secret in the exact sense: something which is not necessarily bad in itself but which (if disclosed) will bring her into disrepute in 'the little world in which she figures'.

More than one kind of disrepute is involved. First, there is the disrepute of being the consenting object of such a passion as Keats felt. Here it seems to me that, in the middle-class world of 1829, Fanny's fears were abundantly justified; and although she hoped that very few of the very few who knew that she was the object of Keats's passion would read the book containing the poems to herself, she was courageous indeed in giving Brown permission to publish them. Second, there is the disrepute of being connected, as she had been, with one who was struggling against poverty and obloquy. Fanny's aversion to this is harder to sympathize with. But again there is cause for admiration in her courage in admitting to Brown that she had changed from the girl of ten years before and that now, though she could endure it, she would not like the public association. Thirdly, there is the disrepute of having loved one whose character was represented as that of a weakling. She thinks she may have overrated Keats's manly qualities, but even his would-be defenders go too far in underestimating them. She would be glad if Brown could correct the picture, and vindicate her choice.

The most astonishing change that has taken place in regard to Keats in the last hundred years is the change in the estimate of his character. That has been nothing less than a revolution. From having been regarded as the weakest and most morally deplorable of the romantic poets, he has come to be regarded as the bravest and sanest: so that it is peculiarly difficult for us to realize how low his character stood even among the few who had not known him personally yet admired his poetry. The nearest we can get to an accurate description of his reputation as a man in 1829 is the passage in the preface to Monckton Milnes's *Life and Letters*. That was published in 1848, when Keats's poetical genius was beginning to be more widely recognized — nearly twenty years after Fanny Brawne's letter.

> I had to consider what procedure was most likely to raise the character of Keats in the estimation of those most capable of judging it. I saw how grievously he was misapprehended even by many who wished to see in him only what was best. I perceived that many, who heartily admired his poetry, looked on it as the product of a wayward, erratic genius, self-indulgent in conceits, disrespectful of the rules and limitations of Art, not only unlearned but careless of knowledge, not only exaggerated but despising proportion. I knew that his moral disposition was assumed to be weak, gluttonous of sensual excitement, querulous of severe judgment, fantastical in its tastes, and lackadaisical in its sentiments. He was all but universally believed to have been killed by a stupid savage article in a review, and to the compassion generated by his untoward fate he was held to owe a certain personal interest, which his poetical reputation hardly justified.

The very fact that someone of the social eminence of Monckton Milnes had undertaken the task of rehabilitating him was indicative of a change for the better in the twenty years that followed Fanny's letter. In 1829 Keats's character stood even lower than Milnes described it. Can we wonder that Fanny's chief concern was for the vindication of his character rather than his genius, or that she shrank from the odium of being associated with him, otherwise than in the secrecy of her own memories? If the main concern of Milnes was to 'raise Keats's character' — how much more must it have been the concern of Fanny, and how hopeless the enterprise must have appeared to her, in 1829. To be known even to the few as having loved and been loved by such a man was a daunting prospect. Keats was no aristocrat like Shelley and Byron, he did not belong to the respectable middle class like Wordsworth and Coleridge. He was vulgar and lax and low.

Nevertheless, in spite of all these misgivings, which Fanny sets down with such care and accuracy of language, she was giving Brown the permission for which he asked. She was willing to take the risk. And the risk was great. In the little world in which she figured nearly all of Keats's poems to Fanny — probably all — would have been regarded as absolutely shocking, and completely compromising to the girl to whom they were addressed. Even until quite recently devoted admirers of Keats's poetry have withheld their admiration from these, with the possible exception of the *Bright Star* sonnet. Matthew Arnold, who was the first boldly to set Keats as a poet with Shakespeare, could not do away with this Shakespearian element in Keats the man.

No doubt the letter comes at first with a shock to us who know that Keats was one of the *great* poets of the world and who feel that the mark of his genius, the sign of the dedicated nature, is in nearly all that he expressed. But the greatness of Keats the poet was very far from being apparent in 1829. Even in 1835 his publisher, friend and enthusiastic admirer, Taylor, did not believe that a complete edition of Keats's poetry would sell two hundred and fifty copies. It was perhaps beginning to appear possible that his poetry would not be forgotten. The Galignani volume of Coleridge, Shelley and Keats was just about to be published; it was indeed the occasion of Brown's letter. But, in any case, this was a matter on which Fanny Brawne had no conviction at all. It would have been highly gratifying if she had said to Brown that she was convinced that one day Keats's poetic genius would be recognized. But Keats would not have expected that of her, and

why should we? She, and she alone, knew the judgment Keats
had passed on himself in a mood of clarity and resignation.

'If I should die', said I to myself, 'I have left no immortal
work behind me — nothing to make my friends proud of my
memory — but I have lov'd the principle of beauty in all
things, and if I had had time I would have made myself
remember'd.' Thoughts like these came very feebly whilst
I was in health, and every pulse beat for you — now you
divide with this (may *I* say it?) 'last infirmity of noble minds'
all my reflection.

These words must have been graven in Fanny's memory. She
took them for gospel. Keats *had* left no immortal work behind
him: but if he had had time he would have made himself remembered. How could she have believed differently? Only if she had
possessed a power of poetic appreciation to which she laid no
claim at all. We can see plainly from her letters to Fanny Keats
that she deferred entirely to Keats's poetic taste and critical judgment. These were high things and beyond her, and concerning
them her lover was her oracle.

Don't you or do you admire *Don Juan*? [she wrote to
Fanny Keats]. Perhaps you like the serious parts best, but I
having been credibly informed that Lord B. is not *really* a
great poet, have taken a sort of dislike to him when serious
and only adore him for his wit and humour. I am by no
means a great poetry reader — and like few things *not* comic
out of Shakespeare. Comedy of all sorts pleases me.

Again she says, 'I go on, as usual, reading every trumpery
novel that comes my way'.
All that seems eminently natural, and so far from indicating
that she would not have made a suitable wife for Keats, it suggests
that Keats's choice in the human sense was an admirable one.
Fanny with her instinctive distaste for tragedy, her obvious 'relish
for looking on the bright side of things', and her equally obvious
willingness to be taught by Keats in matters where she professed

no judgment of her own, would have provided an excellent counterpoise to what he called his 'horrid morbidity of temperament'. Together they would have embodied that 'light and shade' in which Keats's imagination rejoiced.

But in Fanny's view the die had been cast. Keats had not had time to make himself remembered. She could not possibly have foreseen that he would one day be recognized as the most original poetic genius of his age. To her it was the simple truth that Keats's name had been 'writ in water'. What more natural than that she should have often 'wished most intensely that his name, his very name, could be forgotten by every one but myself'? Those are the only words of her letter in which her suppressed emotion is plainly audible. They ring true. And they are loyal to Keats — not to the immortal Keats, but to the living Keats whom she knew and loved, to the living Keats who knew and loved her.

It is we who take him out of life. We cannot do otherwise. We have our own, quite different loyalty to him, in obedience to which we probe and penetrate, and force our way into the secret places of his heart, and unveil that 'which he would rather die than share it with anybody's confidence'. We take upon ourselves the privilege (which Keats would have accorded only to Shakespeare) of looking upon and judging his correspondence with his beloved. That Fanny shrank from the exposure in every fibre of her being, while she was alive; that she affirmed: 'Without claiming too much constancy I may truly say he is well remembered by me and that, satisfied with that, I could wish that no one but myself knew he ever existed' is natural, and it is right. It comes from the very nature of the girl whom Keats loved and who deserved to be loved by him.

This essential loyalty and reluctance are mingled with other considerations, more worldly, and those also are natural. Fanny was not born to be an old maid or sit like Patience on a monument. She was thinking of marriage, and no doubt desired to be married. What had been between her and Keats belonged to another life, frozen in the irrevocable past, living still in her memory and (if Fanny could have had her way) in her memory alone. She had now her own life to live.

The more I study her letter — and to meditate it line by line is to come close to the heart of a mystery — the more impressed I am with Fanny Brawne's extraordinary integrity: her determination to tell the truth of her feeling to herself and to Brown. And it leaves me with the persuasion that it was her integrity, as much as her beauty, which captured the heart and mind of Keats.

CHAPTER II

FANNY KEATS

IT is strange to think that Fanny Brawne at the moment when she replied to Charles Brown's letter was living in Brown's old house, and that she was living there with Fanny Keats. Very likely she pondered her reply in the front parlour where Keats had his 'sopha bed' in February 1820, from the windows of which he had looked out to describe what he saw from his sick-bed for the entertainment of his little sister, held captive by the Abbeys in unprofitable idleness at Walthamstow. There is something remarkable in the destiny that united the two girls whom Keats loved, and who loved him, during the years from 1821 to 1833 — the interregnum between Keats's physical death and the beginnings of his acknowledged immortality.

Keats's last letter to his sister was written to his dictation by Fanny Brawne, on September 11th, 1820, two days before he left Mrs. Brawne's house. 'It is not illness that prevents me from writing but as I am recommended to avoid every sort of fatigue I have accepted the assistance of a friend, who I have desired to write to you when I am gone and to communicate any intelligence she may hear of me.' The strange handwriting filled his sister with foreboding, as though a dark curtain were descending to hide from her the one being who was all the world to her, who loved her and whom she loved with a child's unquestioning faith. The light was going out of her life. In another week a second letter in the unknown hand came to her, in which Fanny Brawne revealed her identity. It was delicately written in terms designed to put a shy and now bewildered girl at her ease. If there were nothing else to impel us to become Fanny Brawne's 'champions for ever', these early letters of hers to Fanny Keats would make that claim upon us. One at least of her lover's deep human concerns — undoubtedly the deepest, after his love for herself — she had made entirely her own. She would be to Fanny Keats what John had been, what John desired her to be.

Fanny Keats responded instantly to the new offer of affection, and Fanny Brawne interposed herself between Fanny Keats and the full impact of the tragedy. She protected her and confided in her. She spontaneously obeyed the letter and the spirit of Keats's own first letter to his sister. 'We ought to become intimately acquainted in order that I may not only as you grow up, love you as my only Sister, but confide in you as my dearest friend.' Fanny Brawne opened her heart to Fanny Keats as to no one else, wrestled with the Abbeys to gain some little freedom for her just as John had done, but even more pertinaciously and diplomatically, and slowly won the day. It must have been wonderful for Fanny to know not merely that she had a friend whom she could trust, a champion on whom she could rely, but to feel that what had brought and bound them together was the love they felt for their dead but ever living man. This was the secret which they shared, and which no one shared with them.

When this relation was quickly and firmly established between the two Fannys, there suddenly arrived, like a Prince in a fairy-tale, an elegant and distinguished young Spaniard, a liberal refugee from the Bourbon tyranny of Ferdinand VII, who had met Keats in Rome not long before his death, and on coming to England had sought out Keats's friends. His meeting with the dying poet must have impressed him deeply. Señor Valentine Maria Llanos y Guiterez was almost exactly the same age as Keats himself. He seems to have met Fanny Keats, who was then eighteen, at Hampstead and to have been immediately attracted by her: so much that he arranged to stay with a friend at Walthamstow in the hope of improving the acquaintance. Fanny Brawne aided and abetted the growing attachment. She wrote to Fanny Keats in October 1821.

Guiterez dined with us yesterday and told me he had seen an acquaintance of mine. After guessing for an hour to no purpose, for though I thought of you it seemed so improbable I did not mention it, my Mother found out; of course we laughed at him finely for his polite offer of calling on you. However, I have informed him your guardian is particular and cautioned him against letting the family see you are acquainted. Don Valentine Maria Llanos Guiterez is a pretty name, is it not? he himself is everything that a Spanish Cavalier ought to be. You need not be afraid of speaking to him for he is extremely gentlemanly and well-behaved.

That this tall distinguished-looking Spaniard should have known her brother in Rome and come to seek her out at Walthamstow must have seemed to shy and simple Fanny like a destiny. With Fanny Brawne's delighted assistance, she began to read Spanish poetry, *Don Quixote* and *Gil Blas* — vastly preferring Cervantes to Lesage — took lessons on the guitar, and mystified her brother George in America by inquiring of him whether he thought she had a Spanish face. It was a fairy-tale romance, the converse of the tale which her brother had told her in his first letter to her.

Perhaps you might like to know what I am writing about. I will tell you.
Many Years ago, there was a young handsome Shepherd who fed his flocks on a Mountain's Side called Latmus — he was a very contemplative sort of a Person and lived solitary among the trees and Plains little thinking — that such a beautiful Creature as the Moon was growing mad in Love with him — However so it was.   (*Letter 19*)

And so it was that not long after Fanny Keats came of age and was free of her guardian she married Señor Valentine Llanos y Guiterez, on March 30th, 1826, and lived happy ever after — or at any rate until his death at the ripe age of ninety in 1885. Fanny survived him four years and died in 1889 at the age of eighty-six.

Valentine Llanos, as he was called in England, returned to Spain with his wife in 1833, when the tyranny was over-past.

But for the twelve previous years he lived mainly in England. He became sufficiently skilful in the language to write two novels which were published and paid for. Immediately after their marriage Fanny and he lived for a time in Paris, where their first child was born; but by September 1828 they had taken Brown's old house at Wentworth Place. The old confraternity of Brown, Keats and the Dilkes was replaced by a new one of Fanny Keats and Fanny Brawne. When Mrs. Brawne met with her fatal accident in December 1829, Fanny went to live with Mr. and Mrs. Llanos next door.

Though it is hardly to be doubted that Fanny Brawne showed Fanny Llanos Brown's letter, it is not very likely that she showed her her reply. Their attitude towards Keats seemed to be much the same in that it was an intense personal attachment to the man; but, at the same time, it was bound to be vastly different. Fanny Llanos could marry and have children without any diminution of her devotion to her brother. On the contrary, since she had met her Spanish cavalier as one who had spoken with John three days before his death, her marriage was a sort of natural fruition of her love for him. There was no such chance for Fanny Brawne. Probably, Fanny Llanos had taken it for granted, from the beginning of her friendship, that Fanny Brawne could not marry anybody else. She had given her heart to John; she was his betrothed; if he had returned from Italy, they were to have married and lived in the house next door. John's lover was set above John's sister in the hierarchy of devoted women; but, of course, she must pay the price for her privilege. In any case, Fanny Brawne was getting on. She was nearly thirty now, and John himself had looked on an unmarried woman of twenty-seven as already on the shelf. So it seemed to Fanny Llanos that Fanny Brawne could not dream of marrying. After all, she had claimed, and Fanny Llanos had had no thought of disputing it, that in their love of John, she came first and Fanny Llanos second.

But Fanny Brawne, naturally enough, did dream of marrying. She would hardly have been the kind of woman whom Keats would have loved at first sight if she had not been impelled that way. But this was a thought which she did not confide in Fanny Llanos. There was no room for it in Keats's little sister's idea of the relation between Fanny Brawne and her brother. And when Fanny Brawne, at the age of thirty-two, did show signs of marrying, Fanny Llanos was shocked. She seems to have severed all relations with the friend who had done so much for her. Possibly the severance was mutual. The ideal, or romantic, basis of their relation was broken. John could continue to be the sum of all perfections to his sister, who could unite an ideal devotion to him with a complete love of her husband. But Fanny Brawne was bound to suffer damage in her eyes. Either she failed in devotion to Keats, or she failed in not making a marriage of love. There was no escape for her. She was doomed to be a fallen angel.

It is sad to think of the parting of the two Fannys. But they held together longer than any others of Keats's friends. Like another, it was his destiny to bring not peace but a sword. Nearly all those who had known him intimately in his life were at odds with one another long before the two Fannys had parted. And Fanny Brawne had at least fulfilled her unspoken compact with Keats. She was the one who had justified to the full his word of encouragement to his sister, when he foresaw his approaching end.

Keep yourself in as good hopes as possible: in case my illness should continue an unreasonable time many of my friends would I trust for my sake do all in their power to console and amuse you, at the least word from me — You may depend upon it that in case my strength returns I will do all in my power to extricate you from the Abbies.

(*Letter 221*)

That Fanny Brawne did, and did completely. I do not believe that any service to his memory would have pleased Keats better — nor any half as well.

For Keats's concern for his sister was deep and abiding. When we have made every allowance for George, the contrast between his attitude and John's towards their sister is marked. It took a great deal to drag from John any breath of criticism of his brother. The only instances I can remember relate to Fanny. When George returned to England in January 1820, Mr. Abbey complained to him about Fanny's behaviour. She was withdrawn and silent. George wrote her, before he left, a mild encomium on Abbey.

> Mr. Abbey behaved very kindly to me before I left, for which I am sure you will feel grateful. He is attentive in his commerce with his fellows in all essentials. He observes with pleasure the pleasure communicated to others; he says you sometimes look thin and pale but he thinks you have been better since you ran about a little ... A man of coarse feelings would never notice these things. He expressed surprise that neither you nor Miss A. spoke at meals, so you see it is not his wish that you should be moped or silent.

Fanny passed George's letter on to John; he would not have it. The blame was Abbey's, not Fanny's. 'George mention'd, in his Letters to us, something of Mr. Abbey's regret concerning the silence kept up in his house. It is entirely the fault of his Manner.' Later in the year, while Keats was at the Brawnes' house before leaving for Italy, Fanny complained that George had not written to her. Keats replied, in the last letter to her written in his own hand: 'George certainly ought to have written to you: his troubles, anxieties and fatigues are not quite a sufficient excuse. In the course of time you will be sure to find that this neglect is not forgetfulness.'

George's troubles, anxieties and fatigues may have been great; but they could not have been one half so great as John's. Yet in little more than a fortnight after the haemorrhage of February 1820, Keats found time and strength to write six letters to his sister, to amuse, console and hearten her in her anxiety. I doubt whether George wrote her a dozen in the whole period that passed between his leaving England in 1818 and his death in 1841. It was all the difference between an ordinary affection and a tender, imaginative love for the little girl. No wonder Fanny was prepared to believe the worst of George. He had come over from America and taken John's little bit of money just when he most needed it.

I do not think George can be acquitted of behaving insensitively both to John and Fanny. That his financial intentions were strictly honourable, there is no doubt. Dilke's verdict on this matter is conclusive, as it was to Fanny herself. But that George, when he saw his brother so often in the month immediately before the haemorrhage, should have had no inkling that he was seriously ill — this, I confess, is hard to reconcile with the kind of affection which we suppose to have existed between them, and which on John's side certainly did exist. And George's rather easy dismissal of Fanny's unhappiness at the Abbeys' is of the same order. He believed what he wanted to believe. Mr. Abbey had treated him relatively well; indeed he had added a small loan of his own to George's fresh stock of capital. George had always got on better with Mr. Abbey than John did. Being in trade, he and his ambitions were altogether more comprehensible to Abbey than John.

But not all John's conscious loyalty to George could prevent him from speaking the truth to Fanny in February 1819, when he had incurred Mr. Abbey's particular displeasure by trying, pertinaciously but in vain, to persuade him to let Fanny remain at school as she ardently desired. Mr. Abbey's mean-spirited reaction to John's rightful intervention had been to tell Fanny that John must not write to her so often. Keats replied to her letter:

Your Letter to me at Bedhampton hurt me very much. What objection can there be to your receiving a Letter from me? . . . I had always a presentiment of not being able to succeed in persuading Mr. Abbey to let you remain longer at School — I am very sorry that he will not consent. I recommend you to keep up all that you know and to learn more by yourself however little. The time will come when you will be more pleased with Life — look forward to that time and, though it may appear a trifle, be careful not to let the idle and retired Life you lead fix any awkward habit or behaviour on you — whether you sit or walk — endeavour to let it be in a seemly and if possible a graceful manner. We have been very little together: but you have not the less been with me in thought. You have no one in the world besides me who would sacrifice anything for you — I feel myself the only Protector you have. In all your little troubles think of me with the thought that there is at least one person in England who if he could would help you out of them — I live in hopes of being able to make you happy — I should not perhaps write in this manner if it were not for the fear of not being able to see you often or long together.

(Letter 113)

That is the constant spirit of John's letters to Fanny Keats. Some of the best of his letters are written to her out of the fullness of his imaginative sympathy. I think, in particular, of the letter written to her during his tour in Scotland, when he was very tired, which contains *Meg Merrilies* and *There was a naughty Boy*, and ends:

My dear Fanny I am ashamed of writing you such stuff, nor would I if it were not for being tired after my day's walking, and ready to tumble into bed so fatigued that when I am asleep you might sew my nose to my great toe and trundle me round the town like a Hoop without waking me.

(Letter 74)

It might reasonably be held that this letter, with its poems written for Fanny, is the finest thing Keats did during his Scottish journey. He lavished himself on his little sister, and his letters must have opened magic casements to her in her dull and decorous confinement. From the beginning of their correspondence he had a presentiment of their future importance to her.

You will preserve all my letters and I will secure yours — and thus in the course of time we shall each of us have a good Bundle — which, hereafter, when things may have strangely altered and god knows what happened, we may read over together and look with pleasure on times past — that now are to come.

(Letter 19)

That was in the first letter of Fanny's bundle. As she read it over in the time to come when she lived her strangely altered life in Spain, it seemed to her mysteriously prophetic, and the wonderful brother who wrote it, and all the rest of the letters ending at last in the one in a strange hand, appeared to her as something more than mortal. By a queer chance this emerges in the only contemporary description of Fanny Llanos which we have: that of Frederick Locker-Lampson, who was introduced to her in Rome in 1861 by Joseph Severn.

Whilst I was in Rome Mr. Severn introduced me to M. and Mme Valentine de Llanos, a kindly couple. He was a Spaniard, lean, silent, dusky and literary, the author of *Don Estehan* and *Sandoval*. She was fat, blonde and lymphatic, and both were elderly. *She was John Keats's sister!* I had a good deal of talk with her, or rather *at* her, for she was not very responsive. I was disappointed, for I remember that my sprightliness made her yawn; she seemed inert and had nothing to tell me of her wizard brother of whom she spoke as of a mystery — with a vague admiration but a genuine affection. She was simple and natural — I believe she is a very worthy woman. She most kindly gave me one of her brother's letters addressed to herself.

The portrait is undeniably clever. Locker-Lampson was no mean literary artist. As an impression of what Fanny Keats appeared to be at fifty-eight or so to a semi-aristocratic man of leisure and taste who admired Keats's poetry it is veracious and convincing. Between the persons there was a gulf, and a gulf also between their conceptions of Keats: but the genuineness of Locker-Lampson's admiration of her brother's poetry must have touched Fanny's heart. He had little idea of the sacrifice she was making in giving him one of her precious letters, or of the reason why she had nothing to tell him of her 'wizard brother'. What would her childish adoration and her treasured memories have meant to this literary man of the world? They would have seemed to him petty and trivial and unworthy. But in spite of her silence and unresponsiveness the essence of her attitude to her brother was conveyed in his portrait of her. 'She spoke of him as of a mystery.'

A mystery apparently quite different from the mystery of his poetic genius — the mystery that broods over

> Thou still unravish'd bride of quietness,
> Thou foster-child of silence and slow time . . .

The mystery of her brother to Fanny Llanos, grown stout and middle-aged and oddly like Queen Victoria, was the mystery of a brother who had poured his genius and his humanity into the task of irradiating her solitary childhood with love, who had promised her her own happiness and fulfilled his promise, who had given her the clue to life and then been taken away. But it was the same mystery.

A whole book has been written about the life of Fanny Keats by Marie Adami. It seems a great deal to devote to a life so uneventful, in the ordinary sense, so taken up and fulfilled by a simple domesticity in a foreign land. Yet it is not inordinate. One feels that some quintessence of Keats's spirit is being faithfully translated into the even tenor of a humdrum life. Fanny Llanos kept the fire of love quietly burning on the altar of her heart, so that her children and her children's children turned to her as to a fixed and certain refuge. What her brother had been to her in her solitariness, she became, to the measure of her capacity, to the children who surrounded her. Their mother's and grandmother's mysterious brother, the young English poet who suffered so much and died so young, whom their father and grandfather had spoken to on his death-bed, became as it were the tutelary deity of the Llanos household. When in 1935 Mrs. Adami, on her pious pilgrimage to Madrid, sought out Fanny's grandchildren and entered the flat where Fanny Llanos had lived

so long, there on the top of a mahogany wardrobe in her bedroom
was a copy of Haydon's life-mask of Keats which Fanny had
brought with her to Spain a hundred years before. During her
lifetime, it had always occupied the same place, opposite her bed,
and her grandchildren had faithfully kept it there. On Mrs.
Adami's farewell visit part of the entertainment offered her was
a rich plum cake, dark with cherries and raisins. 'I made it this
morning', said Fanny's granddaughter, 'from the recipe my
grandmother used and which she taught me — the recipe for the
cake she had watched Mrs. Jennings bake at Edmonton.'

'English must be kept up,' wrote Keats at a crucial moment in
his poetic life. Fanny Llanos had not read the letter and would
not have understood it if she had. Yet it was the same purpose
and spirit which she translated into her own idiom by handing
on Grandmother Jenning's recipe for a rich fruit cake — the one
she had helped to mix and bake at Edmonton in the happiest days
of her childhood, when John was serving his apprenticeship to
Hammond the surgeon at the big house on the other side of the
green, and she could see him every day starting off on the round
with Hammond in the gig: on hot summer days 'when the apothecary's apprentice, with a bitterness beyond aloes, thought of the
pond he used to bathe in at school', on snowy winter ones when
the schoolboys pelted Keats from behind with snowballs as he
sat in the gig waiting outside the patient's house: in the days
before Keats had begun his voyage among the realms of gold or
Fanny been led away captive to Walthamstow and Pancras Lane,
when she was still 'the little girl at her grandmother's cottage
door watching the coaches going by with her hand held up over
her sunny forehead'.

In the same spirit Fanny Keats throughout her life in the heart
of Spain remained an Englishwoman. Mrs. Adami, who devotedly
gathered up her grandchildren's recollections of her, writes:

Though she had spent fifty years in Spain she never read
or spoke the language easily, and she had kept up her own
and John's early antipathy to French. She had insisted that

her children should learn her language, and Juan, Rosa and Luis all spoke and wrote it ... Now when the grandchildren made little progress in English Señora Llanos allowed them no concessions; she always spoke to them in her own language, and those who did not make efforts to learn it had to get on with her as best they could. But they did not find her difficult to understand and the effort was always worth while; the longer they lived beside her the more fascinating and unusual their English grandmother became to them all.

After her husband's death in 1885, Señora Llanos became 'if possible, more English than ever'. She wrote to Mrs. Buxton Forman asking her to send her an English widow's bonnet. It came and she was enchanted with it. 'It delights everyone', she wrote to the sender, 'by its neatness and taste. So great a contrast to that worn by the elderly ladies here, who fancy that to be in the fashion is all that is required.' In the year of her death she asked her correspondent for a white muslin widow's cap with two streamers at the back, exactly like that worn by Queen Victoria. It came to her in a white moiré bandbox from Jay's, and she was so pleased with it that she decided to have a black one made to the same pattern for morning wear while she kept the white one for evenings. Before the copy was made she died; but her grandchildren had preserved the box and the white cap, and Mrs. Adami had the odd sensation of seeing it taken out from its box, forty-five years afterwards — 'both as fresh as if they had only just left London'. It was, in its own order, as authentic a manifestation of Keats's spirit as the manuscript of the *Ode to Autumn*.

Keats's letters to Fanny Keats began in September 1817, when she had just turned fourteen. It was a deliberate beginning of a correspondence intended to be preserved, not indeed for the delight of posterity at large, but to be a tangible bond between them, to knit them more closely together, and above all to be a permanent assurance to Fanny of her brother's presence in her life. If she could not have him, she could have his letters. One may conjecture why Keats began to write to her at this particular moment. There were several reasons. Fanny was now of an age at which she could take her part in a correspondence; Keats had begun to realize that Abbey would put difficulties in the way of their being much together; George was meditating his emigration to America, Tom's illness was increasing, it was becoming evident that Keats would be her 'only Protector'; and Keats had begun a series of long absences from London. All these considerations counted; but, I think, the final fillip was given to his purpose by his work upon *Endymion*. In that poem Endymion's 'little Peona sister' is his confidante; and Keats desired to make his imagination a reality. 'We ought to become intimately acquainted in order that I may not only, as you grow up, love you as my only Sister, but confide in you as my dearest friend.' That is exactly the relation between Endymion and Peona in the poem.

It would take time to establish, and Keats's sympathy with his sister was far too sensitive for him to try her capacity beyond her power. For the first eighteen months he simply set himself to amuse, entertain, console and encourage her. But by the spring of 1819, when troubles and perplexities came thick upon him, the tone and content of his letters begins to change. It may be simply that he could no longer detach himself so completely from his own anxieties that he could wholly surrender himself to his sister's concerns; and he could not help communicating his own to her. Or it may be that, despite his love for Fanny Brawne, he felt an increased need to confide in a girl whose love for him, he knew, was entire. Probably, it was both together. Anyhow it is notable that in several of his letters to his sister in 1819, he no longer makes the complete adjustment to her which he made spontaneously before. Whether he tried her beyond her capacity, we cannot know for certain; but I should think he did.

The more serious note enters in when we should expect it — in May 1819, when the *Odes* were written, and Keats was facing the beginning of his separation from Fanny Brawne. News had come from George — 'all things considering, good news' — and Keats promised to bring his sister the letter to Walthamstow and read it to her. By an unfortunate accident the letter, while going the rounds of those concerned, was destroyed by Haslam; so Keats would have to tell her all he could from memory.

> I want also to speak to you concerning myself. Mind I do not purpose to quit England as George has done; but I am afraid I shall be forced to take a voyage or two.
>
> (*May 26th, 1819*)

He went to see her the next day, and explained to her that he had now to make a living, and that his choice seemed to be between going as a surgeon on an Indiaman and making another attempt to produce a successful book of poetry; and he promised to come to see her again within a week to tell her his decision. On June 9th he wrote his excuse for failing.

> I shall be with you next Monday at the farthest. I could not keep my promise of seeing you again in a week because I am in so unsettled a state of mind about what I am to do. I have given up the Idea of the Indiaman; I cannot resolve to give up my favorite Studies: so I purpose to retire into the Country and set my Mind at work once more.

But on the Monday, too, he had to write his excuse. His sore throat is too bad to permit his walking the six miles, and he cannot now afford to come by coach. He will come on Wednesday. Again, he fails and explains why.

> Still I cannot afford to spend money by Coach hire and still my throat is not well enough to warrant my walking. I went yesterday to ask Mr. Abbey for some money; but I could not on account of a Letter he showed me from my Aunt's Solicitor — You do not understand the business — I trust it will not in the end be detrimental to you. I am going to try the Press once more and to that end shall retire to live cheaply in the country and compose myself and verses as well as I can . . . I was preparing to enquire for a Situation with an Apothecary, but Mr. Brown persuades me to try the

press once more; so I will with all my industry and ability.

(Letter 132)

On July 6th he writes to her from Shanklin. Another letter has come from George, but he cannot send it because it is full of matters of business, to which he must refer.

> I think I told you the purpose for which I retired to this place — to try the fortune of my Pen once more, and indeed I have some confidence in my success; but in every event, believe me my dear sister, I shall be sufficiently comfortable, as, if I cannot live that life of competence and society I should wish, I have enough knowledge of my gallipots to ensure me an employment and maintenance.

Naturally he felt it impossible to tell his sister that he had fallen desperately in love, and he had told her no more of his troubled situation than she could understand. He was still able to fill the rest of his letter with a charming account of his journey to the Isle of Wight and the attractions of Shanklin. To her, too, he gave the benefit of Jem Rice's characteristic mot about the ham. 'He bought a ham the other day for says he "Keats, I don't think a Ham is a wrong thing to have in a house".'

But as the tension within himself increased, he found it impossible to keep it out of his letters even to Fanny. On August 28th he wrote to her from Winchester that he had completed the tragedy of which he thought he had told her, though he had not. 'But there I fear all my labour will be thrown away for the present as I hear Mr. Kean is going to America.' Then he shows Fanny what must have been to her a quite unfamiliar aspect of himself.

> I some time since sent the Letter I told you I had received from George to Haslam with a request to let you and Mrs. Wylie see it: he sent it back to me for very insufficient reasons without doing so; and I was so irritated by it that I would not send it travelling about by the post any more: besides the postage is very expensive. I know Mrs. Wylie will think this a great neglect. I am sorry to say my temper gets the better of me — I will not send it again.

John irritable must have been a new and rather astonishing phenomenon to her. But it breaks out again.

Why have you not written to me? Because you were in expectation of George's letter and so waited? Mr. Brown is copying out our Tragedy of Otho the great in a superb style — better than it deserves — there as I said is labour in vain for the present. I had hoped to give Kean another opportunity to shine. What can we do now? There is not another actor of Tragedy in all London or Europe. The Covent Garden Company is execrable. Young is the best among them and he is a ranting, coxcombical tasteless actor — A Disgust A Nausea — and yet the very best after Kean. What a set of barren asses are actors!

That outburst must have been clean above Fanny's head. And his next letter written to her on October 16th, immediately after he had abandoned Westminster and journalism and returned to Wentworth Place and Fanny, is in a totally unfamiliar tone.

My Conscience is always reproaching me for neglecting you for so long a time. I have been returned from Winchester this fortnight and as yet I have not seen you. I have no excuse to offer. I should have no excuse.

From beginning to end it is devoid of the affectionate gossip with which he was wont to entertain his sister. It is easy to account for his inability at this time to enter into her world. He had just surrendered to his love for Fanny Brawne, as to a destiny. It is the most preoccupied and detached of all his letters to his sister. By December 20th he had regained his poise in writing to her. Although the letter he wrote to her on that day is a very grown-up letter, in which he tells her of his concerns, it is suited to her capacity, and he has not forgotten that she is an anxious and bewildered girl of sixteen. He puts as brave a face as he possibly can on his situation, even at the cost of seeming to have neglected her.

When I saw you last [apparently on November 18th] you ask'd me whether you should see me again before Christmas. You would have seen me if I had been quite well. I have not, though not unwell enough to have prevented me — not indeed at all — but fearful lest the weather should affect my throat which on exertion or cold continually threatens me.

(Letter 170)

He has, on his doctor's advice, got a warm great-coat and ordered some thick shoes. So furnished, he will come to see her, if it holds a little fine, before Christmas Day. 'My hopes of success in the literary world', he assures her, 'are now better than ever.' Keats certainly did not believe that; but it would help to make Fanny happy. Towards the end of his letter he sets himself to do so.

This moment Bentley brought a Letter from George for me to deliver to Mrs. Wylie — I shall see her and it before I see you. The direction was in his best hand, written with a good Pen and sealed with a Tassie's Shakespeare such as I gave you — We judge of people's hearts by their Countenances; may we not judge of Letters in the same way? If so, the Letter does not contain unpleasant news — Good or bad spirits have an effect on the handwriting. This direction is at least unnervous and healthy. Our Sister is also well, or George would have made strange work with Ks and Ws. The little Baby is well or he would have formed precious [queer?] vowels and Consonants — He sent off the Letter in a hurry, or the mail bag was rather a warm birth, or he has worn out his Seal, for the Shakespeare's head is flattened a little. This is close muggy weather as they say at the Ale houses.

That is in the characteristic vein of his letters to his sister. But he could not make it good with the promised visit. Two days later he was sorry to say 'I have been and continue rather unwell'. His next letter to her was written three days after the haemorrhage.

There could be no more convincing evidence of the depth of his concern for her than the fact that he wrote her no less than six letters between February 6th and February 26th, 1820 — all to reassure her, and to warn her to take care of her health. He tells her, in his most delightful manner, all that he sees from his sopha bed in the front parlour — the pot-boy, the old women with bobbins and red cloaks and unpresuming bonnets, the gipsies, the old French émigré, the man with the wooden clock.

How much more comfortable than a dull room upstairs, where one gets tired of the pattern of the bed curtains. Besides I see all that passes — for instance now, this morning, if I had been in my own room I should not have seen the coals brought in. (*Letter 175*)

But he is forced to acknowledge that it will be a long time before he will be able to walk six miles again.

Meanwhile, Fanny was becoming more and more miserable. She was worrying about her beloved brother, who was all the world to her; and, as was inevitable, she chafed more and more at her treatment by the Abbeys, and became more silent and withdrawn. Mrs. Abbey no doubt it was who chose this moment to insist that Fanny should get rid of her dog — a spaniel. Keats found a home for it, where it was 'attended like a Prince'. But he no longer had the strength to comfort her in her miseries. He had to ask her to excuse him 'from endeavouring to give you any consolation just at present for though my health is tolerably well I am too nervous to enter into any discussion in which my heart is concerned'. Just before he left Hampstead for Kentish Town, he tried to explain more fully and to prepare her for the event which he now foreboded.

You will forgive me I hope when I confess that I endeavour to think of you as little as possible and to let George dwell upon my mind but slightly. The reason being that I am afraid to ruminate on any thing which has the shade of difficulty or melancholy in it, as that sort of cogitation is so pernicious to health, and it is only by health that I can be enabled to alleviate your situation in future. For some time you must do what you can of yourself for relief, and bear your mind up with the consciousness that your situation cannot last for ever, and that for the present you may console yourself against the reproaches of Mrs. Abbey. Whatever obligations you may have had to her you have none now as she has reproach'd you. I do not know what property you have, but I will enquire into it: be sure however that beyond the obligations that a Lodger may have to a Landlord you have none to Mr. Abbey. Let the surety of this make you laugh at Mrs. A's foolish tattle. Mrs. Dilke's brother has got your dog. She is now very well — still liable to Illness. I will get her to come and see you if I can make up my mind on the propriety of introducing a stranger into Abbey's House. Be careful to let no fretting injure your health as I have suffered it — health is the greatest of blessings — with *health* and *hope* we should be content to live, and so you will find as you grow older.   (*Letter 211*)

Keats, with neither health nor hope remaining, was speaking from his heart. Keep health and keep hope are the twin themes of all his remaining letters to Fanny. He insists upon them again and again. And in his letters to her, which are disinterestedly devoted to doing what he can to secure her future happiness, he shows more clearly than elsewhere, how deeply he was convinced that his own disease was due to his despondency and his worrying. He was mistaken. The chief cause of the anxieties that had worn him down had been the undermining of his health. It was not until August 1818, when he began his three months' vigil by the side of the dying Tom, that his confidence in life showed signs of being profoundly shaken; and that, according to the medical witness of the late Sir William Hale White, was the time when he was fatally infected with tuberculosis. He mistook cause and effect, as tubercular patients do even today when the knowledge of the disease is exact. In Keats's day the ignorance of it was abysmal. There was no means whatever of detecting the onset of the disease. The stethoscope and the clinical thermometer were unknown. Keats's illness, as he himself experienced it, must have appeared to him to be the direct effect of the psychological conditions that were its consequence. In this conviction he wrote to Fanny during his last days at the Brawnes' house.

> Do not suffer your Mind to dwell on unpleasant reflections — that sort of thing has been the destruction of my health. Nothing is so bad as want of health — it makes one envy Scavengers and Cinder-sifters. There are enough real distresses and evils in wait for every one to try the most vigorous health. Not that I would say yours are not real — but they are such as to tempt you to employ your imagination on them, rather than endeavour to dismiss them entirely. Do not diet your mind with grief, it destroys the constitution; but let your chief care be of your health, and with that you will meet with your share of Pleasure in the world — do not doubt it. If I return well from Italy I will turn over a new leaf for you. I have been improving lately, and have very good hopes of 'turning a Neuk' and cheating the Consumption. (*Letter 235*)

The optimism was assumed to comfort Fanny. Apart from that, it was Keats's farewell charge to her, though she did not know it. When, after his death, she realized that it was his last message, she seems to have obeyed it to the utmost of her power: for in Fanny Brawne's letters to her there is no indication that she grew despondent over her unpleasant situation at the Abbeys'. That it was unpleasant, even intolerable, is taken for granted by both of them; but it is a practical difficulty which they set themselves to overcome as best they could.

The last words of Keats's last letter are about his sister. He begs Brown to write a note to her. 'She walks about my imagination like a ghost — she is so like Tom.' No more than those of Fanny Brawne could he bear to have her letters opened or read. They touched the anguished nerve of unavailing love.

And yet, it seems to me, Keats's love for his little sister was not unavailing. It had awakened love in her, as it is in the nature of true love always to do. The love which Keats had called forth in her sounded in her a note to which she must always be faithful, and gave her the clue to living. 'For love alone can lend you loyalty.' Fanny's loyalty to her brother was simple and exquisite. It was something to be lived. By being lived, it brought her marriage; it brought her happiness in a serene acceptance of life; and it brought her the same quality of devotion from her children and her grandchildren.

There was in her quiet life one marvellous period. She had left England with her husband and family in 1833, and lived a secluded domestic life in Valladolid and Madrid for twenty-eight years — three years more than the whole lifetime of Keats. She was now a grandmother. Then her son-in-law was made engineer-in-chief to the new railway-system which was being built in the Papal States, and he proposed that the whole Llanos family should move with them to Rome.

Fanny's heart must have leapt at the proposal that she should live for some years in the immortal city where her brother had gone to die. The Llanos family settled there in March 1861. In that same year Joseph Severn had been appointed English Consul in Rome, and early in April Fanny Llanos and he met, by accident, in the Piazza di Spagna, apparently in the house in which Keats died. On April 6th Severn wrote to his brother.

Just now I have had a most affecting meeting with the sister, the only sister of Keats: we discovered each other this morning. For a long time we remained without being able to speak. 'Twas like a brother and sister who had parted in early life meeting after forty years. How singular that we should meet in the very place where Keats died.

They became close friends. It does not need much imagination to understand how marvellous and mysterious it seemed to Fanny to have had this meeting with the one living soul with whom her brother's life had been passed after he had faded out of her sight. The torso was completed.

For nearly four years Fanny lived in Rome. She planted two bay trees at her brother's grave, and considered with Severn the desirability of a new inscription; but only in the last year of her stay did she bring herself to allow Severn to take away her bundle of letters. Lord Houghton had asked him to read them to see whether any ought to be added to the new edition of the *Life and Letters*. Severn's report is astonishing. 'I have well examined them and cannot find anything for publication as they were all addressed to a little girl, and constrained in style.' Locker-Lampson showed more discernment than the man 'of cheerful yesterdays and confident tomorrows', and Fanny Keats rewarded it. For all his sprightliness he glimpsed something of Fanny's attitude to her brother which Severn did not see. 'She spoke of him as of a mystery.' Like another woman, she had pondered all these things in her heart.

CHAPTER III

KEATS AND ISABELLA JONES

MR. ROBERT GITTINGS'S book, *John Keats: The Living Year*, contains so much that is novel, interesting and valuable concerning Keats's life, as man and poet, during the *annus mirabilis* which began, in September 1818, with *Hyperion* and ended, in September 1819, with the *Ode to Autumn*, that it may appear ungrateful to subject an important part of it to a rigorous critical examination. But, in fact, it is such an intricate and bewildering mixture of probable and improbable conjecture, of brilliant 'detective work' and wild hypothesis, that some systematic attempt to separate the grain from the chaff must be made. Moreover, because Mr. Gittings's most revolutionary and most questionable theories have been light-heartedly endorsed by well-known literary critics, there is a very real danger that they may become current.

In the first part of this chapter I shall briefly examine, as a preliminary test of the critical method Mr. Gittings chiefly employs, the strength of the evidence on which he bases his assertion that Keats's reading of Burton's *Anatomy of Melancholy* during this year had a constant and immediate influence upon his thought and writing: so constant and so immediate, indeed, that we — or rather Mr. Gittings — can tell at any moment from Keats's poems or letters of this year, the precise point he had reached in his reading of Burton. I shall also examine, merely by way of specimen, two of Mr. Gittings's applications of this critical method to the composition of *Hyperion*.

In the second part I shall examine the evidence for the still more novel contention (which, if true, would have serious consequences for Keats's character) that the first version of the *Bright Star* sonnet was written in October 1818, and not in 1819; and that the woman about whom it was written was not Fanny

Brawne but Mrs. Isabella Jones: and I shall conclude by examining the evidence for his consequent, and even more sensational theory that Keats, in January 1819 — that is, after he had fallen in love with Fanny Brawne — was involved in a love-intrigue with Isabella Jones, the success of which he first celebrated in the verses *Hush, hush, tread softly*, and immediately afterwards in his great poem *The Eve of St. Agnes.*

In the first of these matters Mr. Gittings deals very honestly with us. Not only does he set out in an Appendix all the passages of Burton — forty in all — together with the passages of Keats which, he claims, are immediately derived from them; but at the very outset of his book (p. 5), he puts before us an example of the critical method on which he relies in this matter. He quotes three passages from Keats's journal-letter to George Keats of February-April 1819, and sets beside them three passages from Burton, from which he says they are so obviously derived that we must conclude that Keats was actually reading them at the time he wrote to George. The first is:

Friday, February 18th, 1819: Other wines of a heavy and spirituous nature transform a Man to a Silenus ... I said this same Claret is the only palate-passion I have I forgot game — I must plead guilty to the breast of a Partridge, the back of a hare, the backbone of a grouse, the wing and side of a Pheasant and a Woodcock passim.

This, Mr. Gittings says, obviously derives from

Yet these are brave men, Silenus Ebrius was no braver ... a chicken, a rabbit, rib of a rack of mutton, wing of a capon, the merry-thought of a hen, etc.

Mr. Gittings does not say that some seven hundred words separate these two phrases in Burton, or that the first comes from a denunciation of immoderate drinkers, the second from a denunciation of finicking eaters: and that there is no connection at all between them. Not that it matters very much. Had Keats never before heard of Silenus, that he had to borrow him from Burton? Had he not written about him in *Endymion?* And what has Burton's list of valetudinarian foods to do with Keats's eulogy of game?

The second parallel is this:

Friday, March 19th, 1819: This is the world — thus we cannot expect to give way many hours to pleasure — Circumstances are like Clouds continually gathering and bursting — While we are laughing the seed of some trouble is put into the wide arable land of events.

This, Mr. Gittings says, obviously derives from Burton's

Even in the midst of all our mirth, jollity and laughter, is sorrow and grief; or, if there be true happiness amongst us, 'tis but for a time: a fair morning turns to a lowering afternoon.

What greater commonplace of human experience is there than this? *Medio de fonte leporum Surgit amari aliquid.* Are we really to assume that Keats could not have thought of it for himself? Above all, when we know — for Keats himself tells us — that his reflection directly arose from the news of a specific misfortune to one of his friends. If Burton had anticipated one of Keats's peculiar felicities of expression — circumstances like gathering clouds, or the wide arable land of events — one might reasonably suppose a relation. But to suppose Keats was indebted to another for the commonplace itself is surely unsound.

The third parallel is this:

Wednesday, April 21st, 1819: La Belle Dame sans Merci.
> O what can ail thee knight at arms
> Alone and palely loitering?
> The sedge has withered from the lake
> And no birds sing.

This, says Mr. Gittings, derives from Burton's

As Bellerophon in Homer
That wandered in the woods, sad, all alone
Forsaking men's society, making great moan,
  they delight in floods and waters, desert places, to walk
alone in orchards, gardens, private walks, back lanes ...

Burton is writing of the melancholy man's love of solitude.
Even if we add to the quoted verse of *La Belle Dame*, the line
'And made sweet moan' (which is said not of the knight, but of his
enchantress) I find it impossible to believe that Keats's verses owe
anything whatever to Burton's words.

Yet these three examples of derivation Mr. Gittings puts forward as a sort of *experimentum crucis*. The connections in
each case are, apparently, self-evident to him; and he is, presum-
ably, confident that they will be self-evident to us. They are
entirely unconvincing to me.

He has gathered thirty-seven more such parallels, of which
only one is more cogent than the most cogent of these three
chosen examples, and many of which are less compulsive than the
least compulsive of them. Some, indeed, are positively incomprehensible. One example of these may be given: four lines from
The Eve of St. Agnes:

      While Porphyro upon her face doth look,
      Like puzzled urchin on an aged crone
      Who keepeth clos'd a wondrous riddle-book,
      As spectacled she sits in chimney nook.

I had supposed this might well be a memory of Keats at his
grandmother's knee. Not so, according to Mr. Gittings. It
derives from this of Burton's:

They [Fairies] are sometimes seen by old women and
children. Hierom Pauli, in his description of the city of
Bercino in Spain, relates how they have been familiarly seen
near that town, about fountains and hills; Nonnunquam
(saith Trithemius) in sua latibula montium simpliciores
homines ducunt, stupenda mirantibus ostendentes miracula,
nolarum sonitus, spectacula, etc.

Except for the mention of old women and children in Burton, and an old woman and a child in Keats, I can discover no relation of any kind between these two passages.

Mr. Gittings finds three other such 'parallels' between *The Eve of St. Agnes* and Burton. They are duly set out on p. 216 of his book, numbered 4 to 6. Not one of them, I believe, could possibly convince any unprejudiced reader. *Securus judicet orbis terrarum.* Yet on this fragile evidence Mr. Gittings assures us that 'the magic and superstition with which [Keats] loaded ... [the] original suggestion are obviously to be found in an early chapter of the *Anatomy*, precisely where we should expect to find them, in the subsection of the book entitled *A Digression of the Nature of Spirits*'. I can only suggest that Mr. Gittings has hypnotized himself into believing in resemblances which do not exist. He has, for some reason, made up his mind beforehand that because Keats undoubtedly did read Burton during the summer of 1819, he was reading him constantly throughout the year, and is determined to find evidence that he was. Further, he has made up his mind that whatever book Keats was reading during this year had a direct, immediate and visible influence upon his writing. In his own words: 'Keats's life, his letters, his words, thoughts, and his poems themselves take on the character of whatever book he is studying.' But instead of proving this he assumes it. His whole catena of 'parallels' between Burton and Keats is so neutral or inconclusive or illusory that it leaves us precisely where we were before. We knew already that Keats took the fable of *Lamia* from Burton and that he was reading Burton avidly in the late summer of 1819; we knew already that the influence of a striking phrase of Burton's is visible in the *Ode to Fanny*. But Mr. Gittings's novel proposition that the influence of Burton on Keats was continuous and visible from September 1818 onwards is neither demonstrated nor demonstrable.

Mr. Gittings's critical method is radically at fault. Let us take another example of it. We know that when Keats began *Hyperion* in September 1818, he was deeply impressed by the beauty and manner of Miss Jane Cox, whom he called Charmian. Therefore, according to Mr. Gittings, the influence of this experience of Charmian must be immediately detectable in his poem. And, of course, he detects it (p. 12)

> He had plunged in and out of love, and into the start of his poem; the cause is apparent in the blank verse lines he began to write. Twenty lines of the new strong vein, which Keats was to work deeper and deeper this year, have barely passed when there enters the figure of Thea, the 'Goddess of the infant world'. She gives at once a sensation of magnificence, of size and power, and her face suggests not the creature of Greek mythology she is supposed to be, but of another civilization altogether
>
> > When sages looked to Egypt for their lore.
>
> Keats, like the artist Joseph Severn and many of his young friends, was influenced by the Egyptian acquisitions of the British Museum, which had been described that year in a new catalogue. Yet at this particular moment it is more probable that he had a woman in mind and not an exhibit or a catalogue. That is why his goddess looks not Greek but Egyptian. The impression of dignity and grace, 'an imperial woman', the Egyptian face, 'at least a Charmian', the 'deep organ tone' and 'large utterance' of Thea, the 'tune of Mozart's' and 'the rich talk of a Charmian' all combine in the same picture. So too do the words of the poem and the phrases of his letters. Thea's feeling about her heart
>
> > > as if just there
> >
> > Though an immortal she felt cruel pain:
>
> is Keats's 'There is an awful warmth about my heart like a load of Immortality.'

But, in soberness, is there even the faintest resemblance between Thea and Charmian? Further, it is very unlikely that the name Charmian suggested the image of anything specifically Egyptian to Keats: she was the lively waiting-woman of Shakespeare's Cleopatra. By calling Miss Jane Cox a Charmian, Keats

meant simply that she was a minor Cleopatra. And in any case
Cleopatra and Charmian were Greeks, not Egyptians. So, too,
there is a gulf between 'the rich talk' of Charmian and the 'deep
organ tone' of Thea. And Mr. Gittings's final assertion that

> One hand she press'd upon that aching spot
> Where beats the human heart, as if just there,
> Though an immortal, she felt cruel pain.

is Keats's 'I feel an awful warmth about my heart like a load of
immortality', seems positively perverse. The ideas themselves
are antipodal. Keats's pain is like a 'load of immortality';
Thea's pain is in spite of her immortality. And the pain was felt
by Keats, not by Charmian. In this kind of critical prestidigita-
tion anything may become identical with its opposite.

Again, it was observed long ago (originally, I think, by De
Selincourt) that there was perhaps an echo of Lear's speech, 'Doth
any here know me? This is not Lear ...' in Saturn's words,
'Look up, and tell me if this feeble shape Is Saturn's ...' That is
natural enough. In some respects the two realmless kings were
similar. And we know that Keats was re-reading *King Lear*
intensely at a moment when the idea of *Hyperion* was already in
his mind, namely, on January 23rd, 1818. Then he wrote the
beautiful sonnet, *On sitting down to read King Lear once again.*
Mr. Gittings, very rightly, draws attention to the fact that Keats
was reading *King Lear* yet again on October 4th, 1818, when he
underlined and dated 'Poore Tom' in his folio Shakespeare, probably with his dying brother before his eyes. He declares accordingly that this part of *Hyperion* is 'full of echoes' of *King Lear*.
Naturally, I conclude that he has made some new discoveries over
and above the well-known parallel to which I have referred. I
look up his note for the evidence, and this is what I find:

> These lines include a memory of one of the most famous
> speeches in *King Lear*
> > Men must endure
> > Their going hence even as their coming hither:
> > Ripeness is all.

Saturn's words

> it must — it must
> Be of ripe progress

were first written

> it must — it must
> Be going on.

Both versions echo Shakespeare's words.

Neither 'version' echoes Shakespeare's phrase, if the word 'echo' has any positive meaning in criticism. There is no relation between Shakespeare's 'Ripeness is all' and Saturn's 'It must be of ripe progress', unless it be in the mere word 'ripe'. Nor is there any relation between 'We must endure Our going hence' and 'It must be going on', unless it be in the word 'going'.

But Mr. Gittings improves still further. Obviously, he says, Keats when re-reading *King Lear* on October 4th, 1818, must have re-read his own sonnet, which he copied in his folio Shakespeare. (We do not know when he copied it into his book: but no matter.) He goes further still, and says 'Keats must have actually written [the opening lines of *Hyperion*] with the folio beside him' (p. 14). Mark you, his absolute 'must'. And the justification for this peremptory statement is the usual 'echoes'. He must have had his own sonnet before his eyes, because he 'echoes' it in *Hyperion*. (One would have thought anyhow that Keats might possibly have remembered his own sonnet.)

> O golden-tongued Romance with serene lute!
>   Fair plumed siren! Queen of far away!
>   Leave melodizing on this wintry day,
> Shut up thine olden pages, and be mute:
> Adieu! for once again the fierce dispute,
>   Betwixt damnation and impassion'd clay
>   Must I burn through; once more humbly assay
> The bitter-sweet of this Shakespearian fruit.
> Chief poet! and ye clouds of Albion,
>   Begetters of our deep eternal theme,

When through the old oak forest I am gone,
  Let me not wander in a barren dream,
But when I am consumed in the fire,
  Give me new phoenix wings to fly at my desire.

Says Mr. Gittings (p. 14):

Thea's line about the new terror of Jove's lightning, which
        Scorches and burns our once serene domain
echoes this; but, more than that, Keats's mind hovered over the
haunting and completely Keatsian line
        When through the old oak forest I am gone
to make of it four of the finest lines in the whole range
of his poetry, the image of the oaks.
        As when, upon a tranced summer-night,
        Those green-rob'd senators of mighty woods,
        Tall oaks, branch-charmed by the earnest stars,
        Dream, and so dream all night without a stir.

Those, be it remembered, are the 'echoes' of his *King Lear*
sonnet which prove that Keats *must* have been writing with the
folio Shakespeare and his sonnet beside him. Once again, if
'echo' means something positive, these are not 'echoes' at all.
What connection is there between

        And thy sharp lightning in unpractis'd hands
        Scorches and burns our once serene domain.

and the sonnet, save the two words 'burns' and 'serene' in widely
separate and quite different contexts? And why should it be necessary for Keats to have the line 'when through the old oak forest I
am gone' before his eyes, in order to write the quite different lines
about 'those green-rob'd senators of mighty woods'?
  To follow this critical method of Mr. Gittings in operation
throughout his book would demand another volume much longer
than his own. We have been at pains to make a scrupulously fair
selection for this preliminary test of it. We find it entirely
unconvincing.

We now pass to an examination of his elaborate chain of proof concerning the *Bright Star* sonnet. Mr. Gittings begins this by attempting to demonstrate that Keats wrote the first part of Book II of *Hyperion* with the first three of his Scotch letters to Tom Keats before his eyes. He says that 'the first hundred lines of the second book of *Hyperion* are full of direct quotations from these letters' (p. 24). Direct quotations, this time, not mere 'echoes'. Naturally, it seems strange that no one has remarked them before. Once again I turn to the explanatory note, which runs thus:

> *Hyperion* Book II, 5-17 are based on the description of the Ambleside waterfalls; lines 34-38 describe the 'Druid temple' of the Vale of St. John; Saturn's ascent in line 85 'with damp and slippery footing' takes its wording from Keats's experience on the same day when he 'was damped by slipping one leg into a squashy hole'.

It is, of course, a commonplace of Keats criticism that in the first two of these passages Keats was drawing on his experiences in the Lake District. One of the chief purposes of his northern journey was 'to load his mind with finer images of nature', and thus 'to learn poetry'. Why should Mr. Gittings suppose that Keats could not trust to his memory for these images, but had to have recourse to the actual text of his letters? Any quite ordinary person could be counted on to remember after four months, without reference to his diary, such impressive experiences as his first close encounter with a famous and beautiful waterfall, or his sight of a prehistoric stone circle that he had climbed up a mountain specially to visit. Why must Keats alone be presumed incapable of this very commonplace achievement?

If the first hundred lines of *Hyperion* II were indeed full of 'direct quotations' from his letters, as Mr. Gittings says they are, there might be some justification for supposing that Keats was writing with the letters before his eyes. But these 'direct quotations' exist only in Mr. Gittings's imagination. Here is the first passage from *Hyperion* II:

Scarce images of life, one here, one there,
Lay vast and edgeways; like a dismal cirque
Of Druid stones, upon a forlorn moor,
When the chill rain begins at shut of eve,
In dull November, and their chancel vault,
The Heaven itself, is blinded throughout night.

Here is the relevant passage from Keats's Letter 73:

On our return from this circuit we ordered dinner, and set
forth about a mile and a half on the Penrith road, to see the
Druid temple. We had a fag up the hill, rather too near
dinner time, which was rendered void by the gratification of
seeing those aged stones, on a gentle rise in the midst of
Mountains, which at that time darkened all around, except
at the fresh opening of the Vale of St. John.

Are those lines, in any sense whatever, 'a direct quotation' from
that letter?
Here is the second passage from *Hyperion* II:

where their own groans
They felt, but heard not, for the solid roar
Of thunderous waterfalls and torrents hoarse,
Pouring a constant bulk, uncertain where.

I will not copy the passage in Letter 71 describing the Fall of
Lodore, simply because of its length. But anyone who will look
it up will corroborate my statement that so far from being a
'direct quotation' from the letter, the lines of *Hyperion* have no
direct relation to it at all.
There remain the lines:

Of Saturn, and his guide, who now had climb'd
With damp and slippery footing from a depth
More horrid still.

This, says Mr. Gittings, is a 'direct quotation' from this passage
in Letter 73:

I had an easy climb among the streams, about the fragments of rocks, and should I think have got to the summit, but unfortunately I was damped by slipping one leg into a squashy hole. There is no great body of water, but the accompaniment is delightful; for it [the Fall] oozes out from a cleft in perpendicular Rocks, all fledged with Ash and other beautiful trees.

If it be argued in Mr. Gittings's defence that he did not really mean 'direct quotations', but used the phrase loosely for 'reminiscences', or 'echoes', the reply is simple. Nothing less than 'direct quotations' will serve Mr. Gittings's turn. He is engaged in *proving* that Keats *must* have had three particular letters written to Tom Keats before his eyes at the time that he wrote the first hundred lines of *Hyperion* II. Here are his words (p. 24):

It can only have been letters 1, 2 and 3 [i.e. the first three of his letters to Tom Keats: nos. 71, 73, 75] which he re-read and sent across the Atlantic in these last ten days of October 1818. What was contained in those letters would be strongly associated with these ten days, and thereafter vanish from anything but his unconscious memory. This indeed proves to be the case. The first hundred lines of the second book of *Hyperion* are full of direct quotations from those three letters, as he looked them over before sending them to America. Such quotations never occur again.

Now it so happens that there is one memorable phrase in the quotation from Letter 73 above — one truly poetic and imaginative word: 'perpendicular Rocks, all *fledged* with Ash and other beautiful trees'. And this very distinctive and beautiful word was used six months later by Keats in the *Ode to Psyche*:

> Far, far around shall those dark-cluster'd trees
> Fledge the wild-ridged mountains steep by steep.

This is far more like a 'direct quotation' than anything Mr. Gittings has produced (though I do not believe it to be anything of the kind). And it makes nonsense of his categorical statement

that 'such quotations never occur again'. Both his positive statement: that the first hundred lines of *Hyperion* II are full of 'direct
quotations' from the first three letters to Tom — and his negative
statement: that 'such quotations never occur again', that is after
the end of October 1818 — are untrue.

It is important to realize that there is no solid foundation for
Mr. Gittings's assertion that Keats's mind was full of the actual
words of his letters to Tom in the last ten days of October 1818,
and that then, because the letters were sent to America, they
passed completely out of his conscious memory. For Mr. Gittings
is about to erect an astonishing edifice on this demonstrably false
proposition. He is going to assert that because the first version of
the famous *Bright Star* sonnet contains what appears to be a
reminiscence of Keats's rapt experience on first seeing Windermere, as described to Tom in his Letter 71, it *must* have been
written in the last week of October 1818, before the letters were
sent away. Here are the first eight lines of the first *Bright Star*:

> Bright star! would I were steadfast as thou art!
> Not in lone splendour hung amid the night;
> Not watching, with eternal lids apart
> Like Nature's devout sleepless eremite,
> The morning waters at their priestlike task
> Of pure ablution round earth's human shores;
> Or gazing on the new soft fallen mask
> Of snow upon the mountains and the moors . . .

Here is the passage from Letter 71:

> There are many disfigurements to this Lake — not in the
> way of land or water. No; the two views we have had of it
> are of the most noble tenderness — they can never fade
> away — they make one forget the divisions of life; age,
> youth, poverty, riches: and refine one's sensual vision into a
> sort of north star which can never cease to be open-lidded
> and steadfast over the wonders of the great Power.

In that passage, it is important to note, Keats says that his first views of Windermere 'can never fade away': he will never forget his experience. Surely, we ought to take his word for it. Not at all, says Mr. Gittings. He would have forgotten it altogether, and in fact he had already forgotten it, but that he happened to be reminded of it by re-reading his letter to Tom. Then, having sent away his letter, he forgot it completely again. Because of this extraordinary insensibility of Keats, this utter incapacity to remember his deepest experiences, this absolute inability to do the very thing for which he took his northern journey — 'to load his mind with finer images', it follows that Keats was able to write the octave of the first *Bright Star* only while he had the letter to Tom before his eyes — only in the last ten days of October 1818. Says Mr. Gittings (p. 26):

> It can only be while he had this passage actually before his eyes that he wrote the first eight lines of his sonnet; *the likeness is so close that there can be no question of memory.* [The italics are mine.]

Keats, in fact, was by a whole dimension more stupid than the Bourbons: he learned nothing and forgot everything.

Why could Keats not have remembered, at any period whatsoever in his after-life, the striking phrase he had coined to describe the effect the first sight of Windermere made upon his eager imagination? Must he be made a semi-imbecile? Mr. Gittings cavalierly brushes aside the only piece of positive evidence we have as to the date of the first version of the sonnet. Our only source for it is a transcript by Charles Brown, which definitely dates it 1819. That is not the date of the sonnet, says Mr. Gittings: it 'only shows the year in which Brown copied it' (p. 25). There is, as far as I know, no justification whatever for that statement: which is, if we reflect a moment, highly improbable. Why should Brown, who aimed to be Keats's biographer, think it of the slightest importance to record the date on which he *copied* the sonnet? Can Mr. Gittings point to a single other instance in which Brown behaved in this inexplicable way when copying a poem of Keats?

Thus, by a chain of evidence of which every single link is too weak to bear scrutiny, Mr. Gittings reaches the desired conclusion (p. 25):

> The first version was composed as early as the last week in October 1818, when Keats was finishing the first book of *Hyperion*, before he had met Fanny Brawne, and at a time when his changeable and excitable nature was occupied with quite another lady.

Neither Mr. Gittings nor anyone else knows positively whether or not Keats had met Fanny Brawne before the end of October 1818. But it is, of course, necessary for him to say so; otherwise the whole object of his flimsy 'proof' that the first version of *Bright Star* was written in the last days of October 1818 would be lost: which is to persuade the unwary that the sonnet was not written about Fanny Brawne, but about another woman.

Feeling, apparently, that his chain of proof needed a little strengthening, Mr. Gittings supports his contention that Keats could not have written the first eight lines of the first *Bright Star* except with his own letter about Windermere before his eyes, with two other pieces of 'evidence'. First, he says that the last eight lines of the first book of *Hyperion* also could not have been written except at this same moment. The relevant lines are these:

> Hyperion arose, and on the stars
> Lifted his curved lids, and kept them wide
> Until it ceas'd; and still he kept them wide:
> And still they were the same bright, patient stars.

'This evidence alone', says Mr. Gittings, 'seems to show that Keats wrote the octave of the sonnet *Bright Star* between Books I and II of *Hyperion*, at the end of October 1818' (p. 26). I can discover no connection between these lines and the octave of the sonnet. Hyperion is looking at the stars; in the sonnet the star looks on the world. The evidence is nugatory, unless we are to take it as a critical axiom that a great poet can think of stars and eyelids together but once in his life.

The second piece of additional 'evidence' is derived from Shakespeare's *Troilus and Cressida*, 'which he [Keats] was reading at the time' (p. 26). But, before we consider it, it is as well to ask: *Was* Keats reading *Troilus and Cressida* at this time? In his letter to George, sent on October 31st, he wrote:

> No sooner am I alone than shapes of epic greatness are stationed around me, and serve my Spirit the office which is equivalent to a King's body guard — then 'tragedy with scepter'd pall, comes sweeping by'. According to my state of mind I am with Achilles shouting in the Trenches, or with Theocritus in the Vales of Sicily. Or I throw my whole being into Troilus, and repeating those lines, 'I wander, like a lost Soul upon the stygian Banks staying for waftage', I melt into the air with a voluptuousness so delicate that I am content to be alone.

That certainly does not prove that Keats was reading *Troilus* at this time, unless we assume, once more, that Keats could remember nothing of Shakespeare without the book before him. Besides this occasion, he quoted *Troilus and Cressida* in his letters on September 21st, 1817; on November 22nd, 1817; on January 30th, 1819; in July 1820. Are we to conclude that on each of these occasions he was reading the play? The conclusion is absurd. Keats's letters are packed with quotations from memory of Shakespeare. And this is surely one of them, for it is verbally very inaccurate. Shakespeare wrote 'I stalk about her door like a strange soul' ... But Mr. Gittings says, 'the likeness between what he was writing in *Hyperion* and this play' are a further proof that he was reading it. I turn to his note for these likenesses. Here they are:

> There is sad feud among ye, and rebellion
> Of son against his sire.
>> *Hyperion* I. 321-2
> And the rude son should strike his father dead.
>> *Troilus* I. iii. 15

My life is but the life of winds and tides.
Hyperion I. 341
The sea and winds, old wranglers, took a truce.
Troilus II. ii. 75

Do these far-fetched resemblances prove that Keats was reading *Troilus* when he wrote his lines in *Hyperion?* Surely not. On the contrary, it seems obvious that there is neither necessary nor probable connection between them.

Thus there appears to be no solid ground at all for saying that Keats was reading *Troilus and Cressida* at this time, and making that a datum in a critical argument. He *may* have been reading it, just as (on precisely the same evidence) he *may* have been reading *Measure for Measure*, Milton's *Il Penseroso*, Chapman's *Homer*, or a translation of Theocritus. We simply do not know.

But Mr. Gittings, having assumed that Keats *was* reading *Troilus*, turns to the passage (III. ii) from which he inaccurately quoted to George. Troilus cries to Pandarus:

> O be thou my Charon
> And give me swift transportation to those fields,
> Propos'd for the deserver . . .
> I am giddy; expectation whirls me round
> Th' imaginary relish is so sweet
> That it enchants my sense: what will it be
> When that the watery palate tastes indeed
> Love's thrice repured nectar? death, I fear me,
> Swooning destruction, or some joy too fine,
> Too subtle-potent, turn'd too sharp in sweetness,
> For the capacity of my ruder powers:
> I fear it much . . .

And Pandarus replies:

> She's making her ready, she'll come straight: you must be witty now. She does so blush and fetches her wind so short, as if she were frayed with a sprite: I'll fetch her. It is the prettiest villain: she fetches her breath as short as a new ta'en sparrow.

On this, Mr. Gittings says (p. 27):

> There is no doubt how much the sestet of the sonnet is like this passage, in emotion and expression, and especially when we look at the last couplet, even in particular words. The parallel words 'swoon' and 'death' are made even more distinct by the alteration of the former in the Folio being actually in Keats's own hand, while the last sentence of Pandarus's last speech, 'she fetches her breath so short as a new ta'en sparrow', is beautifully echoed by the 'tender-taken breath', a phrase itself so Shakespearean, in the sonnet. It seems positive, from his reading alone, that Keats wrote the whole sonnet while he had the three Scotch letters in his hand and was reading *Troilus and Cressida* — that is, at the end of October 1818.

It is as well to have the original sestet of the sonnet before our eyes.

> No; — yet still steadfast, still unchangeable,
> Cheek-pillow'd on my Love's white ripening breast,
> To touch, for ever, its soft sink and swell,
> Awake, for ever, in a sweet unrest,
> To hear, to feel, her tender-taken breath,
> Half-passionless, and so swoon on to death.

I do not, in this case, say it is absolutely impossible to imagine *any* connection between the passage in *Troilus* and the sonnet. It is certainly not compulsive; but I should not care to deny categorically that Keats may have had a memory of Shakespeare's words in his mind when he wrote the sestet. But to suggest that Keats needed the help of a simultaneous reading of this passage in *Troilus* to conceive the idea of swooning to death in the ecstasy of possession of his love is absurd. Book IV of *Endymion* is full of the idea. And further, when in his letter to George, Keats actually does quote from memory the most beautiful lines of this passage of *Troilus* — lines which linger in the memory of any sensitive person who reads them — he specifically says that the imaginative delight of his identification of himself with Troilus is such that he is 'content to be alone'.

All this is really a minor matter: for even if Mr. Gittings had convinced us that Keats wrote the sestet of his sonnet under the influence of a memory of the passage in *Troilus*, it would be absolutely nothing to his purpose. Memories are of no use to him; of so little use, indeed, that in defiance of the superabundant evidence of Keats's letters, he virtually denies that Keats could draw upon memories of his experiences or his reading, unless he had the letters or the book before him. Keats must have had his letter to Tom before his eyes in order to write the octave; he must have had *Troilus* before his eyes in order to write the sestet of his sonnet. On this arbitrary and, in the case of Keats, quite incredible *must*, his whole argument depends. Keats probably sent his first three Scotch letters to Tom away to George in America before October 31st: therefore Keats must have written his octave before that date. Deny the validity of that conclusion — and we are bound to deny it, if only to vindicate the at least normal intelligence of Keats — and the whole house of cards falls to the ground. The only solid datum there is in this construction is that Keats did send the three letters away to America at the end of October 1818. That indeed is a deduction, but it is a reasonable one. Nothing else in the argument is either reasonable or plausible; and every step in it depends upon denying Keats the mental endowment of an averagely sensitive man.

No doubt Mr. Gittings is unaware of the consequences of his constant assumption, which is summed up in the words 'the likeness is so close that there can be no question of memory'. If the likenesses were many degrees closer than they are, still in the case of Keats — a phenomenal poetic genius — there would always be the possibility of memory. In likenesses of the order Mr. Gittings adduces, memory must always be infinitely more probable than a consultation of documents. All unwittingly, Mr. Gittings reduces Keats to a person incapable of writing an original nursery rhyme.

And why are Keats's capacities sacrificed to the exigences of

Mr. Gittings's argument? Because he wants to persuade himself and his reader that the *Bright Star* sonnet, which is traditionally supposed to have been written about Fanny Brawne, was really written about a lady about whom he has discovered some new and interesting information: Mrs. Isabella Jones.

Mrs. Isabella Jones, whom we previously knew only as the lady who gave Keats the idea of writing a poem on the legend of the eve of St. Agnes, and as friend enough to Keats to be added, apparently as an afterthought, to the list of those who participated in the share-out of his books after his death, has been convincingly identified by Mr. Gittings as the lady Keats originally met and kissed at Hastings in May or June 1817, met again a year later when he was on the way to the theatre in company with George, and met for the third time at the end of October 1818, in an encounter which he describes vividly in his first letter (94) to George in America. All that Mr. Gittings has found out about her is interesting; but for reasons of his own he tries to exaggerate her importance in Keats's life. His major effort to that end is to try to prove that the *Bright Star* sonnet was originally written about her. We have examined in detail Mr. Gittings's process of proof that the *Bright Star* sonnet was originally written before October 31st, 1818, and find it worthless.

But, even if it were valid and he had proved what he claims to have proved: that the sonnet was originally written before Keats had met Fanny Brawne, and at the time when he renewed his acquaintance with Mrs. Isabella Jones, it would still be impossible to believe that it was written about her. On any showing, the sonnet was written about a woman with whom Keats was passionately in love. There is no evidence at all that Keats was passionately in love for a single moment with Mrs. Isabella Jones. If Mr. Gittings had chosen Miss Jane Cox (Charmian) for the lady of the sonnet, the choice might have seemed psychologically plausible. If we needed to find a woman to replace Fanny Brawne (as we emphatically do not), Charmian would have to be the woman, not Mrs. Isabella Jones. Keats told his brother something of his feelings about Charmian; he told Reynolds more: 'Poor Tom — that woman — and Poetry were ringing changes in my senses', and it was very probably with her in his mind (or his senses) that he wrote the magnificent version of the Ronsard sonnet, with its haunting final lines, which owe very little to Ronsard.

> My heart took fire, and only burning pains
> They were my pleasures — they my life's sad end;
> Love pour'd her beauty into my warm veins.

Nevertheless, Keats did not deceive himself into believing he was in love with Charmian. Still less did he deceive himself into believing he was in love with Mrs. Isabella Jones. He is explicit about it to George:

> As I had warmed with her before and kissed her — I thought it would be living backwards not to do so again — she had a better taste: she perceived how much a thing of course it was and shrunk from it — not in a prudish way but in as I say a good taste. She contrived to disappoint me in a way which made me feel more pleasure than a simple Kiss could do — She said I should please her much more if I would only press her hand and go away. Whether she was in a different disposition when I saw her before — or whether I have in fancy wrong'd her I cannot tell. I expect to pass some pleasant hours with her now and then: in which I feel I shall be of service to her in matters of knowledge and taste: if I can I will. I have no libidinous thought about her — she and your George are the only women à peu près de mon age whom I would be content to know for their mind and friendship alone.

The tone of that cannot be mistaken, particularly when it is compared with the tone of what he had written shortly before about Charmian. Keats is emotionally detached. It is psychologically inconceivable that she was simultaneously the object of the *Bright Star* sonnet.

Mr. Gittings's theory, so far, does violence to every kind of evidence that there is.

But we must continue our examination of the process by which Mr. Gittings establishes to his own satisfaction that the *Bright Star* sonnet was written about Mrs. Jones. In his letter to George, immediately after his account of his meeting with her, Keats goes on to say:

> I shall in a short time write you as far as I know how I intend to pass my Life — I cannot think of those things now Tom is so unwell and weak. Notwithstanding your Happiness and your recommendation I hope I shall never marry. Though the most beautiful creature were waiting for me at the end of a Journey or a Walk; though the carpet were of Silk, the Curtains of the morning Clouds; the chairs and Sofa stuffed with Cygnet's down; the food Manna, the Wine beyond Claret, the Window opening on to Winander mere, I should not feel — or rather my Happiness would not be so fine as my Solitude would be sublime. Then instead of what I have described, there is a Sublimity to welcome me home. The roaring of the wind is my wife and the Stars through the window pane are my Children. The mighty abstract Idea I have of Beauty in all things stifles the more divided and minute domestic happiness — an amiable wife and sweet children I contemplate as part of that Beauty — but I must have a thousand of those beautiful particles to fill up my heart. I feel more and more every day, as my imagination strengthens, that I do not live in this world alone but in a thousand worlds. No sooner am I alone than shapes of epic greatness are stationed around me, and serve my Spirit the office of a King's bodyguard — then 'tragedy with scepter'd pall, comes sweeping by' . . . (The passage already quoted, containing the quotation from memory of *Troilus and Cressida*, follows).

Mr. Gittings says of this (p. 34):

Here is the occasion with which the *Bright Star* sonnet

must be associated — the time when the passage from Letter One to Tom and the scene from *Troilus and Cressida* were present together in Keats's mind. The references to the two are obvious especially when the Troilus quotation is coupled with the strange expression 'Cygnet's down' (instead of, say, swansdown); for this also is a phrase underlined in his Folio, from Act I, scene 1:

> to whose soft seizure
> The Cygnet's down is harsh

To clinch this certainty, 'Winander mere' from Letter One is seconded by something else, which chimes with another of the letters to Tom, Letter 3. In that letter, Keats had copied his lyric *Meg Merrilies*, with its description of old Meg staring at the moon, the hills and the trees, so that

> Alone with her great family
> She lived as she did please.

This is the same thought and practically the same expression as 'The roaring of the wind is my wife and the Stars through the window pane are my Children'. This is the time when the first three Scotch letters and the play of *Troilus and Cressida* were vividly present to Keats's mind. It is the time when he composed the first version of *Bright Star*, and it is also the time, during the week-end of October 24-25, when he was so deeply stirred by his meeting with Isabella Jones.

The very first thing to remark, in this particular connection, about the passage from Keats's letter is that he is, for the time being anyhow, definitely rejecting marriage and love. How on earth is this mood and temper to be reconciled with the mood and temper of *Bright Star*? They simply will not mix. It requires a very great effort of mental contortion to declare that the sonnet *must* have originated from this contrary mood and temper. It is a violent psychological paradox. On the other hand, Keats's rejection of love and marriage is perfectly in accord with the tone of the detached and detailed description of his meeting with Mrs. Jones, and his assurance to George that his passions were in no way stirred by her. True, Mr. Gittings tries to weaken this impression by saying that when Keats wrote to George about Mrs. Jones, he was 'in a state of great excitement'; that he walked home with her 'in the same excited state'; that he was 'deeply stirred by his meeting'. But all this is his own imagination, indulged in defiance of the tone of the description.

In order to establish this gratuitous paradox — 'to clinch this certainty', to use his own phrase — what evidence does Mr. Gittings bring forward? It consists of three items.

First, that Keats could only write of 'a window looking on Winander mere' while he had the Scotch letters to Tom in his hand; second, that he could only write of the softness of 'cygnet's down' — in this case a very probable 'echo' of one of the phrases in *Troilus* that impress themselves on a very ordinary imagination: of the same order of familiarity as 'staying for waftage' — while he was actually reading the play; third, that he could not have written 'The roaring of the wind is my wife and the Stars through the window pane are my Children', unless he had before him the text of *Meg Merrilies* in his Scotch letter, as follows:

> Her brothers were the craggy hills,
>   Her sisters larchen trees;
> Alone with her great family
>   She liv'd as she did please.
> No breakfast had she many a morn,
>   No dinner many a noon,
> And 'stead of supper she would stare
>   Full hard against the moon.

This, says Mr. Gittings, is 'the same thought and practically the same expression' (p. 34) as the sentence in Keats's letter. But what a pity Keats did not write: 'the Moon through the window-pane is my supper'!

What has Mr. Gittings 'proved' by all this? Absolutely nothing at all, unless we grant his two assumptions: the absurd one that Keats could not remember any of the experiences described in his first three Scotch letters to Tom, unless the letters were before his eyes; and the demonstrably false one that this was the only time in Keats's life when he remembered *Troilus and Cressida* sufficiently well to quote it in his letters and echo it in his poetry. When the foundation is unsound, nothing is achieved by adding brick to brick.

But 'there is yet another confirmation', says Mr. Gittings (p. 35). Confirmation of what? we must ask, in order to keep our heads in this critical confusion. It ought to be a confirmation of his hypothesis that Keats wrote the *Bright Star* sonnet in the last week of October 1818 and that the subject of it was Isabella Jones. And what does it consist of? The assertion that Keats's famous letter to Woodhouse on the poetical character (Letter 93, October 27th, 1818) 'contains another series of parallels with the composition of *Bright Star*' (p. 36). That is a curious phrase. What does 'composition' mean here? The 'act of composing' or 'the elements that compose' the sonnet? I do not think the vagueness is deliberate; it seems due rather to a real confusion in Mr. Gittings's mind.

However, the 'parallels' are these. First, a parallel to *Bright Star* itself. Both it and the letter contain the word 'unchangeable'. The poet of the kind to which he belongs, Keats says in the letter, has no 'unchangeable' attribute, as 'the Sun, the Moon and the Sea, and Men and Women who are creatures of impulse' have. In the sonnet he prays to be not remote like the star, but human; yet 'still steadfast, still unchangeable' as the star. The other 'parallel' is that in the letter Keats twice uses the word 'relish', and the word 'relish' also occurs in the passage from *Troilus and Cressida*: 'Th' imaginary relish is so sweet.' Mr. Gittings says he uses the word in the letter 'in just the sense that Shakespeare made Troilus use it'. But how else *can* this very common word be used? It means 'delight' in or 'enjoyment' of something or other. This 'parallel' is surely quite trivial.

The first one may be more serious: but surely only in the sense that we may feel there may be some connection between Keats's thought in the letter and his thought in the sonnet. It may, possibly, have been the germ of the idea expressed in *Bright Star*. But how can we conclude from this that the sonnet must have been written at the same time as the letter? Are we entirely to disregard all the profound and beautiful things Keats himself has told us about his methods of poetic composition? Are we entirely to ignore, for example, 'the innumerable compositions and decompositions which take place between the intellect and its thousand materials before it arrives at that trembling, delicate and snail-horn perception of beauty'? As far as it lies in Mr. Gittings's power to persuade us, we are; in order that we may be hoodwinked into his conclusion: 'That *Bright Star* in its first form was inspired by Isabella Jones seems inescapable' (p. 36).

Mr. Gittings desires to reach that conclusion. I, frankly, do not. I find something very repugnant in the idea that Keats should have written an impassioned and immortal sonnet about one woman and touched it up for another. (For not even Mr. Gittings denies that the second form of *Bright Star* was written about Fanny Brawne.) The piece of cynicism imputed to Keats conflicts violently with my idea of his character. Nevertheless, if it could be proved certain, or shown to be even probable, I would accept it, ruefully indeed, but without intellectual hesitation.

But what are the facts about Mr. Gittings's methods of demonstrating this revolutionary thesis? In order to accept them we are required, first, to dismiss the dating of the sonnet by the man to whom we owe the only copy of it that we have — a man moreover who looked forward to being Keats's biographer; second, we are required to regard Keats as incapable of remembering his own most precious experiences, incapable of remembering (without his diary before his eyes) his sensations at his first sight of Windermere four months afterwards, in spite of his own declaration that he could never forget them, incapable of remembering words and phrases of Shakespeare unless he had the book before him; third, we are required to regard him as incapable of understanding the nature of his own feelings about a woman, and to believe that when he met Isabella Jones in the last week of October

1818, he fell physically and passionately in love with her, in defiance of his own explicit statement that he did nothing of the kind. In short, in order to reach the conclusion that Keats did something which is, by any standards, in deplorable taste, and in contradiction to all we know of his character, we are required in the process to make the assumption that he was intellectually well below the average, and emotionally self-ignorant to an extreme degree.

C'est le premier pas qui coûte. If it could have been established, with any show of probability, that the *Bright Star* sonnet was originally written at the end of October 1818 about Isabella Jones, and not at some time in 1819 about Fanny Brawne, the way would have been made much smoother than it now is towards persuading us that the passionate desire expressed in the sonnet developed in the next three months into a serious love affair between Keats and Isabella. This is what Mr. Gittings attempts to do. But since he has signally failed to make good his preliminary proposition concerning the *Bright Star*, we must examine his arguments for his secondary proposition entirely on their own merits.

We know from Keats's own letters that when he met Isabella Jones again towards the end of October 1818, she gave him a grouse and took his address for the purpose of sending him more game, and that he expected to 'pass some pleasant hours with her now and then: in which I feel I shall be of service to her in matters of knowledge and taste'. He refers to her again in his Letter 123 to George. Writing apparently on February 19th, 1819, he says:

> Talking of game . . . the Lady whom I met at Hastings and of whom I said something in my last I think, has lately made me many presents of game, and enabled me to make as many — She made me take home a Pheasant the other day which I gave to Mrs. Dilke; on which, tomorrow, Rice, Reynolds and the Wentworthians will dine next door — The next I intend for your Mother.

That was written at least a fortnight after Keats had returned to Hampstead after his sojourn in Chichester and Bedhampton, during which he wrote *The Eve of St. Agnes*. Since Woodhouse tells us that the poem was suggested to Keats by Mrs. Jones (that is to say, she suggested his making use of the legend of St. Agnes' Eve, for the main substance of the story apparently comes from Boccaccio) it is a fair deduction that Keats had met her on at least one occasion between his encounter with her in October 1818 and his departure for Chichester towards the end of January 1819; and that he met her again not long after his return from Chichester. We may also fairly suppose that the meetings took place on the condition Mrs. Jones had proposed: that 'they should be acquainted without any of our common acquaintance knowing it'.

Apart from this, Mr. Gittings, cleverly following a trail indicated by Mr. Blunden, has discovered that Isabella Jones was in the habit of staying at Hastings with a short-tempered old gentleman named Donal O'Callaghan, in what capacity we do not know. Quite possibly he was what the Americans call a 'sugar-daddy' to the young and 'beautiful Mrs. Jones', as Reynolds called her, looking back in 1837. In 1819 she seems to have been pretty well known to Taylor and more slightly to Reynolds, who would be the 'common acquaintance' to which she wished her friendship with Keats to be unknown. In the weeks after the news of Keats's death had reached England she was allowed to read Severn's letters about his last days, and at least one of Keats's own letters from Italy to Brown. She was a lively correspondent; fiercely, but unfairly, critical of Severn's letters. She admired *Endymion*, but almost equally Barry Cornwall's poetry.

On this slender basis of fact and reasonable probability Mr. Gittings rears a remarkable construction. Put quite baldly, his thesis is that Keats, having fallen passionately in love with Isabella Jones at the end of October 1818 (as 'proved' by the *Bright Star* sonnet) and having visited her frequently thereafter, stayed with her on the night before he left London for Chichester (which was, according to Mr. Gittings, January 20th, St. Agnes' Eve) and consummated his love. This successful amour he celebrated on the next day, January 21st, by writing to her the verses *Hush*,

hush, tread softly; and, more elaborately, by writing *The Eve of St. Agnes*.

We now examine the evidence for this distinctly sensational story.

First, Mr. Gittings says categorically that 'on Wednesday, January 20th, Keats spent the night in town before catching the early coach the next morning for his long postponed visit to Chichester and Bedhampton' (p. 57). We cannot discover any solid evidence at all for this statement. It contains two assertions: the first, that Keats travelled to Chichester on January 21st; the second, that he stayed the previous night in London.

Concerning the first, Mr. Gittings says, that 'the date . . . can be inferred from a careful study of his [Keats's] letters both before and after the visit' (p. 57). The inference is very dubious. We know from Letter 112 that Keats was back at Hampstead by February 4th, 1819; but the letter does not tell us how long he had been back. In Letter 113 he says he was at Bedhampton a fortnight. In Letter 123 he says, more exactly, 'I was nearly a fortnight at Mr. John Snook's [i.e. at Bedhampton] and a few days at old Mr. Dilke's [i.e. at Chichester] . . . I went out twice at Chichester to old dowager card parties'. In Letter 111, writing from Bedhampton on January 24th, 1819, Brown says 'He [Keats] and I walked here from Chichester yesterday; we were here at 3'. That is the one certain date: Keats left Chichester on January 23rd. If he travelled from London to Chichester on January 21st, as Mr. Gittings says, he was in Chichester not quite two days: which does not fit with 'a few days', and indeed does not allow him time to 'go out twice to old dowager card parties'. The more probable inference is that Keats travelled to Chichester not later than January 19th.

But the second part of the statement — that Keats spent the night of January 20th in town before catching the coach to Chichester in the morning — is the more important, because Mr. Gittings implies that he spent it in bed with Isabella Jones. But he produces no evidence at all that Keats did spend the night in town. It appears to be a mere guess; and it is a very improbable one. For there was no need at all for Keats to spend the night in town in order to catch the Chichester coach the next day. There were stages from Hampstead to London about twice every hour. Nevertheless, Mr. Gittings states it as a fact.

Thus, the evidence dwindles down to that of the transcript of the verses *Hush, hush! tread softly!* in the copy of *The Literary Pocket Book*, which Hunt gave to Keats and Keats gave to Fanny Brawne. The transcript is almost certainly by Fanny Brawne. On the opposite page is a faint pencil note 'Written . . . (illegible) twenty first of January'. It would be difficult to say whether it means that the verses were composed by Keats, or copied by Fanny Brawne on that day. If it is meant for the date of the composition of the verses, it is in direct conflict with Brown's transcript of them, which dates them 1818. Once again, of course, Mr. Gittings brusquely dismisses Brown's as a misdating. But we remember that he dismissed Brown's dating of the first *Bright Star* on the ground that it was the date on which Brown copied the sonnet. Why does he not accept 1818 as the date on which Brown copied *Hush, hush?* The answer is that the previously convenient axiom about Brown's dates is now very inconvenient. In fact, Brown's date is just as likely — I should say, much more likely — to be accurate as the pencil date in the *Pocket Book*.

Further, if we assume that the pencil date is accurate, it means that Keats composed *Hush, hush* while he was with Brown in Chichester. It is very odd, considering Brown's habit of copying Keats's poems immediately, that he should have dated it 1818. It is altogether more plausible to suppose that it was not written on January 21st, 1819, but in 1818, as Brown indicated.

But the date of *Hush, hush* is of importance only if we believe, as Mr. Gittings believes, that the subject of it is Isabella Jones, and that it celebrates a successful amour with her on the night before it was written. Is this credible?

On the face of it, the poem seems to be merely fanciful — a sort of musical comedy lyric; and so it has hitherto been supposed to be. Charlotte Reynolds said that Keats composed it to a Spanish air which she played for him on the piano. Whether or not her memory was accurate, the impression it makes on us is that it may well have been composed to a tune, just like *I had a dove*, which Keats wrote, as he explicitly says, 'to some music as it was playing' in December 1818 (Letter 98). However, Mr. Gittings will not have this. He will have it that the verses describe a real experience. After quoting them, he says positively (p. 58):

> This is not fancy at all; it is an actual description of the place where he had first met Isabella Jones, where they had first 'warmed' to each other and kissed . . . It is based on real events and living circumstances.

That is, the verses realistically describe Keats's first encounter with Isabella Jones at Bo Peep near Hastings about the end of May 1817. They do not sound at all realistic to me. But no matter. Assuming that they are what Mr. Gittings says they are: a realistic description of his flirtation with Isabella, with Mr. Donal O'Callaghan as 'the jealous old bald-pate' in the background, why did Keats wait eighteen months or so to celebrate the occasion — particularly in view of Mr. Gittings's own critical axiom that his experiences were instantly reflected in his poetry? And, still more pertinent, if the verses do celebrate the flirtation of May 1817, how can they also celebrate the hypothetical night of love with Isabella on January 20th, 1819? Mr. Gittings makes no bones about this. After saying (on p. 61) that Keats visited Isabella on the night of January 20th, before his journey, he says positively (on p. 62):

> Keats spent the night of January 20, St. Agnes Eve, in town before catching the early morning coach to Chichester. On January 21 he wrote the lyric recounting the successful love-affair with Isabella, and started writing *The Eve of St. Agnes*. In the latter poem Keats insisted that the love-affair between his hero and heroine on St. Agnes Eve was actually consummated.

If English means anything, this means that Keats was Isabella's lover on the night of January 20th. Absolutely the *only* evidence for that statement is the verses *Hush, hush* themselves, which Mr. Gittings has previously insisted are a description of Keats's flirtation with Isabella in May 1817.

I find this bold hypothetical construction quite incredible. No doubt it is very exciting and revolutionary to suggest that Keats spent St. Agnes Eve, immediately before writing his lovely poem on the legend, in bed with Isabella Jones, and that she gave him the idea for his poem on this auspicious occasion. 'It seems likely enough that she suggested it to Keats on the very night of the legend, January 20th, when he visited her before his journey south' (p. 61). But a theory of this kind is culpably irresponsible unless it is based on a rigorous scrutiny of the evidence. The cynicism of the behaviour thus imputed to Keats — for there is no doubt that by this time he was in love with Fanny Brawne and she with him — may have its attractions for certain minds; but its attractiveness cannot be allowed to overbear the evidence. And, as we have seen, there is neither evidence nor probability that Keats spent St. Agnes Eve in London, or that he spent it with Isabella Jones.

As to *Hush, hush* itself, the theory that it celebrates the successful consummation of a love-affair seems to me grotesquely improbable. It just is not that kind of poem. That it celebrates the original flirtation with Isabella is pure conjecture. Even this is implausible. The use of the name Isabel — in verses very likely composed before Keats had renewed his acquaintance with her — I should say was mere coincidence. After all, Keats had written a long poem called *Isabella* after he first met and kissed Mrs. Jones: but — rather to my surprise, I confess — not even Mr. Gittings suggests that it had anything to do with her.

Mr. Gittings, in the interest of his sensational story, will have it that the flirtation of 1817 was far more serious than there is any reason at all to suppose it was. He is, of course, compelled to this, by his theory that *Bright Star* was originally written about her. But that is demonstrably untrue. We may judge of the seriousness of Keats's entanglement with Mrs. Jones by the fact that, on his own statement, after kissing her at Hastings, he did not

meet her again for a whole year, and then only by accident.
But Mr. Gittings has, by hook or crook, to magnify the affair.
He says on p. 59:

> He romantically portrayed the encounter in the first 140-odd
> lines of *Endymion* Book II, where in similar scenery and
> beside a river in early summer, among the dancing water-
> flies and the wild roses, the hero meets a somewhat enigmatic
> nymph of the stream. Now, eighteen months later, his
> memory revived by this new association with her, he drew
> the picture much more realistically. The same images are
> there. The picture of the wild rose bud which becomes in
> an instant full blown comes from the passage in *Endymion*:
>
> >   a wild rose tree
> > Pavillions him in bloom, and he doth see
> > A bud which snares his fancy: lo! but now
> > He plucks it, dips its stalk in the water: how
> > It swells, it buds, it flowers beneath his sight.
>
> 'The evening's sleepy frown' of the riverside scene in
> *Endymion* has become 'the night's sleepy eye' of the same
> scene in the lyric. In the new poem, however, the love
> affair has become real, warm, and tangible, while behind it
> is the figure of 'the jealous old bald-pate', whose nightcap
> has to be padded — that is, he has to be given, perhaps, a
> stiff dose of late-night whisky — before the lovers can meet
> and creep through the little gate to the meadow and kiss in
> safety.

If anyone will take the trouble to read the first 140-odd lines
of *Endymion* II he will see that the idea that Endymion's encounter with the 'enigmatic nymph' is a 'romantic portrayal' of
any mundane flirtation is distinctly extravagant; that there is no
real similarity at all between the scenery of *Endymion* and that of
Hush, hush; and that the statement that 'the same images are
there' is a very great exaggeration. One can only suppose that
Mr. Gittings was unconsciously pre-determined to find some

influence of the Hastings flirtation in the poetry Keats was writing at the time.

But an even more surprising contention follows:

All this [continues Mr. Gittings, referring to the description of the encounter of 1817 in *Hush, hush*] is exact and vivid; yet the importance of it is not so much that it is a new chapter in Keats's life, but that it is also closely connected with one of his finest poems, *The Eve of St. Agnes*.

Hush, hush, in fact, is a miniature rehearsal for the great poem which Keats began to write directly he arrived in Chichester. There are strong likenesses. A cancelled opening to stanza viii of *The Eve of St. Agnes* shows the lines

> She danced along with vague uneager eyes
> Her anxious lips full pulp'd with rosy thoughts,

which at once recall

> But my Isabel's eyes, and her lips pulp'd with bloom.

In another early stanza of *St. Agnes*, Keats's first draft actually used the exclamation 'Hush, hush!' itself.

It is hard to believe that even Mr. Gittings can be serious here. Angela, in a discarded line of stanza xii of *St. Agnes*, says to Porphyro: 'Child, hush, hush.' It does not seem a remarkable coincidence. That Keats carried over the phrase 'lips ... pulp'd', from *Hush, hush* to *St. Agnes* is probable. But what of it? It was not even original to *Hush, hush*. Keats had written some months before:

> A kiss should bud on the tree of love
> And pulp and ripen richer every hour
> To melt away upon the traveller's lips ...

Moreover, in the very same discarded line of *St. Agnes* he has a phrase, 'anxious mouth', which is carried over from a sonnet written two years before. To assert these are 'strong likenesses' in the diction of the two poems is a critical extravagance.

Yet it is not trivial [Mr. Gittings continues] to see how it [*St. Agnes*] shares the atmosphere of the little lyric.

We are dead if that latchet gives one little clink!

anticipates the hero and heroine of the greater poem, stealing at midnight from the sleeping hall. It is not in the least incongruous to think of Isabella's old O'Callaghan as the ancestor of that 'old Lord Maurice' and the other 'hot-blooded lords', whose presence threatens the safety of the lovers in *The Eve of St. Agnes*: for the poem itself was suggested by Isabella.

In the last few words we reach the solid ground of a fact. Woodhouse noted in his transcript of *St. Agnes*: 'St. Agnes day is the 21st of January. The Poem was written at the suggestion of Mrs. Jones.' But that fact does not make it either congruous or probable that Isabella Jones was the original of Madeline or Mr. O'Callaghan the original of the 'whole bloodthirsty race' of Porphyro's enemies.

We accept Woodhouse's statement that Isabella Jones suggested the poem to Keats, in the sense that she suggested his making use of the legend; it seems probable enough that Keats, meeting her some time before he left London for Chichester, told her that he had in mind to write a poem during his country sojourn, and that she told him that St. Agnes Eve was approaching and outlined the legend to him. There is some evidence (duly adduced by Mr. Gittings) that Isabella Jones was knowledgeable about such superstitions.

Mr. Gittings himself believes that the substance of the story of *The Eve of St. Agnes*, apart from the legend, probably comes from an episode in Boccaccio's romance *Il Filocolo*, as was suggested nearly fifty years ago. He has an ingenious theory that Keats intended to write this tale in prose. On October 16th, 1818, Keats wrote to George:

I shall send you more than Letters — I mean a tale — which I must begin on account of the activity of my Mind; of its inability to remain at rest. It must be prose and not very exciting. I must do this because in the way I am at present situated I have too many interruptions to a train of feeling to be able to write Poetry. So I shall write this Tale, and if I think it worth while get a duplicate made before I send it off to you —

Two months later, on December 18th, he says that he has not been able to write the tale he promised. On the face of it that sounds as though Keats had been contemplating a prose tale of his own invention. But Mr. Gittings believes that what he intended to write was a prose version of the story from Boccaccio. It is a mere conjecture: of which the best one can say is that it is not impossible. However, as usual, it immediately becomes a certainty (p. 61).

That plot, never to be written in prose, had been simmering in his mind for months. The explanation of *The Eve of St. Agnes* not being mentioned previously, in his letters or anywhere else, is that it was identical in plot with the prose tale. Just as the Hastings lady of Keats's letters is one and the same as 'Mrs. Jones' of Woodhouse's note, so the mysterious tale is the same as the poem. The lady and the story are intimately mixed; for it was the legendary subject, suggested by Isabella Jones, which brought Reynolds's suggestion from Boccaccio into life and poetry in Keats's excited brain.

How can this unwritten and entirely hypothetical prose version of Boccaccio's tale in any way *explain* Keats's silence about the poem? Do we really have to seek an explanation why Keats did not mention *St. Agnes* to anybody until it was finished? He was even more silent about the *Nightingale* and the *Grecian Urn*, but his silence has never constituted a problem. In any case there is no warrant for Mr. Gittings's positive statement that Reynolds suggested to Keats this hypothetical prose-tale from Boccaccio. When Reynolds wrote, on October 14th, 1818, urging Keats to publish his 'tale', he was almost certainly referring to *Isabella, or The Pot of Basil*. Whether Reynolds did, or did not, suggest to him to use the story from *Il Filocolo* is a matter of pure conjecture, for which there is no evidence either way.

Finally, Mr. Gittings invokes the evidence of a discussion of *The Eve of St. Agnes* which took place between Woodhouse and Keats nearly eight months after it was written, on September 12th, 1819. Keats then produced an alteration in three stanzas of his poem (which have not survived) and said that he intended to make it clear that Porphyro and Madeline consummated their love. 'His own vehemence on this point,' says Mr. Gittings, 'made it likely that this side of the story was a real experience' (p. 62). But this is very false psychology. In the first place, what Keats thought of and did to his poem in September is quite distinct from, and not to be confused with, what he thought of and did to his poem in January. If Mr. Gittings's theory were correct, he would certainly not have made his poem less realistic in January than he did in September. The love-consummation is part of the Boccaccio story; and, if Keats really used this story, what he did in his poem was to dissolve and sublimate Boccaccio's realism, not insist upon it. Secondly, we have Keats's own comment on his conversation with Woodhouse on *The Eve of St. Agnes*, in a letter to Reynolds and Woodhouse (Letter 152): in which, after saying he persisted in not publishing *Isabella* because 'there is too much inexperience of life, and simplicity of knowledge in it — which might do very well after one's death — but not while one is alive', he says: 'There is no objection of this kind to Lamia — A good deal to St. Agnes Eve — only not so glaring.' That is to say: *The Eve of St. Agnes* (in its original form: the one we have) is almost as unsophisticated as *Isabella*. Keats had tried to sophisticate his poem and shown the result to Woodhouse when he saw him, and Woodhouse had, very rightly, objected. And this Keats had done because, as his letters at the time to Fanny Brawne plainly show, during the summer he had become more cynical (and more despairing) about his love, and his love-poetry. And, of course, thirdly — and most importantly — we have to remem-

ber there is no evidence at all to warrant the identification of
Isabella Jones with Madeline, so that to wrest Keats's subsequent
somewhat cynical sophistication of his poem into evidence for
this identification is really a glaring begging of the whole question.

Mr. Gittings ends his chapter on the subject (p. 63):

> In his 'rhodomontade' about the offending passages in *St.
> Agnes*, he said, according to Woodhouse, that 'he should
> despise a man who should be such an eunuch in sentiment as
> to leave a maid, with that Character about her, in such a
> situation'. If such a situation presented itself to him on the
> evening of January 20th — as we may believe by the lyric it
> did — it is at least possible that he lived up to his words. It
> is certainly one explanation of the mood of heightened and
> sensuous exhilaration in which he began his great poem on
> the following day.

Mr. Gittings has notably hedged on his previous story.
Whereas, only a page before, *Hush, hush* 'recounted the successful
love-affair with Isabella', now it is only evidence that 'a situation
presented itself to him on the evening of January 20th' in which
he could have had a successful love-affair with her, and it is 'at
least possible' that he did. And this 'is certainly one explanation
of the mood of heightened and sensuous exhilaration etc.' Even
here Mr. Gittings is ambiguous. Does the phrase mean it is the
probable explanation, or that it is one explanation among many
possible? Such ambiguity, in such a matter, would be hard to
distinguish from dishonesty, were it not that, henceforward in
his book, Mr. Gittings conducts his narrative as though he had
really proved that Isabella Jones and Keats were lovers on the
night of St. Agnes Eve, on January 20th, 1819.

We have tried to do full, though perhaps tedious, justice to
Mr. Gittings's train of reasoning about *Hush, hush* and *The Eve
of St. Agnes* and Isabella Jones. Of course, if one comes to it
already persuaded that *Bright Star* had been written about Isabella Jones three months before, it becomes more plausible than
it is. But if that theory is quite untenable, as I believe I have

shown, the theory about *Hush, hush* and *The Eve of St. Agnes* becomes very improbable indeed.

And it will become more improbable still. For so far we have considered it in artificial and dangerous isolation from Keats's known situation in January 1819. We must now consider it in relation to this. We know that some weeks before he left London for Chichester Keats had fallen in love with Fanny Brawne. True, Mr. Gittings dismisses Keats's assertion that 'he wrote himself her vassal the very first week he knew her' (Letter 139) on the ground that this is common form among lovers; but he cannot thus dismiss Fanny Brawne's own declaration in 1821 to Fanny Keats that Christmas Day, 1818, was the happiest day she had ever then spent. Though that does not mean, as it has been supposed to mean, that she became engaged to him on that day, it almost certainly does mean that on that day Keats declared his love for her and learned it was reciprocated.

We are thus compelled to ask whether it is psychologically at all credible that Keats should at the same time have been carrying on a love intrigue with Isabella Jones. On the face of it, it seems wildly improbable that four weeks after Fanny Brawne's happy Christmas Day, Keats should have spent the night in bed with Isabella; and indeed almost equally incredible that a responsible critic should put forward such a theory on the sole basis of the verses *Hush, hush*. It seems more incredible still that, if the verses *Hush, hush* really meant what Mr. Gittings says they meant, Keats, shortly after his return to London, should have given Fanny a copy of the verses to transcribe into the *Literary Pocket Book*, which he gave her. Even Mr. Gittings has to contort himself a good deal to explain the astonishing cynicism of this act. He writes on p. 84:

> Before trying to understand why he did this, it must be noticed that she does not seem likely to have taken the poem seriously, nor to have herself fully understood its purport. She wrote it out rather like an exercise, with a good deal of crossing out and rewriting ... Yet the question remains what

Keats thought he was doing in giving or showing to Fanny a lyric which described in literal detail his love-affair with Isabella.

The explanation seems to be the odd mixture of unsure feelings and bravado which, as he himself said, he was always apt to show towards women ... Fanny ... had aroused this antagonism, which was only the other side of a strong attraction, in a flash. His instinct was, in the language of his day, to 'smoke' her. To give her a book which he thought worthless, and to show her a poem which, unknown to her, recorded a love-affair with another lady may not seem admirable conduct; but it was much in the style of his bosom-companion, Brown, who used to put indecent verses among Keats's papers, in order, he said, to prevent young women prying among them.

It is probably the best defence of Keats's behaviour that Mr. Gittings could put up. But it really cannot be made to square with the character of the man who, long before he met Fanny Brawne, hated to have 'to think insults' against women; still less can it be made to square with his own consistent account of the birth of his passion for Fanny Brawne. Mr. Gittings has already, by his argument that *Bright Star* was originally written to Isabella Jones, involved Keats in much the same cynical behaviour. But that theory is baseless. And in this case also, does it not prove to be infinitely more probable that *Hush, hush* is, after all, what it has always been supposed to be, a light-hearted exercise of the fancy, without reference to any real experience at all?

Probably it suits with the temper of much modern criticism to believe, on such remarkably slender evidence as Mr. Gittings puts forward, that Keats behaved, in the matter of his love, with such extraordinary cynicism. I heard a broadcast criticism of Mr. Gittings's book, in which a well-known modern critic said that he found it 'amusing' that Keats should have written his passionate love-sonnet about one lady and then 'polished it up' to serve another; and I have been impressed by the insouciance with which other influential critics have promptly endorsed these paradoxical and improbable theories. I can understand that Keats as a man makes no particular appeal to them, and that they feel no particular obligation to scrutinize closely specious arguments which calumniate his character. Nevertheless, even if the present generation of critics feels no loyalty to Keats himself, I cannot believe it thinks itself exempt from an obligation to the truth, and I can only ascribe the facility with which it has accepted Mr. Gittings's theories about Keats and Isabella Jones to a lamentable ignorance concerning his poetry and his letters.

CHAPTER IV

'THE REALMS OF GOLD'

KEATS'S sonnet *On First Looking into Chapman's Homer*
holds a position of peculiar significance in his work as a
whole: for several reasons: because it is one of the finest
sonnets in the English language; because it is the first entirely
successful poem that he wrote; because he wrote it very early in
his poetic career — in the very month, October 1816, in which he
became twenty-one, and decided, to his guardian's consternation,
to abandon medicine for poetry; because it was to take him many
months, even of his brief and crowded poetic life, to reach such
assured mastery again; and finally because he wrote it very
quickly. There are not many poems so well worth studying as
this one.

But before we study it let us have in mind the story of its composition. We owe the story to the friend of his youth, Charles
Cowden Clarke, his young schoolmaster and intimate. The
poem was written in October 1816. In 1816 Keats had left school
some five years; he had served his apprenticeship to Hammond
the surgeon at Edmonton, and had been living for some time in
the Borough, studying for a diploma in medicine at Guy's
Hospital, and also writing verses.

Keats and Cowden Clarke were in the habit of meeting together
for literary discussion. One day in October Clarke was lent a
copy of Chapman's *Homer* in folio, and Keats was immediately
summoned over in the evening to Clarke's lodging in Clerkenwell
to share the feast. They read Chapman together till dawn; then
Keats went home to his lodgings in the Borough, two miles away.
At 10 o'clock in the morning Clarke found the sonnet on his
breakfast table.

That Clarke's narrative is substantially true seems plain from
the attendant circumstances he gives. The particulars of the

achievement had naturally made a deep impression upon him. He was at the time Keats's most intimate friend, and he had been scarcely less excited than Keats himself by the opportunity of reading Chapman. (There was no cheap reprint in those days — you had your Chapman in folio or not at all.) And Clarke remembered turning up the shipwreck at the end of the fifth Odyssey and Keats's 'delighted stare' at a vivid phrase —

> Then forth he came, his both knees falt'ring, both
> His strong hands hanging down, and all with froth
> His cheeks and nostrils flowing, voice and breath
> Spent to all use, and down he sank to death.
> *The sea had soaked his heart through* . . .

It is the kind of phrase that would have brought a 'delighted stare' into Keats's eyes. The quality of Clarke's memory of this particular occasion is evident: we may rely upon it.

There is no need to make the vain effort to establish precisely how long it took Keats to write his sonnet. The important facts are simple. It was written between daybreak and breakfast-time one day in October 1816, the month when Keats became twenty-one. It is one of the great sonnets in the English language, and it was the first poem of this quality Keats wrote. If the word 'inspiration' is ever to be used in literary criticism it might be used with some propriety here.

Now let us look at the sonnet as Cowden Clarke found it on his breakfast-table that October morning. Three hours before there was nothing: now a masterpiece, a possession for ever, has been dropped into the lap of the world. It has not quite all the perfections of its final form. By one lovely line, and one perfect epithet, it is less than the sonnet with which we are familiar.* But even if these had never been changed the sonnet would still hold a sovereign place in English poetry:

> Much have I travell'd in the realms of gold,
>   And many goodly states and kingdoms seen;
>   Round many western islands have I been

Which bards in fealty to Apollo hold;
Oft of one wide expanse had I been told
   Which deep-brow'd Homer ruled as his demesne.
  Yet could I never tell what men could mean
Till I heard Chapman speak out loud and bold.
Then felt I like some watcher of the skies
   When a new planet swims into his ken;
     Or like stout Cortez, when with wond'ring eyes
He star'd at the Pacific — and all his men
   Look'd at each other with a wild surmise —
     Silent upon a peak in Darien.

What is the impression produced by the sonnet upon us?
Impressions of this sort are hard to define: but here one seems to
be predominant and recognizable.

We receive an impression of excitement so intense that the
declared and actual subject of the poem is as it were dissolved
away by it. It is almost impossible not to forget that it is all about
a book — Chapman's translation of *Homer*. There is a direct
communication of emotion, which grows swifter and swifter, till
in the final picture of Cortez, half visual, half abstract, it touches a
consummation: the image is not merely stamped upon our minds
by the emotional force of the poem, but the image gathers up,
clinches, makes tangible, the emotional content of the poem.
Cortez on the peak — it is the perfect culmination of the sonnet.
All that the sonnet really means is crammed into that final image:
it is the flower of the plant, the purpose and the essence of the
created thing.

Let us leave this for a moment and examine the sonnet more
coldly, putting aside, if we can, the immediate and overwhelming
impression. We observe that the imagery of exploration and discovery is maintained from the beginning.

Much have I *travell'd* in the realms of gold,
   And many goodly states and kingdoms seen;
   Round many western islands have I been . . .
Oft of one wide expanse had I been told . . .

From the first line the poet is a traveller, an explorer, voyaging among islands, discovering the realms of gold: he hears on his travels persistent rumours and reports of a great *El dorado*. The word of the conquistadors is helpful; for the phrase 'the realms of gold' is become so familiar, so much a part of current speech, that we forget that when Keats used it it was original.* And it had come, I fancy, from the same reading whence came his picture of Cortez. '*El dorado*' means simply 'the realm, or the city, of gold'. Keats was, to his own mind, a conquistador, with Chapman's *Homer* for his new-found land.

In the first two lines of the sestet:

> Then felt I like some watcher of the skies
> When a new planet swims into his ken,

the imagery is slightly changed — he becomes the explorer not of earth but of heaven — an astronomer who has discovered a new planet; but the change, instead of weakening the poem, quite definitely strengthens and enriches it: it gives an infinite extension to its imaginative scope — to the yet unlimited earth the illimitable heavens are added, and by the exquisite use of the word 'swims' is created an impression of ethereal stillness, a background of quiet translunary spaces, against which the figure of Cortez on his peak emerges with craggy definition.

So that, on a closer examination, the immediate impression that the image of Cortez on the peak in Darien is the natural and, so to say, organic culmination of the poem, is fully substantiated. At the very outset Keats imagines himself as the explorer in search of *El dorado*, and when finally he likens himself to the mightiest of the conquistadors, at the supreme moment of discovery, he has carried the imagery with which he began to the pinnacle of its potentialities.

It is one of the greatest sonnets in the English language: its immediate effect is startling, and perhaps this cold-blooded analysis has yielded some reason why this is so. The unity of the poem lies deep and is *organic*: in the first line the last is implicit, as a flower is implicit in a seed. And this unity is achieved by what appears, on still closer examination, an almost miraculous subtlety.

Considered in its imagery alone, as we have seen, the poem is a perfect whole — one single and complex metaphor, as intricate as it is clear. There is a real progression, as it were a crescendo, of the imagery which seems to grow out of itself. It completely satisfies Keats's own demand upon poetry which he formulated eighteen months later.

> The rise, the progress, the setting of Imagery should, like the Sun come natural to him [the reader] shine over him and set soberly although in magnificence leaving him in the Luxury of twilight.

Almost certainly Keats, when he wrote these words, was not thinking of this sonnet, and yet there could not be a more exact description of its peculiar magnificence. The quality of his unconscious achievement had become, in eighteen months more, his conscious ideal. That happened often with Keats; it is, indeed, the most profound and persistent trait in his character, and this submission of the consciousness to the unconscious was to become, in his brief and dazzling maturity, not only his declared philosophy, but the means by which he achieved his most consummate poetical perfections. And we may take 'the progress and the setting of Imagery' in this sonnet as a concrete example of Coleridge's penetrating, but more intellectual *dictum*, which is so often misinterpreted:

> Images, however faithfully copied from Nature, and as accurately represented in words, do not of themselves characterize the poet. They become proofs of original genius only so far as they are modified by a predominant passion, or by associated thoughts and images awakened by that passion.

That is to say, imagery must not assume a *raison d'être* of its own; it must exist, not for its own sake, but as subordinated to the predominant emotion, which it has at once to obey, to express and to communicate. Only in so far as it does this will it, in Keats's words, 'come natural to the reader': otherwise it will

merely distract him. In other words, on the side of the poet the
imagery and the emotion must be one: 'rise, progress, and set'
together in a perfect accord.*

This decisive sign of original poetic genius is evident throughout Keats's sonnet. The unity of imagery and emotion is remarkable: in the octave, the imagery and emotion of eager exploration;
in the sestet, the imagery and emotion of breathless discovery.
The rhythm of the imagery precisely corresponds to the rhythm
of emotion: and with a wonderful subtlety. Never have the true
capacities of the Petrarchan sonnet form been more cunningly
realized; the octave and the sestet have each their separate
crescendo. The rhythm of imagery and emotion of the whole
sonnet is reduplicated in either part. In the first the silence of
eager expectation and impotent surmise is triumphantly broken by

Till I heard Chapman speak out loud and bold;

in the second, where a repetition of the actual effect is impossible,
because Chapman's *Homer* has been discovered and the discovery
cannot be undone, its equivalent is nevertheless compassed by a
master-stroke of intuitive genius, by a sort of imaginative parallel-
ism. The silence of infinite space is first suggested, and against
that silence absolute the silence of Cortez sounds like a thunder-
crash.

Analysis will not carry us farther than this revelation of the
intricate structure of the harmony which makes so single and so
signal an effect upon us. Yet, paradoxically, the more the intri-
cacy of the structure is realized the more impossible it becomes to
conceive that the poem was constructed deliberately as a watch-
maker constructs a chronometer. The complexity, the more
closely we comprehend it, the more obviously is the complexity
of an organism. To find an analogue or explanation for it we
are forced to go to the new-born animal, before whose birth there
is indeed a long period of elaboration, but the elaboration is unconscious, and occurs in the darkness of the womb.

Yet, apart from the initial difficulty of applying such a theory
to the genesis of a poem — namely, that if the elaboration is

unconscious, *ex hypothesi* we can know nothing about it, and it must remain a pure conjecture — how is it possible to call such a theory in aid in the present case when we know that Keats had read Chapman's *Homer* for the first time on the evening before he wrote his sonnet, and that he went on reading it till the break of day? Within two or three hours after that the sonnet was written.

Let us begin our inquiry by returning to the immediate impression made by the sonnet. We are conscious of a certain discrepancy between the emotional content of the poem and its ostensible cause: as we have said, for the reader of the poem Chapman's *Homer* is as it were dissolved away in the intensity of the emotion it has excited. That noble book, in its own quiddity, passes out of question; its function is not its own self-existence, but rather to be a symbol of something beyond itself, a point of crystallization for a condition of thought and feeling which existed in independence of it. Chapman's *Homer*, we feel, has served the office of a spark to ignite a highly combustible gas in the poet's mind into a flash of incandescence. The force of the explosion is as great as the flame is beautiful.

Of so much a sensitive reader is conscious through a simple submission of his mind to the isolated sonnet. But if he goes farther and reads it no longer in isolation, but in its native setting among Keats's poetry of this period — that is to say, if he reads it in its place in Keats's first volume of poetry — the immediate impression becomes more definite. He becomes aware, at first perhaps only vaguely, that this particular sonnet, besides being the one perfect poem in that uneven and exciting book, is a crystallization of a mood of thought and feeling which exists in solution throughout the volume. In the sonnet Keats succeeded in expressing, with a strange completeness and concision, a complex condition of thought and feeling which finds imperfect and partial utterance in nearly all his serious poems of the same period.

The condition is not easy to describe, it needs to be demon-

strated; but we may call it, provisionally, the ardour of exploration and the excitement of discovery.

We are first aware of it as a baffled ardour to explore two
different realms — Poetry and Nature. In the *Epistle to George
Felton Mathew*, written in November 1815, Keats cries:

> Far different cares
> Beckon me sternly from soft 'Lydian airs',
> And hold my faculties so long in thrall,
> That I am oft in doubt whether at all
> I shall again see Phoebus in the morning . . .

He was working at medicine in the Borough. The Borough was
a dirty place, and the lodgings of medical students there, to judge
by Dickens's account of Bob Sawyer's rooms in Lant Street, took
the colour of their surroundings. In the same *Epistle* Keats
laments that even if he had the time for poetry he could not write
it there:

> But might I now each passing moment give
> To the coy muse, with me she would not live
> In this dark city.

The darkness and the gloom forbid. From the first quotation it is
already apparent that for Keats Nature and Poetry are one.
'Soft Lydian airs' are the virtual equivalent of 'seeing Phoebus in
the morning'. The idea that he might be the poet of a city of
dreadful night never entered his head. Nature and Poetry are
one; and he is chained prisoner from both. Again:

> O Solitude! if I must with thee dwell,
>   Let it not be among the jumbled heap
>   Of murky buildings; climb with me the steep,—
> Nature's observatory — whence the dell,
> Its flowery slopes, its river's crystal swell,
>   May seem a span . . .

Perhaps he had broken his bonds for a moment and climbed
out of the dingy Borough. His escape is more certain in a sonnet
of the early summer, 1816:

'THE REALMS OF GOLD'

To one who has been long in city pent,
    'Tis very sweet to look into the fair
    And open face of heaven — to breathe a prayer
Full in the smile of the blue firmament.

What had happened? He had found his way to Hampstead Heath; and not merely to Nature and Poetry in the simple sense, but not long after to the company of a poet. Cowden Clarke had shown some of Keats's verses to Leigh Hunt. Hunt had been, as he himself tells us, 'fairly surprised with the truth of their ambition and ardent grappling with nature' (*The Examiner*, December 1st, 1816), and had invited Keats to his cottage in the Vale of Health on the Heath. To Hunt's cottage Keats went often, in the autumn of 1816, and stayed long. (Even his first visit, says Clarke, was prolonged into three morning calls.) He departed reluctantly. Two of his sonnets of 1816 are concerned with his journeys back to the Borough from Hunt's cottage. One describes, with singular charm, his walk back beneath the stars:

Keen, fitful gusts are whisp'ring here and there
    Among the bushes half leafless, and dry;
    The stars look very cold about the sky,
And I have many miles on foot to fare.
Yet feel I little of the cool bleak air,
    Or of the dead leaves rustling drearily,
    Or of those silver lamps that burn on high,
Or of the distance from home's pleasant lair:
For I am brimfull of the friendliness
    That in a little cottage I have found;
Of fair-hair'd Milton's eloquent distress,
    And all his love for gentle Lycid drown'd;
Of lovely Laura in her light green dress,
    And faithful Petrarch gloriously crown'd.

We are fairly safe in dating that in the same month as the Chapman sonnet; and probably another sonnet, definitely entitled *On leaving some Friends at an early Hour*, belongs to the same moment. In the first he had been brimfull of friendly and excited talk of poetry as he shaped the lines on his long walk home; but the excitement was comparatively calm. In the second sonnet it could scarcely be controlled at all:

> Give me a golden pen, and let me lean
>   On heap'd up flowers, in regions clear, and far;
> Bring me a tablet whiter than a star . . .

It is absurd, preposterous; but it comes off. The purity of sheer enthusiasm carries it:

> The while let music wander round my ears,
>   And as it reaches each delicious ending,
>   Let me write down a line of glorious tone,
>   And full of many wonders of the spheres:
>   For what a height my spirit is contending!
>   'Tis not content so soon to be alone.

Such was the ambition with which his contact with Nature and Poetry together at Hampstead had filled him. But we have outrun chronology. We have passed from spring to autumn. Let us go back to the spring.

Hunt had published a poem of his — the sonnet to *Solitude* — on May 6th, 1816, in *The Examiner*. No doubt to Keats, as to any common slave of the inkpot, publication was a tangible evidence of vocation. His mind forsook his gallipots, once and for all. He must be with Nature and Poetry. He walked the Heath; he stood tiptoe upon his little hill, by the gate which leads from the Heath to the field by Ken Wood. It was not enough. He must go away. And away he went, to Margate — to something he had not seen before, the sea. In August he wrote an *Epistle* to his brother George:

> Full many a dreary hour have I past,
> My brain bewilder'd, and my mind o'ercast
> With heaviness; in seasons when I've thought
> No sphery strains by me could e'er be caught
> From the blue dome . . .

Again Nature and Poetry are one: the sphery strains are caught direct from the blue dome. All his three *Epistles*: to Mathew, to George, to Cowden Clarke, are concerned with a single theme, his consuming ambition to write poetry and his conviction that poetry is somehow directly created in the poet's soul by Nature. Nature is poetry — 'The poetry of earth is never dead' — but to his knowledge of Nature one thing is now added — the ocean. 'E'en now,' he writes to George:

> E'en now I'm pillow'd on a bed of flowers
> That crowns a lofty cliff, which proudly towers
> Above the ocean-waves . . .

So in his *Epistle* the simple fact; in his sonnet of the same time to the same brother George, he tells of the significance.

> The ocean with its vastness, its blue green,
> Its ships, its rocks, its caves, its hopes, its fears,—
> Its voice mysterious, which whoso hears
> Must think on what will be, and what has been.

Let us pause to gather together the scattered threads of this tumultuous condition of thought and feeling. A double excitement was fermenting in Keats: the excitement of a discovery of Nature and of a far fuller discovery of poetry. But the excitement is one, and its unity finds utterance in the lovely lines of *I stood tiptoe upon a little hill.*

> Open afresh your round of starry folds,
> Ye ardent marigolds!
> Dry up the moisture from your golden lids,
> For great Apollo bids
> That in these days your praises should be sung
> On many harps, which he has lately strung.

Keats's harp, we may be sure, was the chief of them. He is at once exploring Nature and his own powers of poetry; and the two explorations are a single process. Elsewhere in the same poem his power of poetry is precisely identified with his power of response to Nature. Nature creates her poet. The poet's mind is

> ever startled by the leap
> Of buds into ripe flowers; or by the flitting
> Of diverse moths, that aye their rest are quitting;
> Or by the moon lifting her silver rim
> Above a cloud, and with a gradual swim
> Coming into the blue with all her light.

(There, unmistakably, is the naïve and charming bud of the full-flowered:

> Then felt I like some watcher of the skies
> When a new planet *swims* into his ken.)

And Keats goes on, after an apostrophe to the moon:

> For what has made the sage or poet write
> But the fair paradise of Nature's light?

So the ardour of exploration and the excitement of discovery become threefold: of the beauty of Nature, of the beauty of poetry, and of his own power to utter the beauty of Nature in poetry. And as his excitement gathers, so does his confidence in his own powers. In the sonnet *Great spirits now on earth are sojourning*, there is no mistaking the reference of:

> And other spirits there are standing apart
> Upon the forehead of the age to come;
> These, these will give the world another heart,
> And other pulses.

It is to himself.

Now let us take stock of our materials — what we have gathered towards the making of the Chapman sonnet. The moment is apt, for that spirit 'standing apart upon the forehead of the age to come' is curiously reminiscent of Cortez on his peak in Darien. We have the ardour of exploration, the excitement of discovery: of Nature, of Poetry, and of Keats's own powers of poetry. We have an ocean, that speaks to him unutterable things, upon which he looks down from a lofty cliff. We have, if not a planet, a moon, to whom he cries:

'THE REALMS OF GOLD'

O Maker of sweet poets, dear delight
Of this fair world, and all its gentle livers;

whom he had first described in *Calidore*,

Lovely the moon in ether, all alone,

and later as 'with a gradual swim, coming into the blue with all
her light'.

The discovery of poetry — the thing in itself and his own
powers of it — the discovery of the moon, the discovery of the
ocean. Since Nature and Poetry are one to him, why should not
all these be the same? But how to express these as discoveries?
The moon had been discovered — why not a new planet? The
ocean had been discovered — why not the ocean when it was
unknown?

A good deal seems to be gathered together in Keats's unconsciousness. Can we follow it still nearer to the point of fusion?

Keats's longest and most ambitious poem of this year 1816 was
Sleep and Poetry. It was composed at intervals between the early
autumn and the winter of the year. Part of it, perhaps the greater
part of it, was written before the Chapman sonnet. But in its
entirety it belongs to the same moment, temporal and spiritual;
and its occasion, characteristically enough, was a white night
spent on the sofa at Hunt's cottage, where he lay thinking of
poetry, with a picture of Petrarch and Laura before his eyes.

Most happy they!
For over them was seen a free display
Of out-spread wings, and from between them shone
The face of Poesy: from off her throne
She overlook'd things that I scarce could tell.
The very sense of where I was might well
Keep Sleep aloof: but more than that there came
Thought after thought to nourish up the flame
Within my breast; so that the morning light
Surprised me even from a sleepless night;

> And up I rose refresh'd, and glad, and gay,
> Resolving to begin that very day
> These lines; and howsoever they be done,
> I leave them as a father does his son.

Naturally there is not much about sleep in the poem; as it was conceived in a night without sleep, so sleep in the poem is but the whiffler before the mighty king — Poetry. From the first we are conscious that the poet is straining to utter a conception of poetry too great for his words. He has had an intuition into a mystery, which he seeks again and again to declare. Poetry, he seems to be saying, is the instinctive response of the purified soul to the wonder and majesty of the Universe: through the poet the All finds voice.

> To see the laurel wreath, on high suspended,
> That is to crown our name when life is ended.
> Sometimes it gives a glory to the voice,
> And from the heart up-springs, 'Rejoice! rejoice!'
> Sounds which will reach the Framer of all things,
> And die away in ardent mutterings.

> No one who once the glorious sun has seen,
> And all the clouds, and felt his bosom clean
> For his great Maker's presence, but must know
> What 'tis I mean, and feel his being glow.

Suddenly comes the bitter thought that he may not live to achieve the poetry he dreams of, and he cries:

> O for ten years, that I may overwhelm
> Myself in poesy; so I may do the deed
> That my own soul has to itself decreed.

Then he tries to explain what the deed is. 'First, the realm I'll pass of Flora, and old Pan', which indeed he did pass, though not as the crow flies, in *Endymion*. But that indulgence of his delight in the loveliness of Nature is only the prelude to his real purpose.

> Yes, I must pass them for a nobler life,
> Where I may find the agonies, the strife
> Of human hearts.

Clear enough, it seems; he will leave the world of Nature for the world of men and women. But the reason he gives is startling — 'for lo! I see...a car'. He has a vision of a chariot and a charioteer, who drives from the sky to the mountains, from the mountains to a concourse of 'shapes of delight, of mystery, and fear', to whom he listens, 'awfully intent'. The detail of the vision is obscure; but it is plain that the charioteer is some strange embodiment of the spirit of Poetry, and that the vision meant much to Keats, for his next words are deeply felt:

> The visions all are fled — the car is fled
> Into the light of heaven, and in their stead
> A sense of real things comes doubly strong,
> And, like a muddy stream, would bear along
> My soul to nothingness: but I will strive
> Against all doubtings, and will keep alive
> The thought of that same chariot, and the strange
> Journey it went.

So ends the first movement of the poem — an attempt to declare a mysterious significance of poetry, and a proclamation of his own intention to achieve it.

The second movement begins with the famous apostrophe:

> Is there so small a range
> In the present strength of manhood, that the high
> Imagination cannot freely fly
> As she was wont of old?

It is a vision of the present state of poetry in a country which had been its chosen home.

> Who could paragon
> The fervid choir that lifted up a noise
> Of harmony, to where it aye will poise

> Its mighty self of convoluting sound,
> Huge as a planet, and like that roll round,
> Eternally around a dizzy void?

We note that the great English poetry of the past is imaged as a planet rolling round, and pass to his denunciation of the age of reason that 'blasphemed the bright Lyrist to his face'.

> Ah dismal soul'd!
> The winds of heaven blew, the ocean roll'd
> Its gathering waves — ye felt it not. The blue
> Bared its eternal bosom, and the dew
> Of summer nights collected still to make
> The morning precious: beauty was awake!
> Why were ye not awake?

Again we note that response to ocean, first seen by Keats a bare few weeks before, has become part of the acid test of true poetry. But now, he exults, the time of barrenness is past. There is a rebirth of Poetry, and he hopes that, before he dies, she will regain all her past glories.

So to the third movement. He will be charged with presumption. (He was, and most venomously, by Byron.) He will hide from the thunderbolt, if he hides at all, in the midmost light of Poetry. Against all charges of presumption he vindicates himself by reiterating his claim that he *knows*.

> What though I am not wealthy in the dower
> Of spanning wisdom; though I do not know
> The shiftings of the mighty winds that blow
> Hither and thither all the changing thoughts
> Of man: though no great minist'ring reason sorts
> Out the dark mysteries of human souls
> To clear conceiving: yet there ever rolls
> A vast idea before me, and I glean
> Therefrom my liberty; thence too I've seen
> The end and aim of Poesy.

We note that an ocean rolls, a planet rolls; but hardly an idea.

But ocean, planet, and this idea were, by this time, all one to Keats's imagination. For this is the idea he has been trying to communicate throughout the poem — the idea of Poetry that he has discovered. He says so: 'Thence too I've seen the end and aim of Poesy.' And, though he cannot explain, it shines vast and lucid before him.

> 'Tis clear
> As anything most true: as that the year
> Is made of the four seasons — manifest
> As a large cross, some old cathedral's crest,
> Lifted to the white clouds. Therefore should I
> Be but the essence of deformity,
> A coward, did my very eye-lids wink
> At speaking out what I have dared to think.
> Ah! rather let me like a madman run
> Over some precipice: let the hot sun
> Melt my Daedalian wings, and drive me down
> Convuls'd and headlong!

Better any fate than deny his discovery of the idea, the planet, the ocean. Cortez stands on his peak, and can no other. He looks out before him. What does he see? It is an ocean, after all.

> Stay, an inward frown
> Of conscience bids me be more calm awhile.
> An ocean dim, sprinkled with many an isle,
> Spreads awfully before me. How much toil!
> How many days! what desperate turmoil!
> Ere I can have explored its widenesses.
> Ah, what a task! upon my bended knees,
> I could unsay those — no, impossible!
> Impossible!

By these devious ways we have followed Cortez-Keats while he has climbed the steep to the peak in Darien to discover with wondering eyes the dim ocean before him. With him we stare at the Pacific: it is not exactly Chapman's *Homer*, but rather his vast and rolling idea of poetry, and his own poetry to be; and if we are at all his men we feel the tremor of a wild surmise: surely not less thrilling because the peak in Darien is found in the final inquiry to be situate somewhere between the cliffs of Margate and the heights of Hampstead Heath.

But what can we claim to have accomplished by this investigation? To have explained a great poem? Assuredly not. The act of composing the sonnet on Chapman's *Homer* remains unique and beyond analysis. But we can, I think, fairly claim to have substantiated the theory that the composition of a *great* poem is but a final conscious act supervening upon a long process of unconscious elaboration.*

Can we, with the help of our evidence, more clearly define the nature of this process? What elements can we distinguish in it?

First and foremost, a predominant, constantly recurring complex of thought and emotion. Throughout the period of unconscious elaboration Keats had been continually discovering more and more of what was to him the highest reality: Nature, Poetry, the Nature of Poetry; and the continual discovery was accompanied by an incessant emotional excitement. Whether his successive acts of discovery can properly be called 'thoughts' will depend upon the philosophy of the man describing them; but 'thoughts' they shall be for us, as they were for Keats:

> There came
> Thought after thought to nourish up the flame
> Within my breast . . .

These successive thoughts (which some would call intuitions), accompanied by an incessant emotional excitement, form what Coleridge calls 'a predominant passion' — more exactly a persistent process of thought-emotion.

Second, in the service of this persistent thought-emotion the specific poetic-creative faculty has been continually at work to find means of expression for it. These means of expression are chiefly images derived from a series of particular sense-perceptions. Thus, the poet's first perception of the moon:

> Lovely the moon in ether, all alone

is refined to a subtler perception of her

> Lifting her silver rim
> Above a cloud, and with a gradual swim
> Coming into the blue with all her light.

And this sense-perception is used to enable the poet to grasp his own thought of the nature of poetry. The smooth and lovely motion of the moon is a quality of the poetry he conceives:

> More strange, more beautiful, more smooth, more regal
> Than wings of swans, than doves, than dim-seen eagle.

So the image of the moon becomes an image of his thought of poetry.

Again, he sees the sea for the first time, and that perception of the sea, with its attendant emotion, enables him once again to grasp his main thought with its emotion. The image of the vast ocean also becomes an image of his vast 'idea' of poetry. Nay more, the very sound of the sea,

> which whoso hears
> Must think on what will be, and what has been,

enables him to make audible, as the sight of the sea to make visible his thought. Again, another aspect of his thought is grasped through the vision of himself standing alone on a cliff (at Margate) or on a hill (at Hampstead), staring with wondering eyes at the prospect before him. He is 'a spirit standing apart upon the forehead of the age to come'.

So the poet's mind has been accumulating through successive acts of sense-perception a series of images which can be assimilated into the main process of his thought and act as surrogates for it. And the condition of this assimilation is an emotional and qualitative correspondence. His perception of the moon is a delighted discovery, so is his perception of the ocean — in both the hidden loveliness of an unknown reality is revealed to him; therefore, both in the qualities discovered and in the emotion awakened in discovering them, these sense-discoveries are analogous to the main thought — discovery of the nature of poetry. With his senses he discovers Nature, with his thoughts he discovers the nature of poetry.

His two crowning sense-discoveries were those of the moon and sea, and those are instantly pressed into the service of his thought: the images of the moon and the ocean can serve at will to embody the objects of his thought. And he is able to think more exactly concerning the nature of poetry because the sensuous images of moon and ocean are become true symbols of the reality about which he is thinking. So that in the process of unconscious elaboration the continually progressing thought is given ever fresh definition and substance by the images it is able to assimilate; and, on the other hand, the images acquire a thought-content. The thought steadily gains focus and intensity; the images significance.

Suddenly this complex of thought and images, which is working itself towards an organic unity, is ejected into poetic form. What occasions this sudden birth? The dominant thought, with its attendant emotion, is given a final focus by a particular event. The discovery of the nature of poetry, which had been going on for months, is consummated by the discovery of Chapman's *Homer*. Utterance becomes urgent, necessary, inevitable. The means are at hand — images long since assimilated to that dominant thought-emotion, of which the discovery of Chapman is the final instance and occasion.

But there is a final creative act. If this unconscious preparation were all, we should imagine Keats in his sestet saying: 'Then felt I — as I did when I discovered the moon, as I did when I discovered the ocean.' But the moon was discovered long ago, and so was the ocean. It will not do. It must be: 'Then felt I — as a man who discovers a new planet, as a man who discovers a new ocean.' Then to his need came the memory of Robertson's

America, which he had read as a schoolboy. An inexact memory
— for as Tennyson pointed out, it was Balboa, not Cortez, who
stared at the Pacific — but one definite enough to give the final
perfection to his imagery.

Of the last act of poetic creation there is nothing to say. We
cannot explain it; but it is no longer utterly miraculous. We have
seen at least how the main materials lay ready prepared for the
final harmonious ordering; part, and not the least part, of the final
harmony had already been achieved; we may fairly say that the
actual composition of this great poem was but the conscious last
of a whole series of unconscious acts of poetic creation. And we
may hazard the guess that it is this long period of unconscious
preparation which distinguishes the great poem from the merely
good one; that this is the reason why, in a great poem, the subject
seems to be dissolved away in the incandescence of the emotion it
kindles; and, finally, that this is the reason why the depths of
significance in a great poem are inexhaustible.

CHAPTER V

'THE CAVE OF QUIETUDE'

TOWARDS the end of the Fourth Book of *Endymion*, when the shepherd-prince seems to be as far from his goal of beatitude as he was at the beginning of the First, Keats commiserates with him:

> Endymion! unhappy! it nigh grieves
> Me to behold thee thus in last extreme:
> Ensky'd ere this, but truly that I deem
> Truth the best music in a first-born song.

Even when we have read the poem many times, the last line of that apology strikes us amiss; the more amiss the more we know of the circumstances under which the poem was composed. It was intended, before a line of it was written, to be a poem of four Books of a thousand lines each: and the reason why Endymion, three-quarters of the way through the Fourth Book, had not been 'ensky'd ere this' seems only too obvious. Four thousand lines had to be written before he could be allowed his apotheosis. Why drag in Truth?

But as we grow more intimately acquainted with what Keats called 'his inmost bosom', we become persuaded that it was impossible for him to be disingenuous even in a trifle of behaviour, far less in the conduct of a poem into which for the most of a year he put all his heart and soul. We become convinced that if he said it was Truth that kept Endymion so long from the bliss that was his destiny, it veritably was Truth.

Our dissatisfaction changes into downright difficulty. We take Keats's word for it that Truth is the culprit, yet we cannot see how Truth may be blamed. We conclude therefore, reluctantly and with a certain sorrow, that we do not even yet understand the poem.

Some, who stick to the orderly allegorical interpretation of the poem, and believe that Endymion had to travel through the elements of earth and water and air before his release, may be content with this explanation. I am not, and never was; though it might not be easy to justify my discontent. This discontent is really based, first on an entire dissatisfaction with the systematic allegorical explanation itself, as something alien to the poetic idiosyncrasy of Keats, and second upon a conviction that even had this allegorical purpose been half so present to his mind as its exponents maintain, Keats would never have dreamed of calling its exigencies the exigencies of Truth.

There were moments, above all in the Fourth Book, when Keats was truly identified with his hero. The tale was a tale no longer. And just after he has said that he would have granted him his happiness before, but for the claims of Truth, he brings himself back with a start to the realization that it is a legend that he commemorates:

> Yes, moonlight Emperor! felicity
> Has been thy meed for many thousand years;
> Yet often have I, on the brink of tears,
> Mourn'd as if yet thou wert a forester; —
> Forgetting the old tale.

When that was Keats's attitude to his hero, it was not really possible for him to say that either the necessities of allegory, or the demands of a four thousand line poem, were the Truth which kept his beloved friend, his other self, from felicity. It was something more real and more intimate than that: something that Keats could call Truth, and could not have called by another name.

That *Endymion* has, in the large and general sense, an important meaning has been acknowledged by competent critics now for many years; and most of these would agree with Colvin's judgment that 'The tale of the loves of the Greek shepherd-prince and the moon-goddess turns under Keats's hand into a parable of the adventures of the poetic soul striving after full communion with the spirit of essential Beauty.'

But that description is brief; and *Endymion* is long. Moreover, the description depends for its cogency upon our persuasion of the reality of 'the spirit of essential Beauty'; or at least upon our persuasion that Keats himself believed in its reality. And this is doubtful. For, though Keats does speak, in his letters and with specific reference to *Endymion*, of 'essential Beauty', it is not as 'a spirit' that he speaks of it. On the contrary, in his letter to Bailey (November 22nd, 1817) he says:

> I am certain of nothing but of the holiness of the Heart's affections, and the truth of Imagination — What the Imagination seizes as Beauty must be Truth — whether it existed before or not — for I have the same Idea of all our Passions as of Love they are all in their sublime, creative of essential Beauty. In a Word, you may know my favorite speculation by my first Book [i.e. of *Endymion*]. . . .

That is not an easy passage. Though Keats emphatically disclaimed the title of a philosopher, it is metaphysical, and daring metaphysics. 'What the Imagination seizes as Beauty must be Truth' appears to mean that what the Imagination conceives as Beauty must be actually existent, 'whether it existed before or not'.

No doubt here, as so often in his Letters, Keats is in travail of his own conception; it is struggling to be born in and through him. To pin him down to this tentative enunciation would be disastrous; and almost as dangerous would be the impulse to water his doctrine down. That 'all our passions, in their sublime, are *creative* of essential Beauty' is by no means the same as saying that 'all our passions . . . lead us to communion with the spirit of essential Beauty'.

When Keats wrote to Bailey on November 22nd, 1817, he was nearing the end of *Endymion*. There were only some 500 lines of Book IV still to be written, he said. Therefore he was at about

'THE CAVE OF QUIETUDE'

l. 500 — just before his description of the Cave of Quietude. Perhaps he was wondering how to conclude his poem. Endymion had discovered the Indian Maid and fallen in love with her. Love happened, it was irresistible; and the shepherd-prince could not gainsay it. But he was torn by the thought of treachery to the Moon-Goddess; and torn again by a deep sense of his own innocence. He cries:

> Can I prize thee, fair maid, all price above
> Even when I feel as true as innocence?
> I do, I do — What is this soul then? Whence
> Came it? It does not seem my own, and I
> Have no self-passion or identity.

'I am certain of nothing', the mortal author of *Endymion* was then writing to his friend, 'but the holiness of the Heart's affections, and the truth of Imagination.' Here, in the passion for the Indian Maid, was at least the Heart's affection; and it is possible that in the passion for the Moon-Goddess was that seizing of Beauty by the Imagination which was either a seizing or a creation of Truth.

Endymion and his Indian lady leap on to the winged horses which appear miraculously before them, and they mount together into the empyrean. Endymion sleeps on the journey and dreams of complete bliss among the Immortals. The Moon-Goddess bends towards him in his dream, and he awakes to the loveliness of the sleeping maid beside him. The dream and the reality exist side by side: he turns bewildered from one to the other and utters his perplexity. The mortal pair soar upward on their voyage. Before them the moon rises into beauty. Endymion turns to see if the maid has marked it, and as he looks she fades into nothingness in the cold moonshine.

He passes into a realm of ultimate despair, yet also of final calm.

> The man is yet to come
> Who hath not journeyed in this native hell.
> But few have ever felt how calm and well
> Sleep may be had in that deep den of all.

169

These lines and those which follow them describe a peculiar mood, or rather a peculiar experience, which was recurrent in Keats's brief life, and which was to receive perfect expression in the description of the countenance of Moneta in *The Fall of Hyperion*. In *Endymion* it is thus described:

> Happy gloom!
> Dark Paradise! where pale becomes the bloom
> Of health by due; where silence dreariest
> Is most articulate; where hopes infest;
> Where those eyes are the brightest far that keep
> Their lids shut longest in a dreamless sleep.
> O happy spirit-home! O wondrous soul!
> Pregnant with such a den to save the whole
> In thine own depth.

Here, as so often in Keats, even the careful reader easily passes over the significance of the words. Marvellously, he says, the soul contains this seldom discovered 'cave of quietude' which has the virtue of receiving into itself and regenerating the whole of the pain-tormented human being. Keats was right. Comparatively few men have made this discovery; and those who do are generally called mystics, or more foolish names. But the experience was central to Keats; it belonged to his innermost self.

From this secret cave of strange experience Endymion is borne to earth again. The 'first touch . . . went nigh to kill'. There he finds the Maid, and he vows that he will live in humble happiness with her for ever. He renounces his visionary quest.

> I have clung
> To nothing, lov'd a nothing, nothing seen
> Or felt but a great dream! O I have been
> Presumptuous against love, against the sky,
> Against all elements, against the tie
> Of mortals each to each, against the blooms
> Of flowers, rush of rivers, and the tombs
> Of heroes gone! Against his proper glory
> Has my own soul conspired: so my story

Will I to children utter, and repent.
There never liv'd a mortal man, who bent
His appetite beyond his natural sphere,
But starv'd and died.

But the Indian Maid replies that it is forbidden he to become his love. His superhuman and his human quests alike have failed. He leaves her with his sister Peona; but something bids him return, and when he returns, it is to watch the Indian Maid transfigured before his eyes into his ethereal mistress, the Goddess of the Moon.

The main defect of *Endymion*, once we have learned — and we should learn it early — to pass lightly over the cloying language of his lovers in ecstasy, is disproportion in structure. But if we are patient enough it is not difficult to disengage the pattern from the excessive detail under which it seems at first sight to be smothered. The general pattern of events in Book IV, which we have related, is certainly significant; it has meaning. The metamorphosis of the Indian Maid into the Moon-Goddess has an obvious bearing upon the relation between 'the holiness of the Heart's affections' and 'the Truth of the Imagination'. Since that relation cannot be one of simple identity, we must suppose Keats to mean that the sacred affections of the Heart, loyally obeyed, lead to the same ultimate truth which is prefigured to the Imagination as Beauty. It is impossible not to connect this doctrine with that more clearly expounded in a later letter on the world 'as a Vale of Soul-making', where we are told that 'the Heart is the Mind's Bible, it is the Mind's experience, it is the teat from which the Mind or Intelligence sucks its identity'. The Heart, we are told again, is 'the seat of the human passions'. This accords perfectly with the statement, already quoted, in the letter to Bailey. 'I have the same Idea of all our Passions as of Love; they are all in their sublime, creative of essential Beauty.' And it is fairly clear from that passage that the passion of the Imagination for Beauty in some sense belongs, with human love, to the passions of the Heart. The passions of the Heart, in this large sense, Keats says, are sacred. If loyally obeyed they will lead a man to — what? That is hard to say, and no doubt Keats (at least when he wrote *Endymion*) did not know. They were to be trusted, and by trusting them a man would reach the highest, whatever that highest might be. But what if the passions of the Heart are contradictory?

This is precisely the question which Keats strives to answer in Book IV of *Endymion*. The human passion for the Indian Maid, and the imaginative passion for the Moon-Goddess are in fearful conflict. The conflict is resolved. True, it is finally resolved by a miracle; by the actual metamorphosis of the human into the immortal mistress. But Keats gives us more than poetic symbolism; in the passage which describes the Cave of Quietude he makes a brave attempt to portray the actual psychological process of the resolution.

It may be objected that the Cave of Quietude is, no less than the metamorphosis of the Indian Maid into the Moon-Goddess, poetical symbolism; but since any attempt to depict the subtler anatomy of the human psyche must inevitably be more or less figurative, the objection is invalid. And those who, like myself, believe that Keats was a very subtle psychologist indeed will find the Cave of Quietude well worth exploring.

It is as the result of desperate inward conflict that Endymion enters it. Both the Moon-Goddess and the mortal maiden have faded into nothingness. And more than this; not only has his soul been divided between them; but in the cleft, all constant personality seems to have disappeared. 'I have no self-passion or identity.' But we do not have to gather the condition which brought him into the Cave from the story alone. It is definitely described.

> A grievous feud
> Hath led thee to this Cave of Quietude.

The second point to be observed is that Keats, with equal distinctness, asserts that the initial experience is common to men.

> The man is yet to come
> Who hath not journeyed in this native hell.

Keats may have been quite wrong in supposing this; the point of interest is that he did suppose it. How far he was right the reader may judge by reading carefully the description of 'the native hell' which is transformed for some of its visitants into a Cave of Quietude and soul-content.

> There lies a den,
> Beyond the seeming confines of the space
> Made for the soul to wander in and trace
> Its own existence, of remotest glooms.
> Dark regions are around it, where the tombs
> Of buried griefs the spirit sees, but scarce
> One hour doth linger weeping, for the pierce
> Of new-born woe it feels more inly smart:
> And in these regions many a venom'd dart
> At random flies; they are the proper home
> Of every ill: the man is yet to come
> Who hath not journeyed in this native hell.

It is, as the opening lines show, a realm beyond normal (though not outside common) experience. In it old sorrows are clearly but coldly felt. The sting of 'new-born woe' numbs response to the memory of past pains. It is not clear whether any particular meaning is to be attached to the many venom'd darts which fly at random there. But perhaps we may get an inkling of what Keats is trying to describe from the letter to Bailey (October 1817) which was written when he had just begun Book IV. Keats had been ill for a fortnight; the day before, his brother Tom had 'looked very unwell'; his writing of *Endymion* was going painfully; 'in this world', he said, 'there is no quiet — nothing but teazing and snubbing and vexation'. He had felt himself, as so often, unable to write a letter to his friend. It was a moment of Keats's recurrent and peculiar despondency.

> For one thing I am glad that I have been neglectful — and that is, therefrom I have received a proof of your utmost kindness which at this present I feel very much — and I wish

I had a heart always open to such sensations — but there is no altering a Man's nature and mine must be radically wrong for it will lie dormant a whole Month. This leads me to suppose that there are no Men thoroughly wicked, so as never to be self-spiritualized into a kind of sublime Misery — but alas! 'tis but for an Hour ...

A Question is the best beacon towards a little speculation. You ask me after my health and spirits — this question ratifies in my Mind what I have said above — Health and Spirits can only belong unalloyed to the selfish Man — the Man who thinks much of his fellows can never be in Spirits. ...

It seems to me that this 'self-spiritualization into a kind of sublime misery' is the same condition which he is describing in the Cave of Quietude; and I think that probably 'the venom'd darts' which fly at random there are those thoughts of human misery which afflict the unselfish man. In the letter, too, is the torpor of spirit which sees 'the tombs of buried griefs' but cannot weep over them. And perhaps 'the new-born woe' may be that 'sublime misery' into which every man may be 'self-spiritualized', and may proceed precisely from the consciousness of the spiritual torpor which can no longer respond to sorrow or to joy.

In his letter, Keats is led to suppose that there are no men so thoroughly wicked as not to taste this misery; in the poem he more boldly declares:

> The man is yet to come
> Who hath not journeyed in this native hell.

But there is a peace in and beyond this misery of which few men know.

> But few have ever felt how calm and well
> Sleep may be had in that deep den of all.
> There anguish does not sting; nor pleasure pall:
> Woe-hurricanes beat ever at the gate,
> Yet all is still within and desolate.

Beset with painful gusts, within ye hear
No sound so loud as when on curtain'd bier
The death-watch tick is stifled. Enter none
Who strive therefor: on the sudden it is won.
Just when the sufferer begins to burn,
Then it is free to him: and from an urn,
Still fed by melting ice, he takes a draught —
Young Semele such richness never quaft
In her maternal longing. Happy gloom!
Dark Paradise! where pale becomes the bloom
Of health by due; where silence dreariest
Is most articulate; where hopes infest;
Where those eyes are the brightest far that keep
Their lids shut longest in a dreamless sleep.
O happy spirit-home! O wondrous soul!
Pregnant with such a den to save the whole
In thine own depth. Hail, gentle Carian!
For, never since thy griefs and woes began,
Hast thou felt so content: a grievous feud
Hath led thee to this Cave of Quietude.

The main sense of those lines is clear. There is a sudden passing beyond sorrow and joy, which comes unsought for. If it is sought for, it is not found. It comes when misery has reached its extreme point; then the misery marvellously changes into a profound content. Then silence is the fullest utterance, and hope a sacrilege: then, in this calm ecstasy of despair, the whole being of the sufferer is bathed and renewed.

But the return to common things, after this strange experience, is full of pain.

His first touch of the earth went nigh to kill.
'Alas!' said he, 'were I but always borne
Through dangerous winds, had but my footsteps worn
A path in hell, for ever would I bless
Horrors which nourish an uneasiness

For my own sullen conquering: to him
Who lives beyond earth's boundary, grief is dim,
Sorrow is but a shadow: now I see
The grass; I feel the solid ground — Ah, me!

There is a fine piece of subtle psychological description in the phrase: 'Would I bless Horrors which nourish an uneasiness For my own sullen conquering.' The experience which Keats describes may be rare as Keats believed it was; but those who have made some acquaintance with it will recognize the aptness of the phrase which Keats made to fit it.

The importance of this strange experience in *Endymion* lies in the fact that it is the psychological culmination of the poem. With it what we may call the experiential element of the poem ends. There are still events to come, and those events doubtless have their symbolic significance. Endymion utterly renounces his inordinate quest for the Moon-Goddess, and declares that he will live a life of humble earthly circumstance with the Indian Maid. But the Maid refuses: an unknown power forbids. Then once more despondence seizes Endymion; but the despondence is not of the same kind as that which led him to the Cave of Quietude. It is the simple disconsolateness of a fairy-tale. We have passed from the natural to the supernatural, to which order the final metamorphosis of the Indian Maid belongs. It is the poet's declaration of his faith, or of his desire to believe, that the passion of the soul and the passion of the body for Beauty are somehow identical.

But since no axiom was an axiom for Keats till it had been proved upon his pulses, we have a good warrant for distinguishing between the consummation of his mythological tale and the culmination of his own self-exploration; between his faith and his experience. The self-exploration and experience of Keats in *Endymion* end in the Cave of Quietude — in the peace and unity which he suddenly found beyond and through the extremity of despair caused by the self-division which ensued on loyalty to contradictory passions of the Heart.

And the importance of this reaches beyond the under‌.
of *Endymion*. This division and despair and resolution into
forms the recurrent pattern of the inward life of Keats.
process can be traced again and again in his letters and his poem
The travail of incessant rebirth was never far away from him; he
was for ever passing beyond despair. And if at the last he fell into
the clutch of a despair too great for any sullen conquering of his
own, he was not the first hero of mankind who has reached his
final peace through a supreme agony of soul.

But this extended scope of the pattern-process described under
the figure of the Cave of Quietude does not concern us now. We
are concerned with the meaning of *Endymion* alone. To an intimate understanding of that an understanding of the experience of
the Cave of Quietude is essential. Keats had to *live* all his great
poems. The necessity of living them became ever more rigorous
as the years of his brief life drew on. *Hyperion* was lived with a
completeness and intensity with which *Endymion* was not.
Endymion, in comparison with his later poetry, was only half-
lived. In the main it fulfilled the first part of the plan which he
had set before himself in *Sleep and Poetry*:

> O for ten years, that I may overwhelm
> Myself in poesy; so I may do the deed
> That my own soul has to itself decreed.
> Then I will pass the countries that I see
> In long perspective, and continually
> Taste their pure fountains. First the realm I'll pass
> Of Flora, and old Pan: sleep in the grass,
> Feed upon apples red, and strawberries,
> And choose each pleasure that my fancy sees;
> Catch the white-handed nymphs in shady places
> To woo sweet kisses from averted faces . . .
> Till in the bosom of a leafy world
> We rest in silence, like two gems upcurl'd
> In the recesses of a pearly shell.
> And can I ever bid these joys farewell?

Yes, I must pass them for a nobler life
Where I may find the agonies, the strife
Of human hearts . . .

But the life of a great poet does not unroll itself in obedience to
his conscious plan. Though *Endymion* was to be a journey through
the realm of Flora and old Pan, it became inevitably more than
this. Keats could not keep himself out of it, and with himself
there entered his poem the agonies and strife of a human heart.

Herein we find the meaning of the puzzling lines from which
our search began. It was indeed Truth which kept Endymion
from his blessedness. For a resolution into unity had been necessary in the soul of his author. The conflict between the Ideal and
the Real which divided the soul of his hero was too real to Keats
himself to be speciously resolved by a poetic miracle. That might
have been possible when his poem began; but things had happened
since then. The abstract parable had become the painful adventure of his own soul. The resolution of the conflict must be a real
and a lived resolution; to invoke a miracle, simply to tell the
legendary story, was a kind of cheating. But once the conflict
had been resolved in his own experience, the story could
flow onward to its destined and happy end. The necessary Truth
was there.

At a later time, when he came to sing 'the lute-voiced brother'
of Endymion, the correspondence between the progress of his
poem and the process of his own experience was to be still more
close and exacting. *Hyperion* stopped abruptly at the beginning
of the third book. Keats was not then in the mood to allow himself the luxury of prolonged invention; nor, indeed, was he ever
in such a mood again. In *Endymion* he was free enough from the
compulsion of his own veracity to fulfil at least the outward form
of his plan. That was conceived in independence of his own
spiritual history; it was something objective — a work to be done,
and to be done like a workman, with his stint of fifty lines a day.
But the genius who inhabits every man of genius intervened: not
so violently, or so completely, as he intervened in *Hyperion*, but

enough to trouble the substance of what should have been a lovely
fairy-tale, of what still is a lovely fairy-tale, but also is something
more by virtue of that alien vibration — not merely 'the test of his
invention' which he intended, but a trial of his soul.

Endymion is thus something more than a work of that joyful
'first period' which is familiar to us in the work of great poets and
musicians: it is a transition piece. It begins in a first period and
ends in a second.

This first period of Keats was more carefully defined by himself
a few months after he had finished *Endymion,* when the work of
revision was over and the poem put away from himself for ever.

I compare human life [he wrote to Reynolds on May 3rd,
1818, almost exactly a year after the beginning of *Endymion*]
to a large Mansion of Many Apartments, two of which I can
only describe, the doors of the rest being as yet shut upon
me. The first we step into we call the infant, or thoughtless
Chamber, in which we remain as long as we do not think —
We remain there a long while, and notwithstanding the doors
of the second Chamber remain wide open, showing a bright
appearance, we care not to hasten to it; but are at length im-
perceptibly impelled by the awakening of this thinking
principle within us — we no sooner get into the second
Chamber which I shall call the Chamber of Maiden-Thought,
than we become intoxicated with the light and the atmosphere, we see nothing but pleasant wonders, and think of
delaying there for ever in delight: however among the effects
this breathing is father of is that tremendous one of sharpening one's vision into the heart and nature of Man — of convincing one's nerves that the world is full of Misery and
Heartbreak, Pain, Sickness and oppression — whereby this
Chamber of Maiden Thought becomes gradually darken'd,
and at the same time on all sides of it many doors are set open
— but all dark — all leading to dark passages — We see not
the balance of good and evil. We are in a Mist. *We* are now
in that state — we feel the 'burden of the Mystery'.

It is customary to regard this letter as defining two periods in Keats's poetic life. Two Chambers, two periods — the equation is simple. But, in fact, the periods or phases are plainly three. There is the thoughtless delight of pure sensuous experience; there is the delight of awakening thought; and there is the pain and perplexity of fully awakened thought — the torment of the longing to find pattern and purpose in the Universe.

Perhaps Keats's most perfect expression of the first two phases is in *Sleep and Poetry*. There is the sheer delight in pure and thoughtless experience; there is also the sheer intoxication of Maiden Thought. And that is all. There is just a tremor of awareness of the 'dark passages' and no more. But in *Endymion*, there is not only the delight of pure and thoughtless experience, and the intoxication of Maiden Thought (wonderfully expressed in the lines of the Hymn to Pan:

> Be still the unimaginable lodge
> For solitary thinkings; such as dodge
> Conception to the very bourne of heaven
> Then leave the naked brain)

but there is also, in the Fourth Book at least, the pain of fully awakened thought. Even the opening lines of *Endymion* betray an awareness of the 'dark passages'.

> A thing of beauty is a joy for ever . . .
> Therefore, on every morrow, are we wreathing
> A flowery band to bind us to the earth,
> Spite of despondence, of the inhuman dearth
> Of noble natures, of the gloomy days,
> *Of all the unhealthy and o'er-darkened ways*
> *Made for our searching*: yes, in spite of all,
> Some shape of beauty moves away the pall
> From our dark spirits.

In those lines what might be called the musical theme of *Endymion* is given out. Essentially, the poem is the effort to create a thing of beauty before the spirit is darkened; to make the creation of the poem itself a defence against the onset of the doubts and miseries

and feverous speculations, of which he had a clear presentiment.
It is the poem of maiden experience and maiden thought, indeed,
but they are conscious of their doom.

It is as a poem of 'Maiden Thought' that we should consider
Endymion — of thought not yet toughened and tempered by the
grim stress of experience, of surmises that are not yet, and may
never become, certainties.

Endymion is a poem about Love. That, in one restricted sense,
is obvious to the most casual reader. The poem abounds in
luxurious and cloying descriptions of amorous ardours. Keats
had his own word of self-criticism for these indulgences: they
were 'mawkish'. For this 'mawkishness' — this cloying amorous
excess in *Endymion* — there are two causes: one biological, the
other metabiological. The first cause is that *Endymion* belongs
to the young manhood of a physically passionate man, starved of
satisfaction. The poem contains not merely that sensuousness of
the imagination which is the vital substance, and the indispensable
condition of great poetry; it contains also a certain sensuality of
the imagination, which, though not unrelated to the former, must
not be confused with it. This sensuality of the imagination consists in seeking in the creatures of imagination a substitute for that
specific physical satisfaction of which the biological man is in
need. Now there is a sense in which all creations of man's
imagination are a substitution for biological satisfactions; but this
substitution is a transmutation, or in the language of modern
psychology, a sublimation. There is a passing into a different
order. The sensuousness of the creative imagination is biologically disinterested. But sensuality of the imagination is the sign
of a temporary failure in the process of transmutation. The biological desire which was being wholly transformed into metabiological creation now asserts itself as biological desire; the
imagination becomes biologically interested. This distinction can
be clearly illustrated from a letter of Keats himself. In October
1818 he wrote to his brother an account of a beautiful cousin of
his friends the Reynoldses.

KEATS

The Miss Reynoldses are very kind to me — but they have lately displeased me much and in this way ... On my return, the first day I called they were in a sort of taking or bustle about a Cousin of theirs who having fallen out with her Grandpapa in a serious manner, was invited by Mrs. R— to take Asylum in her house— She is an east indian and ought to be her Grandfather's Heir. At the time I called Mrs. R. was in conference with her up stairs and the young Ladies were warm in her praises down stairs: calling her genteel, interesting and a thousand other pretty things to which I gave no heed, not being partial to 9 days wonders — Now all is completely changed — they hate her; and from what I hear she is not without faults — of a real kind; but she has others which are more apt to make women of inferior charms hate her. She is not a Cleopatra, but she is at least a Charmian. She has a rich eastern look; she has fine eyes and fine manners. When she comes into a room she makes an impression the same as the Beauty of a Leopardess. She is too fine and too conscious of her Self to repulse any Man who may address her — from habit she thinks that nothing *particular*. I always find myself more at ease with such a woman; the picture before me always gives me a life and animation which I cannot possibly feel with anything inferior — I am at such times too much occupied in admiring to be awkward or on a tremble. I forget myself entirely because I live in her. You will by this time think I am in love with her; so before I go any further I will tell you I am not — she kept me awake one Night as a tune of Mozart's might do. I speak of the thing as a pass-time and an amusement than which I can feel none deeper than a conversation with an imperial woman the very 'yes' and 'no' of whose Lips is to me a Banquet. I don't cry to take the Moon home with me in my Pocket nor do I fret to leave her behind me. I like her and her like because one has no *sensations* — what we both are is taken for granted.

The quotation is long; but it is always best to understand Keats

by Keats. This condition of 'having no sensations' is precisely
what we mean by being 'biologically disinterested'. The object —
the real Miss Cox in this instance — is an object for disinterested
and sensuous contemplation, which could not be better described
than by Keats's simple sentence: 'I forget myself entirely because
I live in her.' And that disinterested and sensuous contemplation
directed towards not a real human being but a creature of the
imagination is the complete transmutation of biological desire
which, we have said, is essential to the greatest poetry.

Sensuality of the imagination occurs when that process of
transmutation is interrupted. The poet no longer 'forgets himself'; he 'has sensations'. And these 'sensations', of course, are
not the 'sensations rather than thoughts' for which Keats longed.

The author of *Endymion* 'had sensations' more than once while
he was writing his poem. But, though the vicarious satisfaction
of the biological man was the chief cause of the superabundance
and discrepancy of his amorous descriptions, there was another.
Keats was trying to express his faith in love; and his faith in love
was emphatically not limited to 'disinterested' love. He really did
believe in physical passion, no less than in other forms of love;
and he was driven to insist upon it. But to believe in physical
passion without much, and perhaps without any, actual experience
of it is an awkward position for a poet to be in. He can hardly
save himself from a sort of sophisticated innocence, and misplaced
emphasis. The emphasis may be right in intention, but it will be
wrong in tone.

Endymion, we have said, is a poem about love. It is all about
love. And love has many forms.

For Keats all the forms of love belong to the same kind. They
are the response of the Heart or the Mind to Beauty. Though, as
we have seen, a year after writing *Endymion* he could distinguish
clearly between interested and disinterested love, there is no trace
of any such distinction in the poem itself. 'Why may I not speak
of your Beauty,' he wrote to Fanny Brawne in 1819, 'since without that I never could have loved you — I cannot conceive any

beginning of such love as I have for you but Beauty. There may be a sort of love for which, without the least sneer at it, I have the highest respect, and can admire it in others; but it has not the richness, the bloom, the full form, the enchantment of love after my own heart.' At first sight there is a discrepancy between this and his account of his disinterested admiration of Miss Cox. If what he said about Miss Cox was true, it would seem that he might quite well have felt the same disinterested admiration for the beauty of Fanny Brawne; whereas he tells her that he fell in love with her the moment he saw her. But, in fact, the statements are perfectly consistent. He met Miss Cox at a moment when he was not free to love, when the last stages of the lingering illness of his brother Tom depleted his vitality and made thoughts of love a crime. He met Fanny Brawne when he was free again.

For Keats therefore impassioned physical love was a response to Beauty. Probably he would have looked askance at the more cynical wisdom which argues that unconscious desire is the great discoverer of beauty in woman. But even that more cynical wisdom is perhaps not really incompatible with Keats's idealism. It may be that the beauty which unconscious desire discovers is really there, and that it sharpens the senses to a true perception of the uniqueness of one particular thing. Uniqueness, it is true, is not beauty; but it is more beautiful, so to speak, than beauty. In the lover's discovery of the enchanted otherness, the divine idiosyncrasy, of his beloved, we may see prefigured that serene contemplation of existence which high religion theoretically ascribes to God, and which some mortals — Keats himself among them — do occasionally attain. If this prefigurement be true, as I for one incline to believe, then we shall find it hard to say that there is any illusion in even the most romantic love. The enchanting thing was really there: what fails, when the time of disillusion comes, is the power to see it any more. Love is not blind; rather, it sees too well.

Assuredly, such ideas as this were not in Keats's mind when he wrote *Endymion*. He had them afterwards, beyond a doubt. His mind was not yet 'sorted to a pip'; it was, when he wrote

Endymion, like a 'scattered pack of cards', he said — unjustly indeed. He described the condition more truly to Reynolds (February 3rd, 1818), with an evident recollection of a phrase in his own poem: 'Many a man can travel to the very bourne of heaven, and yet want confidence to put down his half-seeing.' There is much 'half-seeing' in *Endymion*.

The great 'half-seen' truth round which the poem wanders is that Love and Beauty are indissolubly united. Love is the response awakened by Beauty in the total being of man. But what was the real connection between them? Was it indeed Beauty which called forth Love, or was it Love which discovered Beauty? Is it the presence of Love within men's hearts — the awakening of a strange emotion — which tells them that Beauty is there; or is it that they perceive Beauty, and the effect of that perception upon them is to awaken Love?

The problem is a real one, though doubtless the solution does not lie in the acceptance of one of the two alternatives. And behind this problem lurks another: What is the status of Beauty? Is it something distinct and definite, so that we can truly say that some things are beautiful and others not, in the same way that we can say some things are red and others not? Or is the perception of Beauty simply a name we give to moments of heightened awareness, of completer perception; and do we distinguish as beautiful not some things which have a peculiar and common quality, but only those things which we happen to see in their completeness, while we happen to be blind to the completeness of others?

These are some of the questions with which Keats's mind was obscurely in travail when he wrote *Endymion*; and they are questions over which the maturest mind might lose itself in pondering. No wonder then that Keats's mind swayed in the winds of self-discovered doctrine. Only when we have grasped the scope and import of such questions are we in some position to understand the depth of meaning, or of surmise, that lies in his seeming-simple statement to Bailey concerning the meaning of his poem. 'I have the same idea of all our passions as of Love: they are all, in their sublime, *creative* of essential Beauty.' We have at least discerned a sense in which the passion of Love may be regarded as creating Beauty: for that Beauty which Love alone discovers, Love may be said to create. But how can this be true of 'all our passions'? Probably the solution is to be found in supposing that Keats restricted Love in his sentence to the passion between man and woman: and 'all our passions' other than Love are simply the other forms of Love — the emotions aroused by the beauty of Art, the beauty of Nature, the perfection of Truth. These, like Love, 'in their sublime', when they are pure and perfectly themselves, discover Beauty where it was hidden, and so 'create' it. And by this road we perhaps approach the meaning of his former sentence:

> What the Imagination seizes as Beauty must be Truth — whether it existed before or not — *for* I have the same idea of all our passions as of Love; they are all, in their sublime, creative of essential Beauty.

The logician might puzzle a long while over the meaning of that 'for' which we have italicized; but now it seems to yield a meaning. What the passion of Imagination apprehends as Beauty must be real; because like all the other passions it conforms to the type of Love, and discovers (and so creates) qualities which were hidden.

Keats was afterwards to refine, or bring closer to earth, this idea of the power of Imagination. Here he seems to regard it as in some sort actually prophetic of, and pregnant with, a corresponding existence. 'I can never feel certain of any truth', he wrote a year later in December 1818, 'but from a clear perception of its Beauty.' It is possible that his meaning was the same in November 1817. 'The Imagination may be compared to Adam's dream,' he said then, 'he awoke and found it truth: — I am the more zealous in this affair, because I have never yet been able to perceive how anything can be known for truth by consecutive reasoning.' But if we suppose, as seems probable from the context and the correspondent (and it was Bailey who had had 'the

momentary start about the authenticity of the Imagination'), that
the discussion concerned some philosophic scheme, there is no
inconsistency. Keats was contending for his belief that 'Beauty
is Truth, Truth Beauty'. He had not yet entered into full possession of his own intuitive certainty; his statement has something
of the vagueness of conjecture.

And we cannot be altogether certain of what Keats meant by
Imagination. Clearly, in his letter, Imagination belongs to Sensation as opposed to Thought. But at other times we may be sure
that what he here calls Imagination is described if not as Thought,
at least as Thinking.

> Solitary thinkings, such as dodge
> Conception to the very bourne of heaven
> Then leave the naked brain —

these, we may be certain, were the work of Imagination — 'Sensations rather than Thoughts'. The difference is between the Thinking which proceeds by a chain of consecutive reasoning, and the
Thinking which moves from 'truth' to 'truth' by 'a clear perception of its Beauty'. Not that this wholly exhausts Keats's concept
of the Imagination; but it certainly covers much of it.

It would be hazardous to attempt to systematize Keats's thinking further. We must call in aid the poem itself.

'You know my favourite speculation from my first Book,' he
had written to Bailey. On January 30th, writing to his publisher,
Taylor, he specified a particular portion of his first book from
which his meaning might be sought. Referring to Endymion's
speech to Peona (ll. 770 sq.), Keats said:

The whole thing must I think have appeared to you, who
are a consequitive Man, as a thing almost of mere words — but
I assure you that when I wrote it, it was a regular stepping of
the Imagination towards a Truth. My having written that
Argument will perhaps be of the greatest Service to me of
anything I ever did. It set before me at once the gradations

of happiness, even like a kind of Pleasure Thermometer, and is my first Step towards the chief attempt in the Drama — the playing of different Natures with Joy and Sorrow.

The importance of the comment and the passage is obvious. Here we actually have an example, in Keats's view one of the chief examples, of the apprehension of Truth by the Imagination under the form of Beauty. The same distinction between this process and the apprehension of Truth by 'consecutive reasoning' is made as in his letter to Bailey. This 'regular stepping of the Imagination towards a truth,' he says, 'must have appeared' to Taylor, who was 'a consequitive man, as a thing almost of mere words'. From this passage therefore we may hope to gain some authentic light on the Imagination, and the meaning of Keats's belief that 'what the Imagination seizes as Beauty must be Truth'.

> Peona! ever have I long'd to slake
> My thirst for the world's praises: nothing base,
> No merely slumberous phantasm, could unlace
> The stubborn canvas for my voyage prepar'd —
> Though now 'tis tatter'd; leaving my bark bar'd
> And sullenly drifting: yet my higher hope
> Is of too wide, too rainbow-large a scope,
> To fret at myriads of earthly wrecks.

So far the prelude. It is worth a moment's paraphrase. Endymion says he has always been ambitious of true fame. The motive of his adventure has been neither base nor fantastic. It has failed; but his hope is of such a kind as to be undimmed by earthly failure far more complete than he had suffered.

> Wherein lies happiness? In that which becks
> Our ready minds to fellowship divine,
> A fellowship with essence; till we shine
> Full alchemiz'd and free of space.

These lines were added by Keats in his revision. They were doubly well considered. True happiness lies in that which draws us, and draws us willingly, into communion 'with essence', whereby we are transmuted and free of bodily limitation. The process, which is certainly mysterious and may be imaginary, is then described.

> Behold
> The clear religion of heaven! Fold
> A rose leaf round thy finger's taperness
> And soothe thy lips: hist, when the airy stress
> Of music's kiss impregnates the free winds
> And with a sympathetic touch unbinds
> Æolian magic from their lucid wombs:
> Then old songs waken from enclouded tombs;
> Old ditties sigh above their father's grave;
> Ghosts of melodious prophecyings rave
> Round every spot where trod Apollo's foot;
> Bronze clarions awake, and faintly bruit,
> Where long ago a Giant Battle was;
> And from the turf, a lullaby doth pass
> In every place where infant Orpheus slept.

We may, without injustice, say that there is a good deal of mere words in that passage. The fancy that hears mysterious music in the winds, or the winding of faint bugles on forgotten battlefields, hardly needed so much elaboration. It would have been better if Keats had remembered the lines of the introduction to his poem, where, among the catalogue of natural beauties which 'move away the pall from our dark spirit', he suddenly and nobly places

> The grandeur of the dooms
> We have imagined for the mighty dead.

For these are included in the thought of his speech to Peona. Not merely faery fancies, but high imaginations are in his mind: the enchantment of all the mysterious beauties of the imagination.

> Feel we these things? — that moment have we stept
> Into a sort of oneness, and our state
> Is like a floating spirit's.

By these raptures of the passive or active imagination we are carried 'out of ourselves', freed from the quotidian consciousness of the outer world and of ourselves. We are 'alchemiz'd', if not fully, at least in part, and 'free of space'.

That is the first gradation of true happiness, on Keats's pleasure thermometer.

> But there are
> Richer entanglements, enthralments far
> More self-destroying, leading by degrees
> To the chief intensity. The crown of these
> Is made of love and friendship, and sits high
> Upon the forehead of humanity.
> All its more ponderous and bulky worth
> Is friendship, whence there ever issues forth
> A steady splendour.

That is, in its kind, clear enough. All we need to remember is that 'friendship and love' are not in themselves 'the chief intensity'; and that 'intensity' and 'intense' are important words in Keats's idiom. Thus he writes to his brothers (December 21st, 1817) that Benjamin West's picture, 'Death on a Pale Horse', though wonderful considering that artist's age, contains 'nothing to be intense upon, no women one feels mad to kiss, no face swelling into reality'; and that comment leads him to make his famous pronouncement that 'the excellence of every art is its intensity, capable of making all disagreeables evaporate from their being in close relationship with Beauty and Truth'. The bearing of this particular use of 'intensity' upon our passage is manifest. When the Truth which is apprehended in the form of Beauty is expressed in a work of art, there is generated an intensity which transmutes the elements of painfulness or ugliness in the thing represented. The work of art is 'intense', and the man who truly experiences it also becomes 'intense'. 'Intensity' thus is, as we say, objective and subjective; and it peculiarly belongs both to the objective identity of Beauty and Truth and to the subjective response to it.

Friendship and Love are the chief of the experiences which lead to 'the chief intensity'. Friendship radiates a steady splendour.

> But at the tip-top
> There hangs by unseen film, an orbed drop
> Of light, and that is love: its influence,
> Thrown in our eyes, genders a novel sense
> At which we start and fret; till in the end,
> Melting into its radiance, we blend,
> Mingle, and so become a part of it.

Now the self is wholly 'destroyed'; there is complete communion.

> Nor with aught else can our souls interknit
> So wingedly; when we combine therewith
> Life's self is nourish'd by its proper pith.

What is this Love that Endymion is describing? It seems clear
enough from the lines which follow that it is impassioned love
between a man and a woman. The intensity of this communion
is so delightful

> That men, who might have towered in the van
> Of all the congregated world . . .
> Have been content to let occasion die
> Whilst they did sleep in love's elysium.
> And truly I would rather be struck dumb,
> Than speak against this ardent listlessness:
> For I have ever thought that it might bless
> The world with benefits unknowingly;
> As does the nightingale, upperched high,
> And cloister'd among cool and bunched leaves —
> She sings but to her love, nor e'er conceives
> How tip-toe Night holds back her dark-grey hood.
> Just so may love, although 'tis understood
> The mere commingling of passionate breath,
> Produce more than our searching witnesseth:
> What I know not: but who, of men, can tell
> That flowers would bloom, or that green fruit would swell

To melting pulp, that fish would have bright mail,
The earth its dower of river, wood and vale,
The meadows runnels, runnels pebble-stones,
The seed its harvest, or the lute its tones . . .
If human souls did never kiss and greet?

Those beautiful lines make it clear that the Love which is 'the
chief intensity' is not intellectual, or imaginative, or in any way
transcendental, but simply passionate (and romantic) love between man and woman. Endymion surmises that it may be very
essential to the economy of the universe; and no doubt, in one
obvious sense, it is as essential to the universe as humanity itself.
But that supplies no reason why it should be 'the chief intensity'.
Its supreme 'intensity' is a matter of experience.

What are we to say of this argument? Even if we are not
sternly consecutive men, and do not simply feel that it is a thing
of mere words, we are bound to say that it is obscure, and that
when its obscurity has been sifted, it does not yield much at first
beyond a few simple assertions: that the supreme happiness lies
in the complete ecstasy of human love; in this ecstasy, the self is
wholly destroyed. There are also various adumbrations and pre-
figurements of this communion — chiefly, the raptures of the
active and passive imagination: the self-dissolution of reverie, and
the self-forgetfulness of contemplation or of the sympathetic
imagination.

But if we want to understand what, in 1817, Keats meant by
saying 'What the Imagination seizes as Beauty must be Truth',
we must look for the answer here. We confess it is not easy to
find. Not for a moment that we believe that the process even then
was not real to Keats, or that his search after truth by this means
was not productive: our doubt is only whether he knew at all
how to express what he had found.

The argument to Peona is but a small part of *Endymion*, however, and though it is worth careful examination in itself, it is in
the context of the poem as a whole that it yields the fullest mean-

ing. Love, we remember, is kindled in the human soul by Beauty. The love that is kindled in the soul of Endymion by the Moon-Goddess is a love of the supreme Beauty — almost, the Idea of Beauty, at any rate something between the perfect type and the archetype of Beauty. In the Third Book (ll. 24 sq.) the Moon is thus conceived; and the passage which begins 'Cynthia, where art thou now' passes, without our being conscious of much incongruity, into:

> O love! how potent hast thou been to teach
> Strange journeyings! Wherever beauty dwells
> In gulf or eyry, mountains or deep dells,
> In light, *in gloom, in star or blazing sun*,
> Thou pointest out the way and straight 'tis won.

Nothing could show more clearly how completely in the poem the Moon-Goddess has lost her particularity, and become simply the symbol of that 'Principle of Beauty' to which alone, along with the Eternal Being and the Memory of Great Men, Keats at this time said he paid reverence.

With this to aid us we may fill out the argument to Peona, somewhat thus. Wherever Beauty is perceived, in Nature, in Poetry — 'all lovely tales that we have heard or read' — in the imaginative comprehension of history — 'the grandeur of the dooms We have imagined for the mighty dead' — or, finally, in a fellow-mortal like the Indian Maid, the Beauty awakens Love in the percipient soul. These various kinds of Love are the Passions, which (Keats says) 'in their sublime are creative of essential Beauty'. The human being surrendering himself to these impulses of pure Love attains finally to some perfect communion; his self is surrendered, or destroyed, in the 'sublimity' of the passion, and he becomes part of this essential Beauty.

Further, the poem as a whole agrees with the argument to Peona, in placing the passion of love for a fellow-mortal at the pinnacle of this process of self-sublimation. The passion for the Indian Maid is the final step in the ascension of Endymion. Again, the faith which he confides to Peona that Love

> might bless
> The world with benefits unknowingly

receives symbolic expression in the Third Book, where by following the impulse of Love, Endymion — unconscious agent though he is — liberates not only Glaucus from bondage but thousands of death-imprisoned souls to happiness. The meaning of the episode is clearly revealed by Glaucus's words to Endymion.

> Aye, hadst thou never loved an unknown power
> I had been grieving at this present hour.

And all this is corroborated by the song of the Indian Maid — *O Sorrow!* — to which Keats referred, equally with Endymion's speech to Peona as giving expression to his 'philosophy' of Beauty. 'In a word,' he wrote to Bailey, 'you may know my favourite speculation by my first Book and the little song I sent you in my last — which is a representation from the fancy of the probable mode of operating in these matters.' The little song was the five opening verses of the song of the Indian Maid. They are self-contained.

> O Sorrow,
> Why dost borrow
> The natural hue of health from vermeil lips? —
> To give maiden blushes
> To the white rose bushes?
> Or is't thy dewy hand the daisy tips?

The fancy is repeated in a way characteristic of Keats, in a new form in each successive verse; but the substance of it is the same, namely, that Sorrow takes away the various beauties of her victim, only to manifest them again as the beauties of nature. The red of vermeil lips descends again upon the white rose or the daisy; the lustre of the bright eye lights the glow-worm or the foam of perilous seas; the songs hushed on the mourner's tongue enrich the nightingale. Thus the passion of sorrowing love is imagined, or feigned by fancy, to be directly creative of beauty.

This is the counterpart of the surmise at the end of the speech to Peona: that the fulfilled love of man and woman helps to sustain the life and beauty of nature.

> Just so may love, although 'tis understood
> The mere commingling of passionate breath
> Produce more than our searching witnesseth . . .

The sorrow of the Indian Maid, and the happy love which Endymion longs for, are twin forms of passionate self-destroying love: and both are conceived as sustaining the spirit of love and life and beauty in all things. This is the simplest and most naïve expression of that faith in the principle of beauty in all things which Keats held to the end of his life. 'I have lov'd the principle of beauty in all things, and if I had had time I would have made myself remembered.' His love for Fanny Brawne was for Keats an example — the supreme example — of his following his faith. That is why he insisted: 'I cannot conceive any beginning of such love as I have for you but Beauty.' His love for her was his own entire personal surrender to the principle of Beauty incarnate in a woman. *Endymion* is prophetic of this personal surrender.

When due allowance is made for the momentary divagations of a luxurious fancy, *Endymion* as a whole faithfully bears out the argument to Peona. To obey Love, to respond to the essential Beauty in all those of its manifestations of which the soul is aware, leads to one end. By his faithfulness to this self-destroying passion, the mortal servant of Love and Beauty adds to the sustaining power of Beauty and Truth and to the spirit and pulse of Good. By virtue of the liberation from Self which the spirit of Beauty works in him by the love which it awakens, he becomes part of the all-pervading all-sustaining creative power.

To some, no doubt, a truth of this sort is not a truth at all, but a mere indulgence of the romantic fancy. And we may readily agree that in the form in which Keats expressed it in *Endymion* it is confused and elusive. He himself would have been the first — he was the first — to make a frank acknowledgment of the failure of his poem; but, he insisted, 'it was as good as he had power to make it'.

Now there is only one way of proving the truth or falsehood of such a surmise as that of Keats. It is, in reality, immune from intellectual criticism. The rationalist may say: There is no such thing as this essential Beauty, to which men's hearts and minds and souls respond by Love, and which by their selfless response to it, they sustain and increase. But the answer is that there is, in men, this response of Love, whether it be caused by 'essential Beauty' or not. The motion, or emotion, of Love, exists and men can follow it, if they will. They can follow it in their lives, and see what happens.

That is what Keats did. He was eminently the man to do it. He had no use for abstract truths. A proverb was no proverb to him until his life had illustrated it. His argument to Peona, how-ever transcendental it may appear, was not a vague speculation, but something to be lived. It was not easy to live. It meant living by a kind of instinctive and intuitive faith, that the 'affections of the Heart' were holy, and that the vision of reality which the Imagination seized as Beauty must somehow be true.

Much of the dynamic of such a faith depends on what is meant by Beauty, and this in turn depends upon the capacity of the par-ticular soul for Love. For Love is the sign of Beauty; Love warns us of, and warrants, the presence of Beauty. The man who has within him the desire, and discovers in himself the power to love all things, and to welcome all experience, finds Beauty where others are blind to it. Not merely this; but Beauty means for him something utterly different from what is generally understood by the name.

This all-embracing capacity of soul Keats possessed. His whole life was determined by the instinctive passion to achieve within himself that intensity which he discerned in the highest art — 'the intensity capable of making all disagreeables evaporate from their being in close relationship with Beauty and Truth'. He took no pride in his idiosyncrasy; but he discovered it, and acknowledged it, in himself. He put it to his friend Woodhouse that the poetical character 'had no character — it enjoys light and shade; it lives in gusto, be it foul or fair, high or low, rich or poor, mean or elevated'. Beauty was everywhere; and Love was possible for everything.

Endymion does not carry us so far as that. In *Endymion* Beauty is, for the most part, the Beauty of convention. Endymion himself does not yet possess the universal capacity of soul which his author had not yet discovered in himself. But the progress of Endymion is in one cardinal respect like the progress of Keats himself. In following the impulses of Love in his heart, Endymion reaches a condition of conflict and despair. The 'burden of the mystery' grows heavy upon his soul. The way to the universal Beauty is dark, all dark; and the faith grows dim. 'We see not the balance of good and evil.' To see 'the balance of good and evil' — that and nothing less is required if faith in a 'Principle of Beauty' is ever to become a real conviction, and not remain a dubious ideal.

This inevitable conflict in the being of the seeker after essential Beauty, of the follower of the holy affections of the Heart, is, as we have tried to show, faced by Keats in the Fourth Book of *Endymion*. In the Cave of Quietude the divided being of the seeker is reborn. There is a region of the soul, reached by submission to the complete despair which ensues on complete inward division, where the miracle of rebirth is accomplished. This Cave of Quietude at crucial moments of his painful life Keats was destined to revisit, and to explore. Always he emerged from it as man, with the courage of his destiny, and as poet, with a more magically natural utterance.

Did he thereby prove the truth of his faith in the Holiness of the Heart's affections and the Truth of the Imagination? The question is hard to answer. What we can say is that his faith was justified. To believe that what the Imagination seizes as Beauty must be Truth, and to believe that the Love which is awakened in the Heart is sacred and must be obeyed, are in reality one and the same belief: for Imagination is the Love of the Mind. To say that what the Mind can love must be True is for some a meaningless statement, for others a secret 'caught from the very penetralium of mystery'.

No ultimate truth is true, except we love it. Unless it awakens love, it is merely a fact and alien to us. Love alone will change fact into Truth. And this, however strange it may sound, is no foolish fancy. For Love is a faculty of understanding, and unless it enters into and transmutes our knowledge of fact, we cannot really know. It is not that the fact is changed by Love; but only by Love can it be fully seen. For the presence of Love in knowledge is the evidence that the total, and not merely the partial, man, responds to the total thing.

That is what Keats meant when he declared that 'Beauty is Truth, Truth Beauty'; and that is what he had glimpsed when he wrote *Endymion*. Nothing could be true unless it could be loved; and nothing could be loved unless it could be seen as beautiful. Without Beauty, therefore, no Truth. To some it is meaningless or mad, to others the only wisdom. Keats lived and died by it. To those who understand his faith, his faith was justified. For to them his woeful and glorious life is a fact, which they needs must love: therefore it is a Truth. Their minds which love that fact, for the beauty which is manifest in it, are no longer simply minds: they are souls. And, in the process of that transmutation, in the despair and suffering which they re-live in his experience, they discover that they also have visited and explored the Cave of Quietude.

CHAPTER VI

'THE FEEL OF *NOT* TO FEEL IT'

KEATS'S walking tour in Scotland with Charles Brown in the summer of 1818 is painful to contemplate. We know what havoc the toil and privation of the journey worked upon him; we know also that it was a desperate attempt to prevent himself from 'having time to be glum', and to escape the burden of his dying brother's presence. Escape was not in Keats's destiny; even the effort after it was an unnatural condition for one who strove instinctively to submit himself completely to experience. Probably to this cause, as much as sheer physical fatigue, is due the comparative poverty of the poems which he wrote on his long journey. Poetry, at that time, did not 'come natural' to him.

But he wrote one sonnet on his journey which has a strange elusive beauty of its own: *On Visiting the Tomb of Burns.* He copied it into a letter to his brother Tom on July 1st, with this comment:

> You will see by this sonnet that I am at Dumfries, we have dined in Scotland. Burns's tomb is in the Churchyard corner, not very much to my taste, though on a scale large enough to show they wanted to honour him ... This Sonnet I have written in a strange mood, half asleep. I know not how it is, the Clouds, the Sky, the Houses, all seem anti-Grecian and anti-Charlemagnish.

The sonnet is this:

> The town, the churchyard and the setting sun,
>   The clouds, the trees, the rounded hills, all seem
>   Though beautiful, cold — strange — as in a dream,
> I dreamed long ago, now new begun.
> The short-liv'd, paly Summer is but won

From Winter's ague, for one hour's gleam;
Through sapphire warm their stars do never beam:
All is cold beauty; pain is never done;
For who has mind to relish, Minos-wise,
    The Real of Beauty, free from that dead hue
    Sickly imagination and sick pride
Cast wan upon it? Burns! with honour due
I have oft honour'd thee. Great shadow, hide
Thy face; I sin against thy native skies.*

It is somewhat obscure; but the obscurity is lessened if we substitute (as I have done) the question mark for the note of exclamation in l. 12. This confusion was fairly frequent with Keats; it
happened several times in *Endymion*. And the change is necessary
to the sense. 'For who', Keats asks, 'has a mind steady and strong
enough to discern and respond to the Real of Beauty, to keep it
unclouded by the dead hue cast upon it by sickly imagination and
sick pride?' Possibly also, as Professor Garrod has suggested, in
l. 7 we should read 'these stars' for 'their stars'. It would be somewhat simpler; but I do not feel any great difficulty about '*their*
stars' — the stars that belong to, and share their dream-being with,
'the town, the churchyard, and the setting sun, the clouds, the
trees, the rounded hills'.

The main interest of the sonnet is psychological. It centres in
ll. 8-12. 'Pain is never done' comes with a strange and unexpected
vehemence. We feel that Keats, at this moment, was really
suffering. And we should like to understand his suffering.

We may turn for a moment to his comment: 'I know not how
it is, the Clouds, the Sky, the Houses, all seem anti-Grecian and
anti-Charlemagnish.' 'Anti-Grecian' we understand from the
lover of the Elgin Marbles, and the poet of the Grecian Urn; 'anti-
Charlemagnish' is not quite so simple. Perhaps a clue to the mood
is given earlier in the letter, in his account of climbing Skiddaw:
'All felt, on arising into the cold air, that same elevation that a cold
bath gives one. I felt as if I were going to a Tournament.' And
another is in his account of Loch Lomond a fortnight later (July

17th): 'The banks of the Clyde are extremely beautiful — the north end of Loch Lomond grand in excess — the entrance at the lower end to the narrow part from a little distance is precious good — the Evening was beautiful nothing could surpass our fortune in the weather — yet was I worldly enough to wish for a fleet of chivalry Barges with Trumpets and Banners just to die away before me into that blue place among the mountains.' There was for Keats at that moment in the clouds, the sky, the trees of Dumfries neither classical nor Gothic beauty. Not that the beauty which they had was of another kind than these. It was Keats's way of saying that he could not respond to their beauty. 'All is cold beauty.'

This was the pain: that Keats found himself unresponsive. To use the idiom of the previous chapter: the beauty which his mind perceived awakened no love within his soul.

> For who has mind to relish, Minos-wise,
>   The Real of Beauty, free from that dead hue
>   Sickly imagination and sick pride
> Cast wan upon it?

The aptest commentary upon this is a passage from Keats's letter to Bailey, four months earlier (March 13th):

I am sometimes so very sceptical as to think Poetry itself a mere Jack a lanthen to amuse whoever may chance to be struck with its brilliance. As Tradesmen say everything is worth what it will fetch, so probably every mental pursuit takes its reality and worth from the ardour of the pursuer — being in itself a nothing — Ethereal things may at least be thus real, divided under three heads — Things real — things semi-real — and no things. Things real — such as existences of Sun, Moon and Stars and passages of Shakespeare. Things semi-real, such as Love, the Clouds, etc., which require a greeting of the Spirit to make them wholly exist — and Nothings, which are made Great and dignified by an ardent pursuit.

Keats is there half-laughing at a mood which he knew well; he was therefore no longer in it. But that 'greeting of the spirit' which was necessary to make certain 'semi-real things' wholly existent is precisely what was lacking in him in the churchyard at Dumfries.

The mood was recurrent in Keats. He described it twice to the same correspondent, Bailey.

> I wish I had a heart always open to such sensations [as that of appreciating Bailey's forbearance and generosity]; but there is no altering a Man's nature, and mine must be radically wrong for it will lie dormant a whole Month. This leads me to suppose that there are no men so thoroughly wicked as never to be self-spiritualized into a kind of sublime misery; but, alas! 'tis but for an Hour. . . .
>
> *(October 1817)*

> I beg now my dear Bailey that hereafter should you observe anything cold in me not to put it to the account of heartlessness, but abstraction — for I assure you I sometimes feel not the influence of a Passion or affection during a whole week — and so long this sometimes continues I begin to suspect myself and the genuineness of my feelings at other times — thinking them a few barren Tragedy-tears.
>
> *(November 22nd, 1817)*

The intensity of this condition, we may suppose, was proportioned to the intensity of the responsiveness which it displaced. A man who believed, as Keats did, in 'the holiness of the Heart's affections' and the creativeness of the 'passions, in their sublime', and whose belief was based on the intensity of his actual experience of these affections and passions, must have suffered deeply when the spiritual torpor came upon him. It is easy to understand how a moment of self-awareness during such a period could bring with it a 'self-spiritualization into a kind of sublime misery'.

This 'sublime misery' was precisely that 'feel of *not* to feel it' which is (as Colvin rightly maintained) the true and authentic reading in the last verse of *In a drear-nighted December*:

'THE FEEL OF *NOT* TO FEEL IT'

> Ah! would 'twere so with many
> A gentle girl and boy!
> But were there ever any
> Writhed not at passed joy?
> The feel of *not* to feel it,
> When there is none to heal it,
> Nor numbed sense to steel it,
> Was never said in rhyme.

This condition is, I think, definitely to be distinguished from another characteristic mood of Keats — the warm, delicious, diligent indolence in which the Thrush spoke to him, and in which 'neither Poetry, nor Ambition, nor Love had any alertness as they passed by him' but 'seemed rather like figures on a Greek vase'. This mood of Keats, this 'state of effeminacy' appears to have been the immediate prelude to a condition of pure creativeness: witness the richness and subtlety of the two letters in which he records it. That of February 19th, 1818, to Reynolds is a perfect thing, culminating in the native magic of 'What the Thrush said'. It has the misted opulence, the unsmutched bloom of ripeness, which is so peculiarly the mark of Keats's genius. In this indescribable stillness our heightened sense seems to hear the secret and simple livingness of Nature. And I do not think it is fanciful to believe that condition which seems to have preceded these magical utterances — 'the state of effeminacy' in which, Keats said, 'the fibres of the brain are relaxed in common with the rest of the body' — was veritably an instinctive self-submission to the creative power of that Nature of which man is part and instrument. Keats, then, indeed re-entered the womb of the great Mother, and surrendered himself to the unspoken thoughts that stirred within. His utterance then became drowsy with a pure plenitude of life.

> Thou still unravish'd bride of quietness,
>   Thou foster-child of silence and slow time . . .
> My heart aches, and a drowsy numbness pains
>   My sense . . .

Season of mists and mellow fruitfulness
    Close bosom-friend of the maturing sun . . .
Deep in the shady sadness of a vale . . .
And the ripe plum still wears its dim attire . . .
For shade to shade will come too drowsily
    And drown the wakeful anguish of the soul . . .

One cannot copy the lines so fast as they pour into the remembering mind. The richness and mystery of life seems to inform the very syllables. 'The fibres of the brain were relaxed'; the conscious mind has yielded to that which is far older, far deeper, and far richer than itself.

All is warm beauty, then; the sonnet in the churchyard at Dumfries records the very antipodes to this condition. 'All is cold beauty: pain is never done.' But in the creative indolence, 'pleasure had no show of enticement, and pain no unbearable power'.

Here, again, the intensity of the one condition seems to have been proportioned to the intensity of the other. They were the polar opposites in the wonderful organism which was John Keats. In the creative indolence his organic continuity with Nature was entire; in the churchyard condition the discontinuity was entire. (These entireties are, of course, relative; but in comparison to any condition experienced by the ordinary sensitive man, they may be fairly called absolute.) The sense of the discontinuity must have been agonizing to one who knew such an extraordinary condition of continuity; it must verily have been a 'sublime misery'.

To determine the sequence of these conditions would be full of interest. There are precious hints to be had from the part of the journal letter of March-April 1819 dated 'March 17th, Wednesday'. It begins:

On Sunday I went to Davenport's where I dined — and had a nap. I cannot bare a day annihilated in that manner — there is a great difference between an easy and an uneasy indolence — An indolent day — fill'd with speculations even of an unpleasant colour — is bearable and even pleasant alone — when one's thoughts cannot find out any thing better in the world; and experience has told us that locomotion is no change: but to have nothing to do, and to be surrounded with unpleasant human identities; who press upon one just enough to prevent one getting into a lazy position; and not enough to interest or rouse one: is a capital punishment of a capital crime: for is not giving up, through good nature, one's time to people who have no light and shade a capital crime? Yet what can I do? — they have been very kind and attentive to me. I do not know what I did on monday — nothing — nothing — nothing — I wish this was anything extraordinary.

There is an obvious connection between this description of 'uneasy indolence' and the letter to Woodhouse of October 27th, 1818, describing 'the poetic character'. In that letter after saying that the poet 'enjoys light and shade, and lives in gusto', he continues:

When I am in a room with People, if I ever am free from speculating on creations of my own brain, then not myself goes home to myself, but the identity of every one in the room begins so to press upon me, that I am in a very little time annihilated — not only among men; it would be the same in a Nursery of children.

To systematize these two accounts would be a preposterous undertaking: Keats was not a 'Godwin-methodist'; but it is worth noticing that this latter kind of 'annihilation' was, in Keats's view, desirable. It belonged to the nature of 'the chameleon poet', and was not an unpleasant condition. It was the condition of 'enjoying light and shade, and living in gusto'. The attention might be directed outwards or inwards, to observing the people in a room or to 'speculating on creations of his own brain'; the light and shade might be found in real or imagined characters.

When we compare this with Keats's condition at Davenport's dinner, we find that 'the pressure of the unpleasant human identities' is very slight. There is no desirable 'annihilation'; no possi-

bility of either outward or inward surrender. And, in consequence, the people are described as 'having no light and shade'.
But it is plain from the former description, where Keats emphatically says that the 'annihilation' would take place 'not only among
men; it would be the same in a nursery of children', that the
change is not in the object. It is not that the particular company
at Davenport's really had 'no light and shade'; but that, in this
condition of uneasy indolence, Keats is unable to discern or
respond to it.

This 'uneasy indolence' is thus virtually the same as the condition in the churchyard at Dumfries; it is the painful 'feel of *not*
to feel it'. There is the same awareness of an absence of 'light and
shade' in the object; for that is exactly the meaning of 'I know not
how it is, the Clouds, the Sky, the Houses, all seem anti-Grecian
and anti-Charlemagnish'. The beauty is cold. And in the sonnet
Keats very clearly recognizes that the apparent defect of the
object is a deficiency in his own power of response. There is, he
says, 'a Real of Beauty', independent of his momentary capacity
of response, though he wonders, and very justly, who among
mortal men has power of mind enough to overcome a momentary
incapacity such as his.

> For who has mind to relish, Minos-wise,
> The Real of Beauty, free from that dead hue
> Sickly imagination and sick pride
> Cast wan upon it?

And perhaps we have a glimpse of the particular meaning of
'sickly imagination and sick pride' in this context. It is the pride
of a preconceived imagination, and it is sick, because it fails to
make the 'self-destroying' surrender to the thing that is. And the
consciousness of this impotence, this inability to be true to 'the
poetical character' — to be true, in the case of Keats, to his own
simple and profound self is an indescribable pain. We may well
believe that

> The feel of *not* to feel it
> Was never said in rhyme.

If we may trust the account of the somewhat analogous condition in the description of 'The Cave of Quietude' in *Endymion*, Book IV, the impotence to respond, when it reached an extremity of pain, suddenly passed into a condition of total responsiveness. This is certainly borne out by the fact that his description of his 'uneasy indolence' at Davenport's is followed two days later by one of the most perfect examples of 'delicious diligent indolence' in all his letters: one to be compared only to that of a year before described in the letter to Reynolds, of February 19th, 1818. And that letter in turn seems to have been preceded by a condition of 'uneasy indolence', for on February 14th we find that he wrote to his brothers:

When once a man delays a letter beyond the proper time, he delays it longer, for one or two reasons — first, because he must begin in a very commonplace style, that is to say, with an excuse; and secondly things and circumstances become so jumbled in his mind that he knows not what, or what not, he has said in his last.

This recalls 'I do not know what I did on monday — nothing — nothing — nothing — ' in the letter about Davenport.

The two letters of February 19th, 1818, and of March 19th, 1819, deserve therefore to be carefully compared, as expressions of the same opulent poetic mood. There are indeed no richer expressions of the peculiar genius of Keats's letters than these. I have considered them in their place in *Keats and Shakespeare*; but it is worth drawing attention again to the pregnancy of the thought in the letter of March 19th, 1819. After his vision of men 'making their way with the same instinctiveness, the same unwandering eye from their purposes, the same animal eagerness as the Hawk', he turns and looks upon himself and his own thinking with the same lucid detachment.

Even here though I myself am pursueing the same instinctive course as the veriest human animal you can think of — I am however young writing at random — straining at particles of light in the midst of a great darkness without knowing the bearing of any one assertion of any one opinion. Yet may I not in this be free from sin? May there not be superior beings amused with any graceful though instinctive attitude my mind may fall into as I am entertained with the alertness of a Stoat and the anxiety of a Deer? Though a quarrel in the Streets is a thing to be hated, the energies displayed in it are fine: the commonest Man shows a grace in his quarrel. [Seen] by a superior being our reasonings may take the same tone — though erroneous they may be fine — this is the very thing in which consists Poetry . . .

With that conclusion the manifestation of the mood of 'diligent indolence' is complete. When the Mind, as it were, behaves as the pure instinct that it veritably is, and becomes the willing instrument of the total being, instead of its separated lord — then Poetry appears. And this is the condition that Keats has already described himself as being in when the letter was begun — the condition when 'the fibres of the brain are relaxed in common with the rest of the body'. In this condition the human organism can act as a whole: then Poetry comes naturally as the leaves to a tree. The Poetry which came naturally on this memorable morning was Prose — the letter itself: with all the animal grace of its unhesitating thought, rich, flexible, swift and unerring, passing at a bound to the detachment which is beyond good and evil. 'Though a quarrel in the Streets is a thing to be hated, the energies displayed in it are fine.' What could have been more 'anti-Grecian and anti-Charlemagnish' than a street-row? But in such a moment of contemplation, all is warm Beauty, and the pain is done.

True enough, Keats could not maintain himself for ever, or even for long, in a state of such lucid comprehension. But once attained, it could never be forgotten. He had seen what he was; and we see what we are. We are all in this sense potential poets, because we are all capable of this complete organic unity. Keats held this faith to the last. In *The Fall of Hyperion* he wrote:

'THE FEEL OF *NOT* TO FEEL IT'

      Who alive can say
'Thou art no Poet — mayst not tell thy dreams?'
Since every man whose soul is not a clod
Hath visions, and would speak, if he had lov'd,
And been well-nurtured in his mother tongue.

It was essentially the same thought that came to him in his mood
of 'diligent indolence' on February 19th, 1818.

> Memory should not be called Knowledge. Many have
> original minds who do not think it — they are led away by
> Custom ... Man should not dispute or assert but whisper
> results to his neighbour and thus by every germ of spirit
> sucking the sap from mould ethereal every human might
> become great, and Humanity instead of being a wide heath
> of Furze and Briars with here and there a remote Oak or
> Pine, would become a grand democracy of Forest Trees!

To yield to Life: this was, for Keats, the secret of poetry and of
human living. To receive, to lie open, to grow; yet also to
strive, to seek, to endure: to strive to the uttermost, and when the
organism can no more, to sink back through numbness, and pain,
and despair, into the warm darkness of Nature's womb, thence to
emerge re-born.

CHAPTER VII

'BEAUTY IS TRUTH...'

Thou shalt remain, in midst of other woe
Than ours, a friend to man, to whom thou say'st,
'Beauty is Truth, Truth Beauty' — that is all
Ye know on earth, and all ye need to know.

MEN'S reactions to this assertion of Keats are strangely various. Take two of the most distinguished literary critics of the older generation. First, Dr. Robert Bridges. His judgment on *The Ode on a Grecian Urn* is individual, and needs to be quoted entire.

> The thought as enounced in the first stanza is the supremacy of ideal art over Nature, because of its unchanging expression of perfection; and this is true and beautiful; but its amplification in the poem is unprogressive, monotonous, and scattered, the attention being called to fresh details without result (see especially ll. 21-4, anticipated in ll. 15-16), which gives an effect of poverty in spite of the beauty. The last stanza enters stumbling upon a pun, but its concluding lines are very fine, and make a sort of recovery with their forcible directness.

Thus, in the judgment of Dr. Bridges, it is these concluding lines which redeem a poorish poem. Sir Arthur Quiller-Couch, on the other hand, finds them worse than mediocre. He quotes the two final lines and says:

> But, of course, to put it solidly, that is a vague observation — to any one whom life has taught to face facts and define his terms, actually an uneducated conclusion, albeit pardonable in one so young. . . .

Parallel to these critics of an older generation we may set two of a
younger: Mr. I. A. Richards and Mr. T. S. Eliot. Mr. Richards
chooses precisely these two lines as an example of what he calls a
'pseudo-statement': while Mr. Eliot, commenting upon this view,
writes as follows:

> I am at first inclined to agree with him, because this state-
> ment of equivalence means nothing to me. But on re-reading
> the whole Ode, this line strikes me as a serious blemish on a
> beautiful poem; and the reason must be either that I fail to
> understand it, or that it is a statement which is untrue. And
> I suppose that Keats meant something by it, however
> remote his truth and his beauty may have been from these
> words in ordinary use. And I am sure that he would have
> repudiated any explanation of the line which called it a
> pseudo-statement. On the other hand the line I have often
> quoted of Shakespeare,
>
> 'Ripeness is all'
>
> or the line I have quoted of Dante,
>
> 'la sua voluntade è nostra pace'
>
> strikes very differently on my ear. I observe that the
> propositions in these words are very different in kind, not
> only from that of Keats but from each other. The statement
> of Keats seems to me meaningless: or perhaps the fact that
> it is grammatically meaningless conceals another meaning
> from me. The statement of Shakespeare seems to me to have
> profound emotional meaning, with at least, no literal
> fallacy. And the statement of Dante seems to me *literally
> true*. And I confess that it has more beauty for me now,
> when my own experience has deepened its meaning, than it
> did when first I read it.

Diversity of opinion could hardly be more extreme than in
these judgments. For Dr. Bridges the final lines redeemed a poor
poem; for Mr. Eliot they spoil a good one; for Sir Arthur Quiller-

Couch they are ignorant and uneducated; for Mr. Richards that still ambiguous entity which he calls a 'pseudo-statement'.*

I have no hope, and no desire, to convert any one of these eminent critics. I call them in evidence simply to show the astonishing variety of opinion which exists at this day concerning the culmination of a poem whose beauty has been acknowledged for many years. Whether such another cause, and such another example, of critical diversity exists, I cannot say; if it does, it is unknown to me.

My own opinion concerning the value of those two lines *in the context of the poem itself* is not very different from Mr. Eliot's. At any rate, I disagree with Dr. Bridges's opinion that by their 'forcible directness' the Ode is enabled to make 'a sort of recovery'. To my sense the lines disturb the subtle harmony of the poem. Their very directness is disruptive, for the Ode as a whole is not, in this sense, direct at all. And therein, I think, lies the cause of Dr. Bridges's surprising condemnation of the poem, which he places 'last, or disputing place with the last' among Keats's Odes. He has looked in it, necessarily in vain, for direct statement of the kind which is in the last lines; and he condemns it for not possessing a quality which, if it were present, would necessarily exclude the subtler richness which it has abundantly.

The direct and enigmatic proposition disturbs the poem, because it does not belong to the same kind of utterance. The poem, as a whole, advances on strong and delicate waves of the pure sensuous imagination. It ends dissonantly with a stark enunciation which, to that part of the human mind which is aroused by stark enunciation, must be a baffling paradox.

Such is my judgment of the poem, even though the paradox with which it ends is full of meaning for me. And I would support it by quoting Keats against himself:

We hate poetry that has a palpable design upon us, and, if we do not agree, seems to put its hand in its breeches pocket. Poetry should be great and unobtrusive, a thing which enters into one's soul, and does not startle it or amaze it with itself, but with its subject.

This condition of the greatest poetry, which the *Ode on a Grecian Urn* for the most part so marvellously satisfies, the last two lines, to my sense, fail to fulfil.

One further point in these conflicting critical opinions deserves to be noticed. Dr. Bridges declares: 'The thought as enounced in the first stanza is the supremacy of ideal art over Nature, because of its unchanging expression of perfection; and this is true and beautiful.' Possibly this thought is, indeed, both true and beautiful. But where in the first stanza of Keats's Ode is it enounced?

> Thou still unravish'd bride of quietness,
>   Thou foster-child of silence and slow time,
> Sylvan historian, who canst thus express
>   A flowery tale more sweetly than our rhyme.

The thought is surely not enounced in those four lines. The beautiful vase, says Keats, can tell 'a flowery tale' more sweetly than poetry can. He says more mysterious things than this; he says whatever it is that he says in the two perfect lines:

> Thou still unravish'd bride of quietness,
>   Thou foster-child of silence and slow time...

But, whatever it is that he asserts in that brooding and mysterious speech, it is certainly not 'the supremacy of ideal art over Nature'. Nor is there any trace of this thought in the remaining lines of the stanza, which ask what is the legend depicted on the frieze which surrounds the vase.

> What leaf-fring'd legend haunts about thy shape
>   Of deities, or mortals, or of both,
>   In Tempe or the dales of Arcady?
> What men or gods are these? What maidens loth?
>   What mad pursuit? What struggle to escape?
>   What pipes and timbrels? What wild ecstasy?

It is remarkable that a fine poet and fine critic should be able to make a statement of fact about the first stanza of a famous poem which simply is not true; and it is perhaps equally remarkable that this statement of fact should never, so far as I know, have been challenged up to this moment. This curious state of things may indicate that there is an element of truth in the theory of Henri Brémond — namely, that 'pure poetry' communicates to the attuned reader a quasi-mystical condition of consciousness.

The amount of truth we allow to this theory will depend upon our explanation of this quasi-mystical condition. Though we will reject the epithet 'mystical' as question-begging, we are inclined to believe that there is something peculiar in the condition of consciousness aroused by the first stanza of a perfectly familiar poem, if Dr. Bridges is able to say that it contains a simple assertion which it manifestly does not contain.

If we speak, provisionally, of the effect produced by the poem as the communication to the reader of a certain 'vibration', we may fairly say that the kind of 'vibration' set up by the first verse of the *Ode on a Grecian Urn* is one which does not easily permit that activity of the intelligence by which abstract propositions are criticized or corroborated. It seems very probable that the 'vibration' induced by the poem is such that it is unusually difficult even for Dr. Bridges to attend to what is asserted in the Ode. There comes a moment, it is true, when a stark assertion is made which neither we nor he find any difficulty in remembering:

Beauty is Truth, Truth Beauty.

We remember it because it excites a sort of intellectual resistance. But even there we do not remember, or do not easily remember, precisely how the assertion is made. We are inclined to forget, in particular, that it is the Grecian Urn which says: 'Beauty is Truth, Truth Beauty', and that it is the poet himself who adds:

That is all
Ye know on earth, and all ye need to know.

This putting as it were to sleep of the logical intelligence by such a poem as the *Ode on a Grecian Urn*, this curious inhibition of which Dr. Bridges's mistaken assertion and his readers' failure to recognize it are examples, is, we believe, an essential and not an accidental effect. We surmise that, if it were examined, it would be shown to have an important bearing on the various difficulties encountered by the critics we have quoted in their attempts to understand the poem. Just as Dr. Bridges makes a mistake in his effort to wrest a clear assertion out of the first stanza of the poem, so the other critics may well be nonplussed by the clear assertion which is indubitably made in the last stanza. Dr. Bridges, it is true, finds no difficulty at all in the last stanza: it is, for him, 'forcible and direct'. Yet his judgment on the poem as a whole seems to be so greatly at variance with the consensus, if not of opinion, of feeling about the poem, that we are dubious of his apparent certitude. And this dubiety is increased by his collocation of 'true and beautiful' in his mistaken assertion with regard to the first stanza. The 'thought of the supremacy of art over Nature, because of its unchanging expression of perfection' is, he says, 'true and beautiful'. And indeed it may be. But the words suggest that Dr. Bridges believes that the relation between truth and beauty which is manifest in that thought (if it is both true and beautiful) is the same relation between the same qualities or essences as is proclaimed by Keats in the last stanza. This, at any rate, we are convinced, is not true. The identity of Truth and Beauty which may, or may not, be manifest in the thought that Art is supreme over Nature because of its unchanging expression of perfection, is emphatically not the same as the identity of Truth and Beauty which is asserted in the last stanza of the poem.

We suspect that Dr. Bridges believes that it is; that he believes that the poem really consists in the enunciation of the 'true and beautiful' thought that Art is supreme over Nature; and that this thought and the assertion that 'Beauty is Truth, Truth Beauty' are the same. If our suspicion is founded, it can be easily understood why the development of the thought in the poem seems to him 'unprogressive and monotonous', and why the last stanza seems to him to make 'a sort of recovery by its forcible directness'.

What has happened is that Dr. Bridges has misinterpreted the last stanza as an assertion of the supremacy of Art over Nature, he has then read this misinterpretation by main force into the first stanza, and has finally judged the poem by its inevitable failure to develop a thought which is not contained in the poem at all.*

That Truth and Beauty of the kind which are manifest in the thought of the supremacy of Art over Nature are not the Truth and Beauty whose identity is asserted in the last stanza is obvious from one simple consideration. The vase whispers, and will whisper, to minds aching with the thought of human misery, 'Beauty is Truth, Truth Beauty' and to the poet this whisper brings the comfort of a great finality. When he hears the words, he cries:

> That is all
> Ye know on earth, and all ye need to know.

That is, of course, in the literal and grammatical sense, untrue. It is not 'all we know'; and some of us do not know it at all. But Keats's meaning is unmistakable. If we know that 'Beauty is Truth, Truth Beauty', we have attained the topmost stretch of human knowledge; we know, as it were, the secret — the one thing needful.

I do not believe that anybody could, and I am quite certain that Keats could not, have found this finality in the mere thought that Art is supreme over Nature, because of its unchanging expression of perfection. Had this been the thought which the Grecian Urn awakened in his mind, Keats would never have written his poem; nor would he have written a poem at all. His mood would have been the mood of

> Though beautiful, cold — strange — as in a dream . . .
> All is cold beauty: pain is never done.

The mood of the *Ode on a Grecian Urn* is the sheer opposite of this. The beauty is warm; the pain is done. Nor again, if his thought had been the simple one of the supremacy of Art over Nature, would he have said:

Thou, silent form, dost tease us out of thought
As doth eternity.

The thought awakened in him by the Grecian Urn is a thought beyond thought. *Ars longa, vita brevis* is not such a thought; nor does it become such a thought even in the form given to it by Leonardo; 'Cosa bella mortal passa e non d'arte'. And, finally, Keats could not have expressed this simple thought by the strange and mysterious assertion that 'Beauty is Truth, Truth Beauty'.

What is it, then, that Keats was saying? We must pick up the clues to his meaning as we can. But one thing is certain. The message of the Grecian Urn is a message of comfort in human woe. That this is no vague and casual assertion, no piece of vulgar and uneducated aestheticism, Keats's life must be sufficient witness. The time at which he wrote the *Ode on a Grecian Urn* was a time of great happiness indeed but greater misery. A brother dead, a brother exiled, the fear that his new-born love would be denied fulfilment, his money gone, his health and perhaps his life in question — such was Keats's part of the human woe to which, he declared, the Grecian Urn brought comfort. It was more than a fair share of the miseries of the world; and those who are tempted to find the message of peace which the Grecian Urn whispered to him vulgar and uneducated must be very sure, before they publicly declare their finding, that they themselves have borne as heavy a load of perplexity and pain.

What meaning, we have to ask, could the words 'Beauty is Truth, Truth Beauty' bear to a man who was suffering as Keats was suffering then, which could bring to him finality and peace? We do not have to ask, coldly, what is the meaning of 'Beauty is Truth'. We have to ask what meaning it could possibly bear to such a man at such a moment in order to assuage his pain. Again, we have to ask this as men to whom bitter experience is not alien and remote; as men aware that comfort in such an extreme of misery is not to be had for a song. It is not some simple panacea which can be had for the asking. If we know anything of human life we know that words which contain a message of peace in moments such as Keats was then enduring will not be easy words. They may be simple, but they will not be easy. And as human beings we know more than this: we know that they must contain a great renunciation. Such a message is in the words: 'Not my will, but Thine be done'; or, in the words of Dante in which Mr. Eliot finds an ever deepening meaning:

La sua voluntade è nostra pace.

It is meaning of this kind, and of this order, that we must seek in 'Beauty is Truth, Truth Beauty', if we are ever to know what they meant to Keats or what Keats meant by them.

The relation between Beauty and Truth was one which exercised the mind and heart of Keats throughout his life. This was the chief form into which his search for a purpose in life was cast. The words recur constantly, and always significantly, in his letters. They are at the core of his famous definition: 'The excellence of every art is its intensity, capable of making all disagreeables evaporate from their being in close relationship with Beauty and Truth.'

The bearing of this statement on the last stanza of the *Ode on a Grecian Urn*, and upon the whole poem, is immediate. The statement was made long before the *Ode* was written, while Keats was still comparatively a happy man. In the ensuing time the 'disagreeables' which his own art had to 'evaporate' had come to deserve a harsher name. He had been 'convinced on his nerves that the world is full of heart-break, misery, pain and oppression'. The evaporating of disagreeables had passed into the lifting of the burden of misery. The tone is deeper, as the experience is more profound. Nevertheless, the words are prophetic of the last stanza of *The Grecian Urn*.

The Urn is such a work of art; it is capable of making 'all disagreeables evaporate from their being in close relationship to Beauty and Truth'. The thought came originally to Keats as he was meditating on the effect of a painting; it was exemplified, he said, throughout *King Lear* — a dramatic poem. And the Grecian

Urn, as it is depicted in Keats's Ode, is something between a painting and a dramatic poem. It is a sculptured drama. And this is as important to remember as it is readily forgotten. The Grecian Urn of Keats's poem is not some actual vase, but the Urn of his imagination. To know what it was, we are not to conceive some hypothetical original, but simply to read his poem.

No doubt, at some time or other, Keats had actually seen and delighted in the beauty of a Greek vase. But that may have been long before he wrote his poem. It probably was long before. The vision lay somewhere in the deeps of his being, to appear at moments before his conscious imagination. In the Third Book of *Endymion* (ll. 29-32) we read:

> Aye, 'bove the withering of old-lipp'd Fate
> A thousand Powers keep religious state,
> In water, fiery realm, and airy bourne;
> And, *silent as a consecrated urn*,
> Hold sphery sessions for a season due.

It appeared more visibly, a year before he actually wrote *The Grecian Urn*, in a letter to Reynolds, where he complained of the ugly visions which haunted him when he lay sleepless. Perhaps, he said, some were more fortunate than himself, and escaped these evil visitations. What these fortunate ones would see, in their happier visions, would be:

> Some Titian colours touch'd into real life —
> The sacrifice goes on; the pontiff knife
> Gleams in the sun, the milk-white heifer lows,
> The pipes go shrilly; the libation flows:
> A white sail shows above the green-head cliff,
> Moves round the point, and throws her anchor stiff;
> The mariners join hymn with those on land.

There is the frieze of another Grecian Urn — manifestly no real one, in the practical and tangible sense, but as beautiful and of the same kind as the vase of the *Ode*. The Greek vase was a form into which Keats's sensuous imagination could naturally be cast.

Later, and near to the time of writing the *Ode*, the vision came
again — on the morning when, he said, 'the fibres of the brain
were relaxed in common with the rest of his body, and to such a
happy degree that pleasure had no show of enticement nor pain
no unbearable power'. 'Neither Poetry, nor Ambition, nor Love',
he wrote, 'have any alertness of countenance as they pass by me;
they seem rather like figures on a Greek vase — a Man and two
women whom no one but myself could distinguish in their
disguisements.' This vision formed the whole theme of the *Ode
on Indolence*.

> One morn before me were three figures seen
>   With bowed necks and joined hands, side-faced;
> And one behind the other stepp'd serene
>   In placid sandals, and in white robes graced;
> They pass'd like figures on a marble urn,
>   When shifted round to see the other side;
>   They came again; as, when the urn once more
> Is shifted round, the first seen shades return;
>   And they were strange to me as may betide
>   With vases to one deep in Phidian lore.

The Greek vase, with its surrounding frieze, was a form congenial to Keats's richly plastic imagination; it was a means by
which he could immobilize, in 'a frozen moment', the beauty of
an imagined action.*

The Grecian Urn may have been in part actual, or wholly an
imaginative creation; that is indifferent. The important thing is
the action depicted upon it — the drama, the thing doing, in the
actual sense of the Greek word. That is evident enough to any
one who simply reads the poem; the vase is primarily a sculptured
frieze, an arrested action, like the Parthenon pediment.

On this arrested action Keats's imagination intensely plays.
He envies the felicity of the participants who are immune from
mortality and decay. But they are human still. Mortality and
decay have slipped from them, like a garment; but that is all. They
are mortals as we are; who have wandered unawares into an en-

chanted land, whence they can never return. Their felicity has its
tinge of sorrow; the poet who began by envying, ends almost
by pitying. They are, as it were, lost to humanity.

> And, little town, thy streets for evermore
> Will silent be; and not a soul to tell
> Why thou art desolate, can e'er return.

The happening is entirely human. It is to misconceive the poem
completely to conceive it as a theorizing on some exquisite piece
of decorative art. It is a drama of the pure imagination. A
destiny falls upon some human beings; they pass into the spell-
bound land of eternity,

> All breathing human passion far above

and the poet who watches them, who indeed himself has cast the
spell of eternal immobility upon them, envies and grieves for
them. The Urn is the record of the lovely and yet fatal enchantment.

More exactly, the Grecian Urn is the symbol of a possibility of
vision. All human action, all human experience, can be thus
arrested in enchantment. All the visible and invisible drama of
human life can be thus seen, or imagined *sub specie aeternitatis*.
That is why the 'silent form doth tease us out of thought as doth
eternity'. It is not that it is incomprehensible as is the abstract
concept of eternity; but that it is simple and lucid as is the eternal
aspect of things of which it is a symbol. This aspect of things is
beyond thought, because it is prior to thought; and beyond
thought because it is the end of thinking. Under this aspect the
innocent vision of the child doubtless beholds existence; the
grown man can recapture it only when he has struggled onward
towards a second innocence. And then he is unable to declare
what it is that he sees; it is too simple for speech. What words can
there be to describe this seeing of the world and of ourselves with
a vision from which all passion has been dissolved away; with a
vision which is unclouded by any desire or any regret; by any

belief or any anxiety: this moment of untroubled lucidity in which we are unmoved spectators of the great drama of human destiny?

For this vision there are indeed no words. Keats declared it in the form: 'Beauty is Truth, Truth Beauty.' The words to many are meaningless. And it is certain that by no poring over the words themselves can the vision which they express be attained. Nor, probably, if we turn them about, like a jewel of many facets, will they reflect a gleam.

We may turn them in many ways. We may say that the Real is Beautiful. The answer straightaway is that the Real is full of ugliness and pain. And this is true: who will deny it? But the Beauty of the Real is a Beauty which resides as surely in pain and ugliness as in beauty itself. There is the sorrow which makes

Sorrow more beautiful than Beauty's self.

But that sorrow may still be called, by our human standards, beautiful. The Beauty of the Real is beyond this. It lies in the perfection of uniqueness which belongs to every thing, or thought, simply because it *is*.

But this is not Beauty. And indeed it is not what men commonly call Beauty, any more than the Love with which all high religion invests its Deity is what is commonly called Love among men, any more than the perfection which, Spinoza said, belonged to every existence is what men commonly call perfection. None the less, the great sayings that 'God is Love', and that 'Omnis existentia est perfectio', have their meaning for those who understand them. Keats uttered another saying worthy to stand with these simple and lucid finalities. 'Beauty is Truth, Truth Beauty' belongs to the same order as they; nor can any one truly understand any one of these sayings without understanding the others.

For the only name for the faculty by which we can discern that element of Beauty which is present in every Fact, which we must discern in every Fact before it becomes Truth for us, is Love.

Whether it is Love which discovers the Beauty in Fact, whereby it becomes Truth; or whether it is the Beauty of Fact which causes the motion of Love to arise in our souls, and so to discern its Truth — to such questions there is no answer, nor any need to answer them. The relation between these things is simple and inextricable. When we love a Fact, it becomes Truth; when we attain that detachment from our passions whereby it becomes possible for us to love all Facts, then we have reached our Peace. If a Truth cannot be loved, it is not Truth, but only Fact. But the Fact does not change, in order that it may become Truth; it is we who change. All Fact is beautiful; it is we who have to regain our innocence to see its Beauty.

But this is inhuman, it may be said. And if it is indeed inhuman to be detached for a moment from all human passion, to see for a moment all things that happen as pure happenings, to cease for a moment to feel what men call love and hate in the peace of a Love that is distinct from, and beyond them both, then it is inhuman. But this ultimate disinterestedness begins at home. It is achieved only by disinterestedness towards the pain and ugliness of one's own experience; and it is achieved chiefly by those to whom the pain of others has been as their own pain. This detachment is reached not through insensibility, but through sensibility grown intolerable.

> None can usurp this height
> But those to whom the miseries of the world
> Are misery, and will not let them rest.

Whether or not it is easily intelligible, there is a meaning in 'Beauty is Truth, Truth Beauty' which satisfies the conditions which we proposed as necessary. It is simple but not easy; and it involves a great renunciation. That the first condition is satisfied is abundantly evident from our efforts to expound it. It is its sheer simplicity which makes it so impossible to explain. In endeavouring to explain it we feel as a man might feel who should try to explain colour to another man born blind; or it is as if we were required to demonstrate the existence of an object that is actually before our eyes — we could only point to it and say 'There it *is*!'

And perhaps it is equally evident that it involves a great renunciation. To attain the vision which Keats describes as the knowledge that 'Beauty is Truth, Truth Beauty' we are required to put away all our human desires and beliefs and anxieties. We have to forget all those cares, delightful or painful, which appertain to our animal existence. Our joys and sorrows must become remote as though they happened to others than ourselves, or to ourselves in some other mode of existence from which we have awakened as from a dream. All the infinite, the all but total activities of man, conscious or unconscious, which are directed towards the maintenance and assertion of the instinctive will to live, must be put away. Cease they cannot, nor can we make them cease; but we must cease to be identified with them. They are the substrate of our vision; without them we cannot see as we desire to see. But when we have become an Eye, the Eye cannot belong to them, or they to it. It sees them with the same utter detachment with which it sees all things else. And this detachment is a real detaching.

Than this no greater renunciation is possible. All we are is become object to the pure vision of this Eye. Our secretest desires, our most precious aspirations, the finest point of our being — all is 'out there', naked to the contemplation of eternity, of which contemplation we are the momentary instruments. A chasm divides the being that we are from the seeing that is ourselves. The renunciation is entire, the spirit is pure.

We must descend. Where we have been we cannot live, but we can always return again. Nor is it by our will that we return; the possibility of this detachment hovers about us henceforward all our lives. We pass into it and out again; we do not know when it may lie in wait for us. A trivial sound or sight may take us there. But if we need it, then it is at our command. We have only to pay the same price for our emancipation.

We are fortunate in that Keats left a record of the actual process of his mind by which he attained the conviction that

'BEAUTY IS TRUTH...'

'Beauty is Truth, Truth Beauty' — That is all
Ye know on earth, and all ye need to know.

The record is examined from one angle in *Keats and Shakespeare*, and from another in the chapter on 'Keats and Blake' in this book, where I try to show how exactly the process to which Keats submitted himself immediately before he wrote the *Odes* corresponds to the process which Blake regarded as the preparation for the apprehension of the final spiritual truth. It is the process by which, in Keats's language, the world of man's experience is seen and used as a School in which the atom of Intelligence becomes a Soul. The Soul, for Keats, is that condition of man in which his Mind and his Heart are reconciled, and Knowledge is transformed by Love: in the idiom of Christian spirituality the condition of the Knowledge and Love of God. The Knowledge which is at the same time Love belongs to a new dimension of experience, in which the conflict of the Mind and Heart are overcome and transcended. The reality and finality of this condition, this new dimension of experience, is what Keats proclaimed by saying 'Beauty is Truth, Truth Beauty'. The Truth — the true Truth — is such that it awakens Love, and the Truth that awakens Love is Beautiful. For the apprehension of that truth, a man must pay the price. It is to see and experience himself, at the moment of his most grievous suffering, as a vehicle of the Truth which is Beauty, to be grateful for and exalted by the privilege of experience, to be filled with love for the world of pains and troubles which schools an intelligence and makes it a soul.

A Place where the heart must feel and suffer in a thousand diverse ways! Not merely is the Heart a Hornbook, it is the Mind's Bible, it is the Mind's experience, it is the teat from which the Mind or Intelligence sucks its identity. As various as the Lives of Men are — so various become their Souls, and thus does God make individual beings, Souls, Identical Souls of the Sparks of his own essence.

That, and more, is behind Keats's declaration. I believe that it is all we know and all we need to know. The only statements of the same order, which seem to other minds more deeply true, will be found at the last to be saying the same thing in other words.

CHAPTER VIII

'THEY END IN SPECULATION'

'SPECULATION' was a favourite word with Keats. It occurs often in his letters and often in very important contexts, with a meaning unfamiliar to modern usage.

I think that Keats almost always used the word 'speculation' either wholly with the meaning (which it had in the Elizabethan poets) of 'contemplation', or 'simple vision', or with a meaning in which the contemplative element predominates. Possibly, he took the word from the memorable use of it in *Macbeth* (III. iv. 95), which Professor Whitehead in *The Concept of Nature* (p. 6) attributes to Hamlet.

> Thou hast no speculation in those eyes
> Which thou dost glare with.

It is interesting to note that Professor Whitehead is anxious to re-establish for the purposes of his philosophy the ancient use of the word; for, if I understand his argument rightly, he is returning to the fundamental philosophic simplicity of which Mr. Santayana is the modern master. This philosophy, or metaphysic, I believe, was always implicit in Keats's thinking; and, as his mind swiftly ripened, it became explicit. A great obstacle in the way of its comprehension is his use of words in senses which are not familiar. One of the most important of these words is 'speculation'.

That he used it in his poetry as the equivalent of 'contemplation' is amply evident from three quotations. One from *I stood tip-toe upon a little hill* (l. 189);

> The pillowy silkiness that rests
> Full in the speculation of the stars . . .

The second from *Isabella* (XXIII), where the stanza needs to be quoted entire:

So on a pleasant morning, as he leant
　　Into the sun-rise, o'er the balustrade
Of the garden-terrace, towards him they bent
　　Their footing through the dews; and to him said
'You seem there in the quiet of content,
　　Lorenzo, and we are most loth to invade
Calm speculation; but if you are wise,
Bestride your steed while cold is in the skies.'

The third is a cancelled line in the manuscript of *Hyperion*
(l. 334). The final text reads:

Now I behold in you fear, hope, and wrath;
Actions of rage and passion; even as
I see them, on the mortal world beneath,
In men who die.

The manuscript originally ran:

even as
In widest speculation do I see . . .

In all these instances — and I know of no other uses of the word
in Keats's poetry — the meaning of the word is, almost precisely,
'contemplation'. It is an act of simple vision; in all these instances,
physical vision, as in the line from *Macbeth*. There is no trace of
the modern meaning. Today we 'speculate about' problems and
possibilities; Keats, it is to be noticed in a following passage from
his letters, 'speculates on', i.e. 'looks on'. I believe I am right in
saying that 'to speculate *about*' occurs nowhere in his writing.

The importance of the distinction is obvious when we consider
the famous letter to Woodhouse on the poetical character
(October 27th, 1818), in which the word occurs twice. First:

As to the poetical Character itself . . . it is not itself — it has
no self — it is everything and nothing — it has no character
— it enjoys light and shade; it lives in gusto, be it foul or fair,
high or low, rich or poor, mean or elevated — It has as
much delight in conceiving an Iago as an Imogen. What

shocks the virtuous philosopher delights the chameleon Poet. It does no harm from its relish of the dark side of things, any more than from its taste for the bright one, because they both end in speculation.

The unprepared reader of the last sentence, who naturally supposes that 'speculation' is being used here in its modern meaning, misses the real point of it. The final state, Keats says, is a state of 'contemplation', of disinterested beholding of the dark and the bright side of things. And that is quite different from speculating about the problem of good and evil.

The word occurs in the same letter a second time:

When I am in a room with people, if I ever am free from speculating on creations of my own brain, then not myself goes home to myself, but the identity of everyone in the room begins so to press upon me, that I am in a very little time annihilated.

Here, perhaps, the nuance of meaning inclines a little towards the modern usage; but I am pretty sure that this 'speculation on the creations of his own brain' is a direct sensuous imagination of them — an experience of the kind which he described at about the same time in his letter to his brother and sister:

No sooner am I alone than shapes of epic greatness are stationed around me, and serve my Spirit the office which is equivalent to a king's body-guard.

Keeping off, one might say, the pressure of the throng of 'unpleasant identities'. The bias of the word 'speculate' is indeed so strong in Keats that I incline to think that his question to Woodhouse: 'Might I not at that very instant have been cogitating on the Characters of Saturn and Ops?' means rather musing on the actual figures present to his imagination than pondering about their psychology.

The word occurs again when, on December 21st, 1817, he writes to his brothers concerning Benjamin West's picture, 'Death on the Pale Horse':

It is a wonderful picture, when West's age is considered; but there is nothing to be intense upon, no women one feels mad to kiss, no face swelling into reality—The excellence of every art is its intensity, capable of making all disagreeables evaporate from their being in close relationship with Beauty and Truth. Examine *King Lear* and you will find this exemplified throughout: but in this picture we have unpleasantness without any momentous depth of speculation excited, in which to bury its repulsiveness.

The meaning of the word 'speculation' is of obvious importance here. Keats is not saying that repulsiveness, in a work of the highest art, is buried in the profundity of the thoughts which it arouses; not the depth of what we think *about* the work of art or about its subject-matter is the sign of its excellence, but the depth of the direct vision which it embodies and which it communicates to us. This 'momentous depth of speculation' is, in fact, almost a synonym for 'intensity'. And, like 'intensity' it is both in the object and the responsive subject. West's picture lacks 'intensity'; it contains nothing for Keats 'to be intense upon'. Likewise, it manifests no 'momentous depth of speculation' and arouses none.

It would not be easy to decide whether 'speculation' or 'intensity' is the more important of these two keywords in Keats's thinking. It is not really possible to define either of them; they have to be studied in their context, and indeed intensely speculated on (not about), before they will yield their secret. Inevitably, they are closely connected with one another, as in the account of West's picture above. Another example is in his letter to Haydon of April 8th, 1818.

I have ever been too sensible of the labyrinthian path to eminence in Art (judging from Poetry) ever to think I understood the emphasis of Painting. The innumerable compositions and decompositions which take place between the intellect and its thousand materials before it arrives at that trembling delicate and snail-horn perception of Beauty. I know not your many havens of intenseness — nor ever can

know them; but for [all] this I hope nought you achieve
is lost upon me: for when a schoolboy the abstract Idea I
had of an heroic painting — was what I cannot describe.
I saw it somewhat sideways large prominent round and
colour'd with magnificence — somewhat like the feel I have
of Anthony and Cleopatra. Or of Alcibiades leaning on his
Crimson Couch in his Galley, his broad shoulders imper-
ceptibly heaving with the Sea.

The word 'speculation' is not there; only the word 'intenseness'. But that description of the imaginary heroic picture is, I
should say, an excellent description of the art which aroused 'the
depth of speculation' which 'Death on the Pale Horse' did not
arouse in Keats. The passage incidentally gives another example
of Keats's very personal use of words. Nothing could well be
more remote from 'an abstract idea' as ordinarily understood than
his imagination of a heroic picture.

To consider these personal uses of words at all fully would
demand a small volume. The idiosyncrasy of language, of course,
has its roots in the idiosyncrasy of the poet's mind. Abstract
thinking, in the ordinary sense, was alien to Keats; the movement
of his thought was richly imaged, and amazingly concrete —
'sensations rather than thoughts'. Hence the recurrence of
'intensity'.

> Verse, Fame and Beauty are intense indeed;
> But Death intenser — Death is Life's high meed.

These four things, as then experienced by Keats, belong to the
order of 'sensations rather than thoughts'. So, to return to our
original word, 'speculation' is a sensation rather than a thought.
From the same origin proceed many of those arresting casual
phrases with which his letters are so richly strewn, such as:

> We no sooner get into . . . the Chamber of Maiden Thought,
> than we become intoxicated with the light and the atmo-
> sphere, we see nothing but pleasant wonders, and think of
> delaying there for ever in delight. However among the

effects this *breathing* is father of is that tremendous one of
sharpening one's vision into the heart and nature of Man —
of *convincing one's nerves* that the world is full of Misery and
Heartbreak, Pain, Sickness and oppression.

I have italicized the two casual phrases that no one but Keats
would have employed: but they are innumerable in his letters.
He 'proves things on his pulses'. Thought *was* sensation with
Keats — a man of 'more than ordinary organic sensibility', if
ever there was one. So far from making him less of a philosopher
than those who do not possess his incapacity for abstract thinking, I am convinced it made him a better one. He might have
made a poor Platonist; but he was a magnificent materialist, in the
full and true meaning of that grossly abused word.

Keats's peculiar use of 'speculation' is intimately connected
with another phrase which played a distinctive part in the workings of his mind: 'light and shade'. This is a key-phrase in his
conception of poetry. The connection appears plainly in his
description of the Poetic Character. 'It enjoys light and shade . . .
it does no harm from its relish of the dark side of things any more
than from its taste for the bright one, because they both end in
speculation.'

He applies it in his remarks on *Paradise Lost* (ll. 527-567)

The light and shade — the sort of black brightness — the
ebon diamonding — the Ethiop Immortality — the sorrow,
the pain, the sad-sweet Melody — the Phalanges of Spirits so
depressed as to be 'uplifted beyond hope' — the short
mitigation of Misery — the thousand Melancholies and
Magnificences of this page — leaves no room for anything
to be said but 'so it is'.

There, too, the end is 'speculation'; and there could hardly be
a better description of what Keats meant by that word than the
recognition that 'no room is left for anything to be said but
"so it is"'.

That is the strictly aesthetic use of 'light and shade' by Keats, in so far as any of Keats's uses of words can be called strictly aesthetic. It is used there to discriminate the peculiar excellence of Milton the poetic artist: and he was, for Keats, the supreme deliberate *artist* among English poets.

'I have but lately stood on my guard against Milton', he was to write later. 'Life to him would be death to me. Miltonic verse cannot be written but in the vein of art.' And again, 'Miltonic verse cannot be written but in an artful or rather artist's humour. I wish to give myself up to other sensations. English ought to be kept up. It may be interesting to you to pick out some lines from *Hyperion* and put a mark X to the false beauty proceeding from art, and one ‖ to the true voice of feeling.' But this significant reaction against Milton does not invalidate his splendid appreciation of Milton's 'light and shade', which he further defined:

> There is a greatness which the *Paradise Lost* possesses over every other Poem — *the Magnitude of Contrast*, and that is softened by the contrast being ungrotesque to a degree. Heaven moves on like music throughout. Hell is also peopled with angels; it also moves on like music, not grating and harsh, but like a grand accompaniment in the Base to Heaven.

Light and shade is what the poet discerns and delights in; it is the proper object of his contemplation, whether in actual existence or the creations of his imagination. We have seen before that the condition of this perception is a kind of surrender, and that when Keats declares that certain people have 'no light and shade', he does not mean that they objectively possess none. Whether or not it is discerned depends on what might be called the focus of the imagination. A man may be as dull as ditch-water, yet seen from the right angle or in the appropriate field of vision, he may be rich in 'light and shade'. To be discerned and delighted in it requires a 'greeting of the spirit'. We might say that for Keats the poetic condition is that in which he is able to discern the light and shade of whatever he contemplates.

But the philosophy of 'light and shade' is more than an aesthetic philosophy, or it is by implication more. It demands to be extended to the most intimate personal experience, and thus becomes a religion. 'Welcome Joy and welcome Sorrow!' How far can the poet carry that will to acceptance? 'We have leisure to reason on the misfortunes of our friends: our own touch us too nearly for words.' So Keats wrote in March 1819, at a moment when he was struggling to achieve such an attitude of acceptance. I believe he did achieve it at this moment, when the glory of his new love was contending with his despair of its fruition: and that the acceptance he won to, the submissiveness of his spirit to the 'light and shade' of his personal experience, gives the peculiar emotional richness to his *Odes*.

But the victory has to be won over and over again, even in the little lives of ordinary men. How much more in the case of Keats, upon whom disasters crowded!

Most painfully, at the very end, Keats applies the phrase directly to his own life.

> There is one thought enough to kill me; I have been well, healthy, alert, etc., walking with her — and now — the knowledge of contrast, feeling for light and shade, all that information (primitive sense) necessary for a poem, are great enemies to the recovery of the stomach.

It is almost inhuman to submit those words to a scrutiny of vocabulary. Yet how impressive it is that Keats's mind keeps its shape and pattern, in the extreme stress of his suffering! His use of 'information' here makes probable the emendation of his description of the Poetical Character. 'A Poet is the most unpoetical of anything in existence; because he has no Identity — he is continually in for — and filling some other body.' Keats may have intended to write 'informing'. This 'information (primitive sense)' is the imaginative activity of entering into the contrast — the 'light and shade' — of experience. At the moment — seeing that the light and shade is that of his own tortured life — the activity is like to kill him.

Keats had another, curiously pedestrian — or rather sub-ironic — phrase for the same activity of mind, the 'informing' of both terms of the contrast. It is to 'pro and con'. He uses it in the same final letter, to Brown. 'I am afraid to encounter the pro-ing and con-ing of anything interesting to me in England.' He means here the working in his mind of the same 'light and shade' of which he speaks later: the contrast of his former happiness with Fanny and his present misery cut off from her. Here 'pro-ing and con-ing' is practically the same as 'the hateful siege of contraries', pushed to an extreme of agony, intolerably proved upon his pulses.

The moment came when Keats's poetical philosophy of 'light and shade' was beyond his mortal endurance, and he could not contemplate the 'light and shade' of his own life, except at the cost (as he felt) of being killed by the contemplation. At this point the task of 'speculation' is transferred from him to us. At this point Keats ceases to be the artist and becomes as it were the work of art, which by its intensity creates in us 'a momentous depth of speculation' and makes 'all disagreeables evaporate from their close relationship with Beauty and Truth'. Then it is we who are 'afraid to encounter the pro-ing and con-ing' and we are required to die a death in imagination as he in bitter reality.

It seems to me that all the key-words and phrases which form the peculiar idiom of Keats's most inward and distinctive experience, pass eventually in this fashion into a new dimension of meaning, and reveal their significance completely only at the mysterious point when to his poetry is added his life and death, and these, in their totality, are the 'poem' to which his phrases are applied. We seem to know, for example, all that was implied in his cry 'Nevertheless, O for a life of Sensations rather than Thoughts' only when we realize that what the total 'poem' of Keats awakens in us is 'Sensations rather than Thoughts'.

I shall be sorry if this idea is too 'mystical' for acceptance, for indeed I do not propound it as an idea. It is no more than an effort to communicate my experience of Keats. That *is* how I experience him. And in my mind this peculiar experience is intimately connected with the fact that the effort to follow the thread of Keats's use of any one of these key-words takes us very quickly into contact with something which, to borrow the phrase from himself, may be called the element of 'lived prophecy' in Keats.

Take for instance as the beginning of such a thread this phrase 'pro-ing and con-ing'. It first appears in a letter to Jane Reynolds of September 1817. There is a friendly dispute between them as to who shall be preferred — Juliet or Imogen. Keats says:

If I did not think you had a kind of preference yourself for Juliet, I would not say a word more about it — but as I know people love to be reminded of those they most love — 'tis with me a certain thing that you are merely fishing for a little proing and conning thereon.

The phrase seems and is quite normal: a little disputation. In his next letter Keats writes:

So now let me put down in black and white briefly my sentiment thereon. Imprimis — I sincerely believe that Imogen is the finest Creature; and that I should have been disappointed at hearing you prefer Juliet. Item Yet I feel such a yearning towards Juliet and that I would rather follow her into Pandemonium than Imogen into Paradize — heartily wishing myself a Romeo to be worthy of her.

Instantly, there comes into mind a phrase which Keats used to Georgiana a year later, after his encounter with Charmian: 'I should like her to ruin me and I should like you to save me'; and yet another, still later, from *Lamia*.

> Thus gentle Lamia judg'd, and judg'd aright,
> That Lycius could not love in half a fright,
> So threw the goddess off, and won his heart
> More pleasantly by playing woman's part,
> *With no more awe than what her beauty gave,*
> *That, while it smote, still guaranteed to save.*

The 'pro-ing and con-ing' of the contrast between the passionate and the patient love represented by Juliet and Imogen, is

continued in the contrast between Charmian and Georgiana.
Then the contrast is reconciled in a creation of Keats's imagination, the Lamia — a very significant figure as I believe. Something
of her significance is indicated below in the chapter 'The Poet and
the Dreamer'. Here it is enough to emphasize that although the
'pro and con' were reconciled in the imaginary woman, the whole
import of the poem is that her beauty *is* imaginary, and that the
beatitude of Lycius, her lover, ends in death, when the spell is
broken. Life, Keats seems to be saying, does not admit of such
felicity. The Lamia, because she was supernatural, could 'unperplex bliss from its neighbour pain'. She brought to Lycius
'unperplex'd delight'; but that is beyond mortality. *Lamia* expresses through a poetic fable the thought of the *Ode to Melancholy*.

> Ay, in the very temple of Delight
> Veil'd Melancholy has her sovran shrine.

One could (it seems) follow the thread on and on until the
whole pattern of the 'poem' of Keats was unravelled and woven
again. 'Light and shade', 'pro and con', are in Keats's experience
the very law and principle of life — and death. Thus it is that
'Death is Life's high meed' — the final shade to the light of Life.

And the Poet is he who is continually aware of and responsive
to the emotional 'light and shade'. The 'light and shade' is Life;
but the light and shade of Life are one light, as against the shade
of Death. Therefore, the Poet must needs be 'half in love with
easeful Death'. One may explain Keats's continuous musing on
Death as due to the 'self-prescience of disease'; but that really
explains nothing, and reduces prophecy to commonplace. For
Death is there, however much the modern consciousness may
seek to hide it away, or itself away from it. Keats's preoccupation
with Death was not morbid, but one more sign of his splendid
sanity. And if, in any degree and at any time, his imagination
took Death too lightly and saw its coming as too easeful, the
balance was terribly righted at the last. The 'light and shade' of
the poem that was Keats in its final intensity is blinding.

CHAPTER IX

THE POET AND THE DREAMER

IN *Keats and Shakespeare* I discussed at some length the lines in Keats's *The Fall of Hyperion* (ll. 187-210 of the text in Professor de Selincourt's, and now in Professor Garrod's, edition of the Poems) which, Woodhouse tells us, 'Keats seems to have intended to erase'. This passage had in fact been excluded previously from the text of the poem by Monckton Milnes, acting, one supposes, on the authority of Woodhouse's statement. On the discovery of the Woodhouse transcript Professor de Selincourt introduced the passage into the text in his fourth edition of the Poems, on the ground that 'it was of the highest importance to the argument of the poem'. To this restoration I objected on the ground that the added lines falsified the argument of the poem.

In a note to his fifth edition of the Poems Professor de Selincourt appears to dispose of my objection. 'Mr. Murry's argument,' he concludes, 'here as elsewhere, is vitiated by his acceptance of what Keats says when it suits his theory, and rejecting it when Keats has the temerity to differ from him.'

This final statement is irrelevant to the issue. No one denies that Keats actually wrote the disputed lines. The sole question is whether we should, or should not, give effect to Woodhouse's statement that 'Keats seems to have intended to erase' them. Professor de Selincourt argued, and still argues, that we should not. He now says that, whatever may have been the mark Keats put against the lines, 'it is at least as likely to have indicated that the lines needed revision as that they were to be cancelled'. In that statement Professor de Selincourt has already deviated from the authority. Whatever the mark was, Woodhouse interpreted it as meaning that the lines were to be cancelled. Woodhouse is our sole authority for the existence of the mark, and for the interpretation of its meaning. It cannot be thus reduced to a mark susceptible of any interpretation. We must not start, as Professor de Selincourt does, from the position that what Woodhouse wrote was that 'Keats seems to have intended to *revise* these lines'. He wrote: 'Keats seems to have intended to *erase* them.'

We may postpone for a moment the consideration of the argument of the poem, to which (according to Professor de Selincourt) the disputed lines are of the highest importance, and confine ourselves to the actual text of the lines. A moment's examination is enough to show that they themselves strikingly confirm Woodhouse's statement that Keats seems to have intended to erase them. Here is the actual passage (included in square brackets) with the one introductory line, and the ten succeeding lines:

So answer'd I, continuing, 'If it please,   186
[Majestic shadow, tell me: sure not all
Those melodies sung into the world's ear
Are useless: sure a poet is a sage;
A humanist, physician to all men.   190
That I am none I feel, as vultures feel
They are no birds when eagles are abroad.
What am I then: thou spakest of my tribe:
What tribe?' *The tall shade veil'd in drooping white*
Then spake, so much more earnest, that the breath
Mov'd the thin linen folds that drooping hung
About a golden censer from the hand
Pendent — 'Art thou not of the dreamer tribe?
The poet and the dreamer are distinct,
Diverse, sheer opposite, antipodes.   200
The one pours out a balm upon the world,
The other vexes it.' Then shouted I
Spite of myself, and with a Pythia's spleen,
'Apollo! faded! O far-flown Apollo!

Where is thy misty pestilence to creep
Into the dwellings, thro' the door-crannies
Of all mock lyrists, large self-worshippers
And careless hectorers in proud bad verse?
Though I breathe death with them it will be life
To see them sprawl before me into graves.]   210
Majestic shadow, tell me where I am,
Whose altar this, for whom this incense curls;
What Image this, whose face I cannot see
For the broad marble knees; and who thou art,
Of accent feminine, so courteous?'
    Then the tall shade, in drooping linen veil'd,
Spoke out, so much more earnest, that her breath
Stirr'd the thin folds of gauze that drooping hung
About a golden censer from her hand
Pendent; and by her voice I knew she shed   220
Long-treasured tears . . .

The lines marked in italic are repeated, and obviously revised at their second appearance. It is inconceivable to me that Keats intended them to stand together in the text of the poem. That, at least, is certain. And it seems to me as near to certainty as we can get in such matters that in ll. 211-20 we have the *actual* 'revision' of ll. 187-210. Professor de Selincourt has asked, 'May not Keats have intended to revise, and not to erase, ll. 187-210?' But if ll. 211-20 are themselves the revised form of ll. 187-210, his question becomes meaningless. Keats *had* revised them; and in consequence of this revision it was inevitable that he should have intended to erase ll. 187-210. I should, myself, have been forced to that conclusion if no such statement of Woodhouse's were in existence. Moreover, I believe that, if ll. 187-210 had been in the accepted text, before the discovery of the Woodhouse transcript, they would have been challenged long ago. Be that as it may, the evidence of the text itself is striking; and it fully corroborates Woodhouse's statement that Keats 'seems to have intended to erase' ll. 187-210.

When these matters — which I took for granted in *Keats and Shakespeare* — have been made plain, it is seen that the prima facie case against the introduction of the lines into the text is far stronger than Professor de Selincourt allows. To overcome this prima facie case against the lines, Professor de Selincourt has to prove that the lines are, indeed, of *vital* importance to the argument of *The Fall of Hyperion*. It is not true to say, as he does, that 'to prove his main contention Mr. Murry would have to prove either that Keats never wrote the lines at all, or that he wrote them at some considerably earlier period'. My main contention is that the lines are (i) not of vital importance to the argument of the poem and (ii) that, in fact, they conflict with the real argument of the poem. My contention is indeed quite simple: namely, that Keats, when he wrote those lines, was saying something which he did not really mean, and that he pulled himself up and began again at the point where he was conscious that he had 'gone off the rails'. That, I submit, is a perfectly natural happening, and one familiar to the experience of writers far less eminent than Keats. To say that, in order to 'prove' that this happened, I must 'prove' either that Keats never wrote the abandoned lines at all, or that he wrote them a long while before he abandoned them, is unwarrantable.

All that I really have to prove is that the lines are not of *vital* importance to the poem; for this is enough to establish the case against the re-introduction of the lines into the text. That I was involved in the effort to show more than this in *Keats and Shakespeare* was due to the fact that I was primarily concerned with the interpretation of the poem. There I wrote:

The argument by which their inclusion in the text is justified is that the thought is necessary. Without these lines, it is said, there is no answer to the great question put to Keats: 'What benefit canst thou or all thy tribe Do the great world?' The question will go by default and poetry be rejected as useless. The situation is supposed to be saved by those lines wherein Keats admits that he is a dreamer, and of the tribe

of dreamers — whereas the true poet is in this sense no
dreamer at all. Keats deleted the lines. The reason of his
doing so is quite clear.

He did not admit that he was a mere dreamer; he knew —
had he not spent those last bitter months, and all his poetic
life, in learning it? — the difference between a poet and a mere
dreamer. Had he not utterly rejected dreams? Did he not
know that he was a true poet? Was he not proving it at the
very moment that he wrote? The first great reason why
Keats cancelled the lines and why they must remain cancelled
is that they were not true of himself. There was no time and
no place for false modesty. To restore those lines is to do
him and his thought an injury, in the interests of an apparent
logic which he himself rejected.

'Why,' Professor de Selincourt asks, 'if these lines were cancelled because Keats did not admit he was a mere dreamer, did he
not also cancel ll. 168-9, where Moneta charges him with being a
dreamer?' This 'logic' is irrelevant. The whole point is that Keats
is now the dreamer, and something besides. And what that something besides is, is indefinable; it can only be suggested, as it is
suggested precisely at this point of the poem, where Moneta
declares to him:

> Therefore, that happiness be somewhat shar'd,
> Such things as thou art are admitted oft
> Into like gardens thou didst pass erewhile,
> And suffer'd in these temples: for that cause
> Thou standest safe beneath this statue's knees.

Keats has endured a vital change. The essential nature of the
change has been already declared.

>   Thou hast felt
> What 'tis to die and live again before
> Thy fated hour; that thou hadst power to do so
> Is thy own safety.

By this power Keats is differentiated from the mere dreamer. The mere dreamer 'rots on the pavement where he rotted half'. But Keats is saved, by an agony of suffering indeed, but saved.

It is surely obvious that the simple dichotomy between the mere poet-dreamer and the true poet has no application to this condition achieved by Keats. The words which he hastily gave to Moneta:

> The poet and the dreamer are distinct,
> Diverse, sheer opposite, antipodes.
> The one pours out a balm upon the world,
> The other vexes it. —

are irrelevant to Keats's new condition. What that condition is cannot be expressed in those terms.

Professor de Selincourt now writes:

But 'had he not utterly rejected dreams?' asks Mr. Murry. The answer is that he had not rejected them *before*, but that he represents himself *now* as learning from Moneta to reject them. It stands to reason that the judgment passed by Moneta, and endorsed by himself, refers to the poetry he had already written and not to the poem he is now writing, in which he expounds the truth Moneta has taught him; a truth which was to guide his future work. Here, then, he is not the 'dreamer', but the poet from whom the dreamer is 'distinct'.

That argument is, in the main, sound: except for the all-important point that the new truth is not merely to guide Keats's future poems, but is actually guiding this one. But, unfortunately, the lines which Professor de Selincourt still hopes to rescue by this argument end with the appeal to Apollo:

> Where is thy misty pestilence to creep
> Into the dwellings, through the door-crannies
> Of all mock-lyrists, large self-worshippers,
> And careless hectorers in proud bad verse?
> *Though I breathe death with them it will be life*
> *To see them sprawl before me into graves.*

Here plainly, Keats counts *himself* involved in the destruction of the 'dreamer-tribe'. To use his former figure, he is now condemned 'to rot on the pavement where he rotted half'. The inward contradiction is plain. How can such lines be saved by an argument which admits that Keats is no longer a 'dreamer'? This argument is merely a new form of my original argument for the rejection of the lines.

I submit that, first, Professor de Selincourt has failed to prove what he must prove, namely, that the lines are vitally necessary to the argument of the poem; and, second, that the argument of the poem, as he now interprets it, is in complete conflict with the plain meaning of the conclusion, at least, of the lines which he still desires, in spite of Woodhouse's statement, and the textual evidence of the lines themselves, to re-introduce into the body of the poem. I see no reason at all to alter my former conclusion:

> The passage which has been unwarrantably restored to the text not only makes Keats do an injustice to himself which he refused to do, but instead of making clear the real nature of his thought, it confuses it. The clarity it adds is merely superficial; therefore Keats rejected it.

Whether or not Professor de Selincourt agrees with the main thesis of my *Keats and Shakespeare* is beside the point. This particular problem must be considered, and must be settled, on its own merits. Professor de Selincourt took the step of introducing the passage into the text of the poem; a valid defence of his action is still to seek.

There is a thread in the argument of *The Fall of Hyperion*, very relevant to this controversy, which emerges at other crucial moments in Keats's thinking, and seems to puzzle other critics of Keats besides Professor de Selincourt.

When the poet reaches the altar-steps, he is told by Moneta that his title to this escape from death is (i) that he had power to endure a death in life, and (ii) that he was one of

> those to whom the miseries of the world
> Are misery, and will not let them rest.

But are there not (the poet asks Moneta) thousands of these? Why, then, is he alone on the altar-steps? Moneta replies that it is because the others are content to labour for the immediate good of their fellow-men. He is here, because he is 'less than they'.

How he is less, she explains. He is 'a dreaming thing, a fever of himself'. Whereas they are not.

> Every sole man hath days of joy and pain,
> *Whether his labours be sublime or low* —
> The pain alone; the joy alone; distinct:
> Only the dreamer venoms all his days,
> Bearing more woes than all his sins deserve.

A new distinction is here introduced; what logicians call a cross-division. The first division was between unimaginative men and the imaginative, 'those to whom the miseries of the world are misery'. In this division Keats belongs to the imaginative men. But the imaginative men are divided into those like Keats, who dream, and those who act for immediate human good. These latter imaginative men are one with the common, unimaginative men, in that they both — 'whether their labours be sublime' (the imaginative active man) 'or low' (the unimaginative active man) — experience their pain and their joy distinct. Only the dreamer (the imaginative, inactive man) venoms *all* his days, that is, experiences pain in all his joys. Therefore such as he are admitted often into the garden, and into the temple, in order that they may taste some pure happiness.

The thought is compressed and pregnant but, it seems to me, perfectly clear. The further superimposed division of the dreamers (the imaginative inactive men) into true poets and dreamers (which, as I argue, Keats rejected for this very reason) confuses everything. In the abandoned lines Keats suggests that there is a distinction between the imaginative inactive man who does not act for immediate human good, but does good by his poetry (the

Poet *par excellence*) and the imaginative poet like himself who does no good by his poetry (the Dreamer). Moneta drives home the distinction.

> The Poet and the Dreamer are distinct,
> Diverse, sheer opposite, antipodes.
> The one pours out a balm upon the world,
> The other vexes it.

Is such a distinction really valid? Does such a Poet *par excellence* really exist? Keats very wisely doubted it, marked the lines for deletion and made a fresh start.

The idiosyncrasy of the imaginative inactive man, by which his joy and pain are not distinct, but always intermingled, appears to derive from the centre of Keats's experiencing nature. He recurs to it in *Lamia*, where the Lamia is said to be

> Not one hour old, yet of sciential brain
> To unperplex bliss from its neighbour pain;
> Define their pettish limits, and estrange
> Their points of contact, and swift counterchange:
> Intrigue with the specious chaos, and dispart
> Its most ambiguous atoms with sure art.

These lines are dismissed by Mr. Ridley in his book, *Keats's Craftmanship*, as 'six lines which have a specious appearance of reflective profundity and in fact mean as nearly as may be exactly nothing'. On the contrary, though they may be poor poetry, they mean a great deal. They mean, like the lines from *The Fall of Hyperion* with which they are intimately connected, that the condition in which joy and pain are distinct was for Keats a condition of beatitude from which he was debarred. He was condemned to 'venom all his days', and in the extremity of his consciousness and his imaginative sympathy to know neither joy nor pain distinct. There are moments when he can regard this as a privilege, and the tense inward struggle from which *The Fall of Hyperion* derives its stern and sombre life is precisely the poet's effort to win the assurance that it *is* a privilege. The point of the lines as applied to the Lamia is that she, ostensibly in virtue of her supernatural origin, is born with the power to conquer this equivocal condition of the conscious poet; she can

> Intrigue with the specious chaos and dispart
> Its most ambiguous atoms with sure art.

This is her essential difference, of which her physical metamorphosis is merely the outward sign. This is what sets the Lamia apart from a mortal like Lycius, or like Keats.

In this respect the Lamia is intimately related to the 'ravished nymph' who appears in the first draft of the final lines of *Hyperion*, which as reconstituted by Mr. Ridley runs thus:

> Thus the God,
> While his enkindled eyes, with level glance
> Beneath his white soft temples, steadfast kept
> Trembling with light upon Mnemosyne:
> Soon wild commotions shook him, and made flush
> All the immortal fairness of his limbs,
> *Into a hue more roseate than sweet pain*
> *Gives to a ravish'd Nymph when her warm tears*
> *Gush luscious with no sob. Or more severe; —*
> Most like the struggle at the gate of death;
> Or liker still to one who should take leave
> Of pale immortal death, and with a pang
> As hot as death's is chill, with fierce convulse
> Die into life: so young Apollo anguish'd.

Keats told Woodhouse that the whole passage describing the inward metamorphosis of Apollo (*Hyperion*, Bk. III) 'seemed to come to him by chance or magic — to be as it were something given to him'. It is well that he deleted the three lines; but they are much more than 'a disastrous spasm of the old fatal Leigh Hunt influence', as Mr. Ridley describes them. The image, however shocking to our taste, was meant seriously. What Keats was struggling to convey by the concrete imagery characteristic of his poetic method, was the mystery of 'dying into life'; and whether or not we like the idea that the climax of this inward metamorphosis should be compared to the moment at which the pain of a ravished girl passes into pleasure, there is no doubt that at a deeper level than that of conventional propriety the image is significant.

The Lamia is the counterpart and opposite of this 'ravish'd nymph'. Love, for the Lamia, means no such 'swift counterchange' of bliss and pain; and because it does not, she is not mortal. Every word she speaks entices Lycius on 'to *unperplex'd* delight and pleasure known'. Therefore she is, in the deepest sense of the word, an illusion and the cause of illusion. She neither knows perplexity in herself nor causes it in her lover; whereas this perplexity is inherent in conscious humanity, and the 'ravish'd nymph' is an extreme physical symbol of it.

Through his acceptance of, and submission to, this perplexity of joy and pain, the poet endures his 'death in life', which is, as it were, the supreme experience of that perplexity — its complete and final embodiment in 'sensation'. This perplexity, this impossibility of keeping joy and pain distinct in the imaginative man, is at the very heart of the *Odes*, and receives perhaps its most triumphant poetical assertion in the final stanza of the *Ode to Melancholy*.

> She dwells with Beauty — Beauty that must die;
>   And Joy, whose hand is ever at his lips
> Bidding adieu; and aching Pleasure nigh,
>   Turning to poison while the bee-mouth sips:
> Ay, in the very temple of Delight
>   Veil'd Melancholy has her sovran shrine,
>   Though seen of none save him whose strenuous tongue
>   Can burst Joy's grape against his palate fine;
> His soul shall taste the sadness of her might,
>   And be among her cloudy trophies hung.

The beauty in truth, the truth in beauty of that, is the proof that Keats was right in rejecting the suggestion of his doubtful mind that the Poet and the Dreamer are distinct: 'the one pours out a balm upon the world, the other vexes it'. The great poet vexes the world, and himself; but in the selfless quality of his vexation is the balm.

CHAPTER X

KEATS AND MILTON

IN his book, *The Miltonic Setting*, Dr. E. M. Tillyard attributes to *Keats and Shakespeare* a considerable influence in the critical depreciation of Milton which has, undoubtedly, been going on during the last twenty years. This critical depreciation Dr. Tillyard regards as excessive and unwarrantable, as perhaps it is; and in order to correct it, he criticizes my book.

But here are involved two critical issues which need to be kept distinct. One is: the right estimate of Milton, intrinsically, as a poet. The other is: the right estimate of the role he played in Keats's experience at a crucial moment. For the first, I admit without demur that I, for reasons of idiosyncrasy, am inclined to underestimate Milton's intrinsic value as a poet. For the second, I maintain that my estimate of the role he played in Keats's experience in 1819 is correct. And it seems to me that Dr. Tillyard tends to confuse these distinct issues. Since it is important that the doing of justice to Milton should not involve the confusion of the clear picture I tried to trace of Milton's significance *for* Keats, at a particular moment of Keats's life, I wish to rebut some of Dr. Tillyard's criticisms of that picture.

The most interesting of these is his contention that, so far from the Miltonic style being inadequate to Keats's experience, Milton himself, some time before writing *Lycidas*, underwent much the same kind of experience as Keats had undergone in the early months of 1819, and that the thought and feeling of *Lycidas* is closely akin to that of the *Ode to a Nightingale*. Unfortunately, this is a matter which hardly lends itself to argument. I can do little more than say that the feeling-tone of the two poems is to my sense altogether different. I can, indeed, bring forward good reasons, from Keats's biography, why the feeling-tone of the two poems, and the 'depth of speculation' aroused by them is so different; but if Dr. Tillyard does not feel this difference, there is no common ground between us. 'Mr. Murry', he says, 'really must not be allowed to confine the great generalities of human feeling to the kind of man he happens to prefer; and if Keats's problem and its solution grew out of "the torment of experience", so did Milton's.'

Dr. Tillyard's phrase, 'the great generalities of human feeling', conceals the rather deep gulf that divides us. For precisely what I was concerned to elucidate in Keats was a great particularity of feeling. To Milton the phrase, 'the great generalities of human feeling', seems to me apt, in the main; but hardly at all to Keats. It is the marvel of Keats that his peculiar genius conveys — sometimes with an almost intolerable intensity — the actual sensation, the private and particular quality, of his deep feeling. It is no part of my contention that Milton did not feel deeply, too: I believe he did, but in other ways, and about a different kind of experience. I should say that Milton's feeling, at its deepest, was of a quality entirely different from Keats's.

The existence and the reality of such differences, elemental and wellnigh absolute, between the quality of feeling in different men is with difficulty recognized in literary criticism, because these differences are so hard to formulate. Yet, I believe, they are of major importance. I would even say that to them are due most of the great divergences in the history of the human mind, and that no approximately true history of the human race can be written without a realization of their existence and an appreciation of their significance. Maine de Biran did not exaggerate at all when he wrote in his *Mémoire sur les perceptions obscures*:

Each individual is distinguished from another of the species by the fundamental manner in which he feels his life, and consequently in which he feels — I do not say judges — his relations to other things, in so far as they can favour or menace his existence. The difference in this respect is perhaps stronger even than that which exists between people's features or the external formation of their bodies.

Nevertheless, though I believe that every individual has his own way of 'feeling his life', I also believe that men of imaginative genius could be classed into feeling-types. Spenser and Milton and Dr. Bridges, for example, belong to the same broad feeling-type; Shakespeare and Keats belong to the same feeling-type. These two classes are not exhaustive. I do not consider that Wordsworth, for example, can be fairly placed in either of these classes. Dr. Jung in his suggestive book, *Psychological Types*, has boldly, but perhaps prematurely, attempted a detailed classification. But he has, at least, conclusively established that 'scientific' psychology — in the peculiar modern sense of reductive psychology — is useless in this realm; by its assumptions it abolishes the very phenomena to be studied.

Probably several major antitheses of 'feeling-types' would have to be established, and a great deal of cross-division endured, if a comprehensive classification were to be made. I believe that Blake's Prophetic Books contain a wealth of precious indications for this purpose. But, no doubt, the history of religion, and pre-eminently the history of the Christian religion (of which Blake's Prophetic Books are an integral part), supplies us with the finest instrument for this investigation. The great distinction, as it has manifested itself in history, between the catholic and the protestant mind, roughly corresponds to one of these elemental antitheses of feeling-type. I use the words for my particular purpose without capitals, because Roman Catholicism has contained many protestant minds (e.g. Pascal and Port-Royal), and Protestantism many catholic minds. In so far as Anglicanism can be called Protestant, it is predominantly catholic. And obviously, previous to the Reformation, protestant and catholic minds lived together in the Western Church without intolerable friction.

Using these terms then in a general rather than a precisely religious sense, I should say that Shakespeare and Keats were of the catholic feeling-type and Milton was of the protestant feeling-type; and that they were very pure examples of their type. In my book, *Heaven and Earth*, I examine in detail the fundamental feeling pattern of Milton, and I contrast him successively with Blake and Keats, and finally with Cromwell, in whose composition were some very potent catholic elements. If I am required to describe the catholic type, at a high level, I should say it is much more conscious than the protestant type of the mystery of existence, and in particular of the mystery of suffering; and much more conscious of the limitations of the human reason. This, I should say, derived from a different quality of primary experience, which comes to the catholic nature immediate, warm, and perplexing.

The difference emerges fairly clearly in a dual attitude towards the central Christian mystery. The protestant type of mind lays more stress on the Atonement, the catholic on the Incarnation; the catholic mind is naturally sacramental, the protestant naturally exegetic. At this point, if not before, the significance of the distinction for poetry is manifest. I should say that Keats's poetry is sacramental, and Milton's is not. Keats's poetry is charged with warmth and mystery, like a pulse in the blood, while Milton's is not. Keats was not a professed Christian, while Milton was; yet Keats, I should say, was much more a naturally Christian poet than Milton.

To elaborate the distinction would take me too far. But I should like to suggest that it underlies the constant effort of the catholic mind, manifest in catholic theology, to vindicate the whole conception of 'the naturally Christian' nature of human existence. For the catholic mind, which is nourished by the catholic feeling-nature, divine Grace is a consummation and perfection of the natural order. For the protestant mind, on the contrary, the natural order is hopelessly corrupt and depraved, and divine Grace is an irruption of the totally other supernatural order into the evil of unredeemed existence. The natural is essentially diabolical.

It would be fantastic to charge Milton with this Lutheran extravagance. On the contrary, his apparent peculiarity is that he is overweeningly confident in the natural man, or at least in the natural reason of man. But it would not be difficult to show how this excessive confidence in human reason derived from a secularized Protestantism, in which the religious sense of human depravity produces its own antithesis in a conviction of secular 'election'. Milton was convinced of his 'election' at a curiously early age — an age at which it is psychologically impossible to believe that he had undergone the very intense spiritual struggle which distinguishes the religious Protestant, and of which Cromwell is so striking an example. Milton's sense of 'election' appears to have been entirely precocious and unnatural (from the *religious* point of view); and it issued in a truly astonishing confidence in human reason, and primarily in his own reason, completely emancipated from the humility of religious faith.

I cannot conceive Keats at any moment of his career, even had it lasted twice as long, thinking of himself as 'a great man' with anything approaching Milton's self-assurance. At his highest pitch of confidence Keats hoped to be '*among* the English poets' at his death. Milton never gives me the impression of wanting to be *among* anybody; Dr. Tillyard's notion that, because Milton's doctrines were Protestant, were he living today, he might need to be 'saved from the Groups' is *very* odd — and as for asking to have it inscribed upon his tombstone that here lay one whose name was writ in water — it is, in Milton's case, just unimaginable. Milton was naturally full of his rather magnificent Self, Keats was naturally self-less.

I can see no essential likeness at all between *Lycidas* and *The Ode to a Nightingale*. I think *Lycidas* a very beautiful poem; but I find in it little trace of suffering, and less sense of the mystery of suffering. In it Milton uses the Christian soteriology as a theme for his austere and beautiful poetic pattern. I am none too sure that he felt the loss of Edward King very bitterly; and I feel certain that as a personal pain it was not comparable with what Keats felt on the death of Tom Keats. Dr. Tillyard's theory that *Lycidas* is the outcome of 'the torment of experience' is incomprehensible to me. For the analogue, in life-experience, in Milton of that which utters itself in Keats's *Odes* we should have to go to a much later period in Milton's life. *Lycidas* is a poem of the intellectual imagination, conceived in the great Renaissance-pastoral tradition: it is, to my sense, perhaps the most magnificent 'exercise' ever written. I should not care to deny that it is one of the very loveliest poems in the English language. But it is not the poem of one who has been oppressed by 'the burden of the mystery'.

The types of feeling and thinking represented by Milton and Keats are generically different. And I should say it was precisely because they were so different that Keats was able to learn, as he did, so much as a poet from Milton. His absorption of Milton's art was undisturbed by any deep affinity of feeling. In this particular and important sense he *learned* far less from Shakespeare and Wordsworth than he learned from Spenser and Milton. Milton, as a thinking and feeling human being, was not near to Keats; and he could learn from him as from a schoolmaster.

But there came a moment in Keats's life when he was tempted to learn more from Milton than his poetic art; when, by the exigencies of his own destiny, he was compelled to adopt, if by any means he might, what he felt to be the Miltonic attitude. I gave a careful account of this moment in *Keats and Shakespeare*. Dr. Tillyard misrepresents this account, no doubt inadvertently, in very important particulars. Thus he says that I represent that Keats's Miltonic period, when he was writing the first *Hyperion*, was 'artificial and inorganic'. I do nothing of the kind. My contention is entirely different: it is that Keats's creative adaptation of the Miltonic style was perfectly natural and perfectly adequate, while he was writing the greater part of the first *Hyperion*, but that there came a moment when his being was convulsed by deeper experiences than any he had hitherto known, and that *thenceforward* his adaptation of the Miltonic style was not natural or adequate to him: thenceforward, the influence of Milton was something which he had deliberately, by an effort of will, to impose upon himself. That attempt to impose the constraint of the Miltonic style upon his changed being was finally intolerable. He had to break free from it, or 'die'. 'Life to him would be death to me.'

Surely, there is a very great difference between this contention and that which Dr. Tillyard imputes to me. I feel that he has not understood my argument at all, although I expounded it patiently enough. For example, in order to prove that Milton did not have the peculiar significance for Keats which I assign to him (at the moment of rewriting *Hyperion*) Dr. Tillyard quotes Keats's letter of August 15th, 1819: 'Shakespeare and Paradise Lost every day become greater wonders to me. I look upon fine phrases like a lover.' That shows, he says, that Keats looked upon Shakespeare equally with Milton as a master of 'the verse of art'. If the letter existed in isolation, it would show this. But it does not exist in isolation. It is rapidly followed by others, which Dr. Tillyard forbears to mention. The sequence of these letters I carefully give in *Keats and Shakespeare*: they culminate in the letter to Reynolds of August 25th, 1819.

All my thoughts and feelings which are of the selfish nature, home speculations every day continue to make me more Iron. I am convinced more and more day by day that fine writing is next to fine doing the top thing in the world, the Paradise Lost becomes a greater wonder. The more I know what my diligence may in time probably effect; the more does my heart distend with Pride and Obstinacy — I feel it in my power to become a popular writer — I feel it in my strength to refuse the poisonous suffrage of a public. My own being which I know to be becomes of more consequence to me than the crowds of Shadows in the Shape of Man and women that inhabit a Kingdom. The Soul is a world of itself, and has enough to do in its own home. Those whom I know already, and who have grown as it were a part of myself, I could not do without: but for the rest of mankind, they are as much a dream to me as Milton's Hierarchies. I think if I had a free and healthy and lasting organization of heart and Lungs — as strong as an ox's so as to be able [to bear] unhurt the shock of extreme thought and sensation without weariness, I could pass my Life very nearly alone though it should last eighty years.

256

KEATS AND MILTON

In my comment on this letter in *Keats and Shakespeare*, I assert that the disappearance of Shakespeare from the sentence: 'Shakespeare and the Paradise Lost every day become greater wonders to me' is of crucial significance.

> What is happening is clear. Keats knows he cannot invoke Shakespeare any more, being what he is become. He has shut Fanny Brawne, he has shut the world of men and women out of his heart; and with them he has shut out Shakespeare ... Shakespeare had endured a bitter love; Shakespeare had accepted the world of men and women; Shakespeare had made his terms with the public; and in these things Shakespeare had shown his greatness. Keats could not follow him ... He was trying desperately to make the remoteness and abstraction of Milton his ideal; to find in the deliberate art of Milton and his proud neglect of human destinies for his majestic but inhuman theological drama a refuge from the torment of life.

I find nothing to change in this: I believe that it is true. Obviously, it is not and was not intended as a judgment of Milton, except in so far as it declares that the theological drama of *Paradise Lost* and *Paradise Regained* is 'inhuman'. I believe it is inhuman, not because it is theological, but because its theology is inhuman. That is a matter of opinion. I am prepared to defend mine. 'Un-Christian' is an ugly word to bandy about; but I am even prepared to maintain that Milton's epic is essentially un-Christian.

What I did not notice at the time I wrote *Keats and Shakespeare* was the interesting fact that in his letter Keats half-consciously identifies himself not merely with Milton, the self-sufficient artist, but with Milton's Satan. 'The more I know what my diligence may in time probably effect; the more does my heart distend with Pride and Obstinacy.' The phrase comes from *Paradise Lost*, Book I, ll. 571-2, where Satan reviews his host.

>   And now his heart
>   Distends with pride, and hardning in his strength
>   Glories.

Keats's use of the phrase incidentally affords some corroboration
of Blake's penetrating identification of Satan with Milton himself,
who was 'of the Devil's party without knowing it'. The influence
of the Miltonic Satan on all Blake's subsequent thinking and feeling was profound. He became for Blake the symbol of human
pride and self-sufficiency — the eternal opponent of the Divine-
Humanity, which was Jesus, who took possession of the human
heart only when it had acknowledged that 'we, in our Selves, are
nothing'.

Of this spiritual and religious order was the conflict that tormented Keats in August and September 1819. It was a struggle
between the impulse to pride and self-sufficiency, with Milton
for the ideal, and submission and humility, with Shakespeare for
the ideal. Keats's rejection of Milton implied, of course, a profound criticism of Milton as a spiritual being (which I believe to
be just); but it likewise implied a tremendously high estimate of
Milton as 'a man of Character' (which I likewise believe to be
just).

>   He above the rest
>   In shape and gesture proudly eminent
>   Stood like a Towr; his form had yet not lost
>   All her Original brightness, nor appear'd
>   Less than Arch Angel ruind, and th' excess
>   Of Glory obscur'd.

But Keats, indubitably, did pass judgment on Milton; or rather
the Divine Humanity in Keats passed judgment on him then —
precisely the same judgment that is passed on him in Blake's
Milton. With that judgment I humbly agree.

Dr. Tillyard does well to defend Milton; but I think he does
ill to misrepresent, as he does, the nature of Keats's judgment on
Milton. Keats's rejection of Milton, like Blake's, really does
Milton more honour than Dr. Tillyard's defence of him. He was

for Keats the *nec plus ultra* of spiritual and poetic self-sufficiency. I believe that this attitude, if persisted in to the bitter end, as Milton persisted in it, has unfortunate results, which are manifest to me in *Samson Agonistes*; but that it is an heroic attitude is undeniable. Nevertheless, *Samson Agonistes* seems to me, by its very perfection in its own kind, a lamentable end to the work of a great poetic genius. It is Christianity without Christ; the Old Testament without the Prophets.

> *Samson* hath quit himself
> Like *Samson*, and heroicly hath finish'd
> A life Heroic, on his Enemies
> Fully reveng'd, hath left them years of mourning,
> And lamentation to the Sons of *Caphtor*
> Through all *Philistian* bounds.

Satan hath quit himself like Satan; Milton like Milton. It is tremendous, and it is terrible. I can only echo Keats's words: 'Life to him would be death to me.'

Dr. Tillyard does not appreciate the real issue. He tends, moreover, to 'take everything literally' — and more than literally. Because I say that the *Ode to Autumn* is Shakespearian (as it surely is) I am represented as 'having seen in the *Ode to Autumn*, as individual a poem as Keats ever wrote, a re-embodiment of the soul of Shakespeare', which is 'fantastic'. It may be; but I did not see, or say, it. I do not think it accords with the principles of responsible criticism thus to misrepresent those with whom one disagrees. Moreover, to assert that because the *Ode to Autumn* is a magnificently individual poem it cannot be 'Shakespearian' in the sense in which I used that word, is absurd.

I am accused of substituting Shakespeare for Chatterton at a crucial point in my argument. Keats wrote:

> I always somehow associate Chatterton with autumn. He is the purest writer in the English Language. He has no French idiom, or particles like Chaucer — 'tis genuine English Idiom in English Words. I have given up Hyperion —

there were too many Miltonic inversions in it — Miltonic
verse can not be written but in an artful or rather artist's
humour. I wish to give myself up to other sensations.
English ought to be kept up.

(September 21st, 1819)

And on the same day, at more or less the same moment, he wrote
in his journal-letter to America:

I shall never become attach'd to a foreign idiom so as to
put it into my writings. The Paradise lost though so fine in
itself is a corruption of our Language — it should be kept as
it is unique — a curiosity — a beautiful and grand Curiosity.
The most remarkable Production of the world. A northern
dialect accommodating itself to greek and latin inversions
and intonations. The purest english I think — or what ought
to be the purest — is Chatterton's. The Language had existed
long enough to be entirely uncorrupted of Chaucer's galli-
cisms, and still the old words are used. Chatterton's language
is entirely northern. I prefer the native music of it to Milton's
cut by feet. I have but lately stood on my guard against Milton. Life to him would be death to me. Miltonic verse cannot be written but in the vein of art — I wish to devote myself
to another sensation.

How can I — Dr. Tillyard asks in effect — represent the outcome of the Milton-Shakespeare struggle in Keats as a victory for
Shakespeare, when Keats himself makes plain that it is a victory
for Chatterton? In order to suit the exigencies of my extravagant
thesis, I brazenly substitute Shakespeare for Chatterton.

To which I must reply that, if Dr. Tillyard is content 'to take
everything literally', I am guilty of a bare-faced (though open and
avowed) substitution. But my theme is not, as Dr. Tillyard seems
to imagine, the conflicting influence of the poetic 'objectivities' —
John Milton and William Shakespeare — on the being of John
Keats, but the conflicting influence of two types of 'poetic character' upon him. These two conflicting types of 'poetic character'
were symbolized, for Keats, chiefly in Milton and Shakespeare —

but not exclusively. The Shakespearian type was represented to him also by Chatterton, whose high place in Keats's imaginative hierarchy is precisely given in his original dedication to *Endymion*, wherein he dedicates his poem, reverentially, 'to the memory of the most English of poets except Shakespeare, Thomas Chatterton'. It was no concern of mine to judge whether Keats was in error, or how far in error, in thus estimating a poet who has fallen from esteem; I was merely concerned to establish the significance of Chatterton *for* Keats. That, I think, is plain. For Keats, Shakespeare is at once the greatest and 'most English' of our poets. Chatterton is the next *in order of Englishness*, for him. Certainly not the next in order of poetic greatness. At least four were greater than Chatterton — Chaucer, Spenser, Milton and Wordsworth — and there may have been a dozen others between Shakespeare and Chatterton in the order of poetic greatness. But, at this particular moment, and from this particular angle, Keats is concerned with 'Englishness'. He is seeking to make articulate, on the linguistic side, his revulsion from Milton.

Milton's verse idiom is for Keats, at this moment, 'a foreign idiom'. He includes in this notion of Milton's 'foreign idiom' both his actual diction, and his rhythms. And he sets over against it, not as intrinsically superior, but as more congenial to himself, Chatterton's idiom, in the same twofold sense. Chatterton's idiom is an English idiom — the next most English after Shakespeare's. Since Keats's deliberate conclusion, in this technical province or aspect of his revulsion from Milton's influence, is that 'English ought to be kept up', Chatterton takes on an importance that may not be intrinsically his. He is, if I may so express it, the representative in the technical province, of the type of poetic character which Keats imputed pre-eminently to Shakespeare.

But Shakespeare, as a type of poetic character, included many things which were not, or were only faintly adumbrated, in Chatterton. He stood supremely for Negative Capability, for the capacity of 'being in uncertainties, mysteries, doubts, without any irritable reaching after fact and reason'. These other more inward and spiritual qualities of Shakespeare, as a type of 'poetic character', were irrelevant to Keats's immediate point. He is talking in terms of technical influences and giving a technical reason why he found it impossible to continue his task of re-casting *Hyperion*. It would have been excessive and presumptuous — in one who set Shakespeare as man and artist on so lofty a pinnacle as Keats did — to write to Reynolds or George: 'I have decided to cease following Milton's idiom, I prefer to follow Shakespeare's.' He said, with an altogether characteristic modesty: 'I will follow Chatterton's.' I do not believe that I am mistaken in this interpretation of the actual process of Keats's mind at this moment. But if it still appears to Dr. Tillyard that I have done no more than commit a brazen and high-handed piece of legerde-main, I shall be sorry, but I shall be impenitent.

There were many reasons why Keats found it impossible to get on with *Hyperion* in the early months of 1819; but I do not think that conscious aversion to the Miltonic style was one of them. His incapacity, as I tried to show, was due to an influx of new and undigested experience. There were, again, many reasons why he found it impossible in August and September 1819 to continue with his attempt to recast *Hyperion* into the *Fall of Hyperion*. It was only then that he felt a conscious aversion to the Miltonic style, which he expressed in his letters of September 21st, 1819. But (as Dr. Bridges pointed out long ago) it is remarkable that *The Fall of Hyperion* — that is to say, the lines which Keats now added to the original *Hyperion* — is very much less Miltonic than the original *Hyperion*. What, to take an example quite at hazard, is there Miltonic about these lines?

> A long awful time
> I look'd upon them; still they were the same;
> The frozen God still bending to the earth,
> And the sad Goddess weeping at his feet.
> Moneta silent. Without stay or prop
> But my own weak mortality, I bore
> The load of this eternal quietude,

The unchanging gloom, and the three fixed shapes
Ponderous upon my senses a whole moon;
For by my burning brain I measured sure
Her silver seasons shedded on the night,
And every day by day methought I grew
More gaunt and ghostly — Oftentimes I pray'd
Intense, that Death would take me from the vale
And all its burthens — Gasping with despair
Of change, hour after hour I curs'd myself . . .

It is a very powerful kind of verse on which possibly Cary's
Dante had had some influence; but it is certainly not Miltonic. It
was therefore less directly in reference to the verse he was
actually writing than in reference to that which he was re-reading
in the hope of revising, that he uttered his judgment of Milton's
style. He could not continue in the style of the original *Hyperion*,
now: he would be adding patches of new cloth to an old garment.

Behind this technical incompatibility, as I tried to show, was
another and tremendous influx of new experience. But Keats's
attitude to Milton was complex and equivocal. Actually, he was
not writing Miltonic blank verse (if we apply that name to the
verse of the first *Hyperion*) but a very powerful blank verse of his
own, at the time when, in August 1819, he was identifying himself
with Milton. It was Milton's spiritual attitude — the attitude of
Milton's Satan — that he was trying to enforce upon himself. He
was trying to achieve, at the cost of great inward suffering, an
attitude of detachment from 'the miseries of the world'. He was
trying to control his pain, subdue his heart, and to write an
'epic'. And Milton was the symbol of all that effort. Milton was,
indubitably, a man who made great efforts; but I do not believe he
ever made an effort of this kind. Milton seems to have had no
great difficulty in thrusting his love out of his heart. So that
Milton was not really an adequate symbol of the effort Keats was
making; and on the other hand, by thus elevating Milton to an
ideal role which he was not fitted to fill, Keats ran the risk, when
the inevitable reaction came, of doing Milton some injustice. I

think, for example, it was unjust to Milton to prefer Chatterton's 'native music' to his. But that injustice will disturb us only if we try to read Keats's sentiments about Milton as grave and *ex cathedra* critical pronouncements. They are not that; but neither are they petulant and negligible. They afford us a precious glimpse of what was happening to Keats; and if they are not pressed too far, an equally precious indication of what Keats had come to feel about Milton.

If we insist on knowing what Keats *meant* by saying that he preferred to follow Chatterton's idiom rather than Milton's, what he *meant* by saying that 'English ought to be kept up', what he *meant* by the significantly repeated phrase: 'wish to give myself up to other sensations' . . . 'I wish to devote myself to another sensation' — we have one concrete piece of evidence: the *Ode to Autumn*. It is a much more adequate answer to those questions than any abstract theorizing could possibly give. We can, in a measure, understand what Keats meant by those three intentions from the *Ode*; and reciprocally, we can understand the *Ode* better by those three intentions.

Keats had returned, not deliberately, but by a necessity of his own being, to his axiom of poetry: that 'if it comes not as naturally as the leaves to a tree it had better not come at all'. That is not an axiom for all poets, but for a particular type of the poetic character, of which, for Keats, Shakespeare was the supreme example. It involved a rejection, not so much of artifice in itself, but of all artifice that could not be absorbed into a second nature: of all artifice that was felt to be a constriction on the creative genius of the poet, and on the creative genius of the English language. Of this dual constriction, in the last resort, the poet's 'sensation' was the sole and authoritative criterion. Hence Keats's emphasis on the word at this moment. Artifice was that which constricted 'sensation'. It demanded the 'artful or artist's humour', which meant an encroachment of the deliberate and self-conscious intellectual will on the necessary freedom of the poet's spontaneity. The creative genius, in this type of poetical character, called for surrender of the conscious self as the condition of its own operation. It called for a delicate poise of the faculties, in which the conscious, intellectual, purposive element was definitely subordinated — to what?

There are many names for this. The religious mind naturally thinks of it as God, declaring Himself through his chosen instrument — a human soul from which, for the moment of inspiration, the impediment of the separated and separating Self has been removed. Blake, who early declared that 'the Poetic Genius is the true Man', finally called it the Divine Humanity. If we are averse to such religious descriptions, we may try to avoid them by giving to the power to which the Shakespearian poet surrenders the Self, the name of Life. But that does not take us very far; for the life of the Self is also Life. Discrimination between the life of the Self, and the truer, deeper, higher life that utters itself only when the Self is in abeyance, is essential to any faithful description of the Shakespearian 'poetical character'; and such a discrimination cannot be made except in terms which have, at some point or other, a religious reference. The notion of the Self as an impediment to true being is fundamental and inescapable; and that notion is the essence of the religious conception of the spiritual life. 'Nevertheless not my will, but Thine, be done.'

That is the supreme type of the attitude to which the Shakespearian poet inevitably points and tends. By that eternal word we understand him and his significance. He is a witness to the reality of the Fatherhood of God, into whose hands he commends his spirit. The Shakespearian poet cannot do otherwise. It is no virtue on his part, as he experiences the motion. He obeys the compulsion of his own total being; if he disobeys it, the discord and dissension within his being become intolerable, and deathly. 'Life to him would be death to me.' In those words speaks the experience itself.

The essential quality of the Shakespearian type of poetic genius is the virtue known to Christian spirituality as humility. One must not force the identity too far, or too rigidly. If we

regard Christian humility as supremely manifest in the attitude of
the Christian mind before the mysteries of the Christian faith, the
clear perception of the kinship between the humility of the
Shakespearian poet and the humility of the Christian will depend
on what we regard as the central mystery of the Christian faith.
But if, as I believe, the life, the teaching, the death, and the
eternal life of Christ are that central mystery, and if the dogmas of
the Christian faith are to be regarded, as I again believe, as
deriving their meaning and truth from the central mystery, and
comprehensible only in 'the momentous depth of speculation' to
which that central mystery awakens the dormant soul: then the
humility of the Shakespearian poet and the humility of the
Christian are continuous with one another. The Negative Capability of the poet achieves its natural consummation in the
humility of the Christian before the Cross.

It is at this level that the conflict between Milton and Shakespeare in Keats's soul reveals its full meaning. I should say that
of all our great poets, Milton was the least naturally inclined to
humility. That he at times achieved it was a noble victory; and
we may be thankful that the *mens conscia recti* sustained him when
his brief humility failed. Milton was a great man and a great
poet. Nevertheless, in one who seems to have believed himself a
Christian poet, and is still generally regarded as one, it is astonishing how little reality the person of Christ or the mystery of
Christianity possessed for him. It was no wonder that Keats
believed that Milton's 'philosophy, human and divine, may be
tolerably understood by one not much advanced in years'. It
was the divinity of an amazingly gifted undergraduate, who has
disposed of all difficulties long before he has experienced what a
difficulty is. As I have said elsewhere, Milton's Protestant theology ends in a complete emancipation from Christianity itself.
The harvest of that sowing is to be sought not in any form of
Christianity but in the confidence of eighteenth- and nineteenth-
century rationalism.

Nor does Milton's poetry make adequate amends. There is, of
course, a wealth of poetic richness in Milton: of which the most

astonishing manifestation is the passionate unconscious sympathy with the rebellious energy of Satan, the most attractive the lovely pictures of the sensuous innocence of our first parents in Paradise, the subtlest and most pathetic the continual mingling of the riches of classical and romantic story with his barren and repugnant theodicy. In Milton the Renaissance struggles with the Reformation; but that which is deeper and richer than either is lost. Whether or not Shakespeare was a professing Christian, his poetry has perhaps more powerfully than any other single influence in our subsequent history, constantly replenished the sources of the religious awareness; so, in a lesser measure, has Keats. In both these poets there is something essentially liturgical and sacramental. The things they contemplate, the words they use, reach out beyond themselves, and become the portals of a mystery. There is no such penumbra of mystery in Milton, and no sense of it in him. With him imagination is a faculty; with them it is a condition. In him there is rich ornament in plenty, but it is not consubstantial with the thought it clothes.

Yet I admit that this is an unsatisfying conclusion. Milton is something, and something big. On the moral and spiritual side I find it easy enough to place him: he is, simply, a bad man of a very particular kind, who is a bad man because he is so sublimely certain of being a good one. That judgment at once condemns him, and allows him all his uniqueness and his power. But, when I consider him, simply as a poet, I cannot compass the corresponding aesthetic judgment, though I feel that there must be one. Keats was groping after it when he said that the *Paradise Lost* was 'a beautiful and grand curiosity'; but that is a long way from the judgment I am seeking — still quite in vain. I think, too, that other modern critics who, like me, participate in Keats's reaction to Milton, find peculiar difficulty in formulating their opinion save in terms that lay them open to defenders of Milton such as Dr. Tillyard. But these defences of Milton teach us nothing; they tell us nothing new. They are irrelevant to our dissatisfaction with Milton: which is that a poet so evidently great, in some valid sense of the word, so magnificent an artist of poetry, should have so little intimate meaning for us. We cannot make him real. He does not, either in his great effects or his little ones, touch our depths. He demonstrates, but he never reveals. He describes beauty beautifully; but truth never becomes beauty at his touch.

CHAPTER XI

KEATS AND WORDSWORTH

'I A M convinced', wrote Keats to Haydon on January 10th,
1818, 'that there are three things to rejoice at in this Age —
The Excursion, your Pictures, and Hazlitt's depth of Taste.'
He repeated his judgment in a letter to his brothers. He had
changed significantly in the year and more since he wrote his
sonnet, *Great spirits now on earth are sojourning* ... Not only had
Hazlitt taken the place of Hunt in the trinity of contemporary
genius (and I think he was to keep it to the end) but a more
general and inclusive praise of Wordsworth seems to be con-
centrating, not indeed on *The Excursion* alone, but upon that
element in Wordsworth's genius of which *The Excursion* is
typical, and of which the first two books of *The Excursion* are
perhaps the noblest expression which Wordsworth achieved.
That this high estimate of *The Excursion* should have coincided
with a new appreciation of Hazlitt's depth of taste is peculiarly
interesting, because Hazlitt himself did not adequately appreciate
The Excursion.

There are delightful passages in *The Excursion,* both of
natural description and of inspired reflection (passages of
the latter kind that in the sound of the thoughts and of the
swelling language resemble heavenly symphonies, mournful
requiems over the grave of human hopes); but we must
add, in justice and in sincerity, that we think it impossible
that this work should ever become popular, even in the
same degree as the *Lyrical Ballads.* It affects a system without having any intelligible clue to one, and instead of unfolding a principle in various and striking lights, repeats
the same conclusions till they become flat and insipid.
Mr. Wordsworth's mind is obtuse, except as it is the organ

and the receptacle of accumulated feelings; it is not analytic but synthetic; it is reflecting rather than theoretical. *The Excursion*, we believe, fell still-born from the press. There was something abortive, and clumsy, and ill-judged in the attempt. It was long and laboured. The personages, for the most part, were low, the fare rustic; the plan raised expectations which were not fulfilled; and the effect was like being ushered into a stately hall and invited to sit down to a splendid banquet in the company of clowns, and with nothing but successive courses of apple-dumplings served up. It was not even *toujours perdrix*!

The judgment is, no doubt, juster than any that was pro-nounced by a contemporary critic. Coleridge alone *might* have done better. There is undoubtedly a contrast, amounting almost to anticlimax, between the magnificent passage from *The Recluse* which Wordsworth quotes in his preface, 'as a kind of *Prospectus* of the design of the whole Poem' (i.e. *The Prelude*, *The Excursion* and the unwritten third part), and *The Excursion* itself. But the prospectus-passage is Wordsworth at the height of his inspiration, a great poet if one ever was; and it is impossible to imagine a poem sustained on such a level. Disappointment, of some kind, was inevitable, in any poem that followed such a preface. Hazlitt seems hardly to have realized quite how superb that invocation was.

The second point to remark is that Hazlitt is criticizing *The Excursion* for not containing an explicit system of philosophy. It was on this matter that his mind directly clashed with Words-worth's, and Wordsworth was bewildering to Hazlitt. For Wordsworth, in his prose-preface, first declared that the poem arose out of 'a determination to compose a philosophical poem', and concluded by saying: 'It is not the author's intention formally to announce a system; it was more animating to him to proceed in a different course; and if he shall succeed in conveying to the mind clear thoughts, lively images and strong feelings, the Reader will have no difficulty in extracting the system for himself.' The evasion was unconscious; but to Hazlitt's mind it must have seemed almost deliberate. In fact, Wordsworth's difficulty was intrinsic. What he was trying to do was partly to communicate a profound spiritual experience, partly to expound a religion based upon this experience; and this religion was in process of identifying itself with Christianity. Unfortunately, the specific Christian mysticism — the experience of the eternal Christ — was not original to Wordsworth's mysticism; so that the transition from his mysticism to Christianity generally appears either elusive or arbitrary. What Hazlitt understood by a philosophical system was very different from anything Wordsworth had to offer.

This failure of Hazlitt's mind to engage with Wordsworth's is notable in itself, for it led Hazlitt to a manifest underestimate of Wordsworth's imaginative powers, and an undue and slightly contemptuous emphasis on that part of Wordsworth's poetry which was most influenced by Wordsworth's conscious poetic theory: namely, his versification of the sentiments of simple people in realistic language. Coleridge made the classical criticism of this Wordsworthian dogma, and since the publication of the *Biographia Literaria* no one, except the late Andrew Bradley, has been tempted to explore the matter further. But there is something more to be said, or suggested. Probably it was not Wordsworth's instinctive practice that was at fault — *Margaret, We are Seven*, and dozens of others are beautiful and altogether successful poems — but some of Wordsworth's practice after it had been made self-conscious by theory. I incline to believe that Coleridge should bear the chief responsibility for this contamination. The planning of the *Lyrical Ballads*, and the definite allotment to the two poets of two separate provinces of the imagination (which was, I suspect, mainly Coleridge's doing) was a chief cause of this theoretical rigidity. If that is so, then Coleridge in tearing the theory to pieces in the *Biographia Literaria* was demolishing what was his own invention rather than Wordsworth's, and removing from Wordsworth's genius an incrustation which was largely deposited by himself.

If that is true, or partly true, it explains why Wordsworth was hurt rather than instructed by Coleridge's criticism. For long before Coleridge's criticism was written Wordsworth had found his own solution to the real problem: of which the character of the Wanderer himself in *The Excursion* was symbolic. The Wanderer was a simple pedlar, but a man of education and imagination — an improbable pedlar maybe, but an easily acceptable one; and certainly a character who enabled Wordsworth to achieve his complex purpose — to express in poetry the religion and the morality and the life-wisdom which, he was convinced, was stored in the hearts of simple folk who lived in the bonds of 'natural piety'. In the first book of *The Excursion* Wordsworth expresses what is in his mind, and explains how the character of the Wanderer was a solution of the problem of expression which had been set him by his own matured conviction concerning the nature of true wisdom.

> Oh! many are the Poets that are sown
> By Nature; men endowed with highest gifts,
> The vision and the faculty divine;
> Yet wanting the accomplishment of verse,
> (Which, in the docile season of their youth,
> It was denied them to acquire, through lack
> Of culture and the inspiring aid of books,
> Or haply by a temper too severe,
> Or a nice backwardness afraid of shame)
> Nor having e'er, as life advanced, been led
> By circumstance to take unto the height
> The measure of themselves, these favoured Beings
> All but a scattered few, live out their time,
> Husbanding that which they possess within,
> And go to the grave, unthought of. Strongest minds
> Are often those of whom the noisy world
> Hears least; else surely this Man had not left
> His graces unrevealed and unproclaimed.

There is, moreover, an affinity between Wordsworth's thought in these lines and that of the opening of *The Fall of Hyperion.*

For Poesy alone can tell her dreams —
With the fine spell of words alone can save
Imagination from the sable charm
And dumb enchantment — Who alive can say,
'Thou art no poet — may'st not tell thy dreams'?
Since every man whose soul is not a clod
Hath visions, and would speak, if he had lov'd,
And been well nurtured in his mother tongue.

Precisely that condition — 'if he had lov'd' — is fulfilled by the
Wanderer, though the word carries a different nuance of meaning
in Wordsworth and in Keats.* But in the essential I believe
Wordsworth and Keats were at one concerning the nature of the
love which is the source of 'the vision and the faculty divine',
whether it finds utterance in poetry or not. For both of them
the essential character of this love was that it was 'self-destroying'. The Wanderer is portrayed as one prepared in boyhood

By his intense conceptions, to receive
Deeply the lesson deep of love which he,
Whom Nature, *by whatever means*, has taught
To feel intensely, cannot but receive.

And to the Wanderer in youth Wordsworth gives perhaps the
most exquisite and magnificent of all his descriptions of his own
mystical beatitude in contemplating Nature.

He looked —
Ocean and earth, the solid frame of earth
And ocean's liquid mass, in gladness lay
Beneath him: — Far and wide the clouds were touched,
And in their silent faces could he read
Unutterable love. Sound needed none,
Nor any voice of joy; his spirit drank
The spectacle: sensation, soul, and form,
All melted into him; they swallowed up
His animal being; in them did he live,
And by them did he live; they were his life.

In such access of mind, in such high hour
Of visitation from the living God,
Thought was not; in enjoyment it expired.
No thanks he breathed, he proffered no request;
Rapt into still communion that transcends
The imperfect offices of prayer and praise.
His mind was a thanksgiving to the power
That made him; it was blessedness and love!

'And in *their silent faces* could he read Unutterable love.' The
expression comes again in Book II, applied to the Wanderer
himself.

And in *the silence of his face I read*
His overflowing spirit.

His spirit was overflowing with love of God's creation. 'He
loved them all.' I believe it was due to something more than unconscious memory that Keats used the phrase at the critical
moment of Apollo's dying into life in Book III of *Hyperion*:

Mute thou remainest — Mute! yet I can read
A wondrous lesson in thy silent face:
Knowledge enormous makes a God of me.
Names, deeds, gray legends, dire events, rebellions,
Majesties, sovran voices, agonies,
Creations and destroyings, all at once
Pour into the wide hollows of my brain,
And deify me, as if some blithe wine
Or bright elixir peerless I had drunk,
And so become immortal.

I do not imply that the experience is identical in Wordsworth
and Keats; but I think it has the same spiritual import, involves
the same depths of being, and is reached by the same means,
namely love, experienced with a self-destroying intensity. The
difference is rather in the province of reality from which the
imaginative intensity derives. In Wordsworth it is primarily and
pre-eminently the world of physical nature, including the folk

whose lives are shaped by natural piety; in Keats it is the world
of history, of human destinies, including his own.

The relation between Wordsworth and Keats is peculiarly
intimate; and probably impossible to unravel. Even after his hero-
worship of Wordsworth had received a shock in personal encounter, when the Wordsworth family came to town in the
winter of 1817-18, Keats still could not help regarding Wordsworth as the great living hero of poetry — the one contemporary
poet who had faithfully explored the mystery of life. He reacted
momentarily against the dogmatic simplicities of Wordsworth's
verse; he urged Reynolds not 'to be rattle-snaked' into 'tender
and true'; they were not 'for the sake of a few fine imaginative or
domestic passages . . . to be bullied into a certain philosophy
engendered in the whims of an Egotist': nevertheless he is constrained to admit 'Wordsworth's grandeur'. This was on
February 3rd, 1818. A fortnight later, on February 21st, he tells
his brothers that he is sorry 'that Wordsworth has left a bad
impression where-ever he visited in town by his egotism, Vanity
and bigotry. Yet he is a great poet if not a philosopher'. The
wound made by Wordsworth's condescension to his Hymn to
Pan as 'a pretty piece of Paganism' was evidently healing. No
doubt it had smarted particularly, since *Endymion* was just on the
point of publication. By March 14th, when he 'can't help
thinking' Wordsworth 'has returned to his Shell — with his
beautiful Wife and his enchanting Sister' — he can make a joke
of it all; and a very good one.

It is hardly possible to sort out the different strains in Keats's
momentary disillusion with Wordsworth. He had looked forward to meeting Wordsworth very ardently, because Wordsworth meant more to him than any living poet; moreover, during
the weeks he spent at Oxford with Bailey in the previous September, Wordsworth had been their constant reading. Within
six weeks, September 14th to November 22nd, 1817, there are no
less than three quotations from the *Immortal Ode* in Keats's
letters — all different, and all appropriate to and illuminative of

Keats's deepest feelings. Yet he was not lost in uncritical admiration. His defence of Wordsworth's *Gipsies* against Hazlitt's criticism, is itself a fine criticism of the poem:

> Wordsworth had not been idle he had not been without his task — nor had they Gipseys — they in the visible world had been as picturesque an object as he in the invisible. The Smoke of their fire — their attitudes — their Voices were all in harmony with the Evenings — It is a bold thing to say and I would not say it in print — but it seems to me that if Wordsworth had thought a little deeper at that Moment he would not have written the Poem at all — I should judge it to have been written in one of the most comfortable Moods of his Life — it is a kind of sketchy intellectual Landscape — not a search after Truth — nor is it fair to attack him on such a subject — for it is with the Critic as with the poet had Hazlitt thought a little deeper and been in a good temper he would never have spied an imaginary fault there.

In temper and penetration it is admirable. Keats is applying to one of Wordsworth's later poems the criterion of an earlier one, which was a favourite with Keats, *The Old Cumberland Beggar*. 'But deem not this Man useless,' cries Wordsworth.

> 'Tis Nature's law
> That none, the meanest of created things,
> Of forms created the most vile and brute,
> The dullest or most noxious, should exist
> Divorced from good — a spirit and pulse of good,
> A life and soul, to every mode of being
> Inseparably linked.

That was written in 1797, and *Gipsies* was written ten years later: when Wordsworth's morality was beginning to get the upper hand of his imagination. But the simple fact that Wordsworth's phrase 'a spirit and pulse of good' is one of the clues to Keats's beautiful letter to Reynolds on 'diligent indolence', on February 19th, 1818, when he was superficially most annoyed with Wordsworth; and that another phrase — 'we have all of us one human heart' — from the same poem, *The Old Cumberland Beggar*, is likewise a key to the lovely passage of his letter of March 1819 ('The creature hath a purpose and his eyes are bright with it') indicates how deeply Wordsworth had entered into Keats's being. In part Keats had, as Goethe said of himself in relation to Spinoza, 'discovered himself' in Wordsworth.

This deep response of Keats to Wordsworth — so intimate that he can use the essential Wordsworth as a touchstone for the moody one — made Keats's meeting with Wordsworth a tremendous event for him. And it must have been no small shock when, on the occasion of his first call, he was kept waiting a long while, only to be hurriedly greeted by a Wordsworth all dressed up for the real event of the day — dinner with Mr. Kingston, one of the Commissioners of Stamp Duties. Wordsworth, of course, had his family to provide for; it was imperative that a mere Collector should be on good terms with a Commissioner, and one would imagine that Wordsworth ran a considerable risk of offending Mr. Kingston at Haydon's party: when Charles Lamb, tipsy and irrepressible, took a candle across the room for the purpose of examining the gentleman's 'organ'. Keats was of an age when young genius finds it difficult to make allowances for old. Mr. Kingston in particular seems to have stuck in Keats's gizzard. He wrote to Haydon on April 8th, 1818:

> I am affraid Wordsworth went rather huff'd out of Town
> — I am sorry for it. he cannot expect his fireside Divan to be
> infallible he cannot expect but that every Man of worth is as
> proud as himself. O that he had not fit with a Warrener that
> is din'd at Kingston's.

But Keats's admiration recovered from the set-back; and Wordsworth became the subject of his conscious meditation, in the letter to Reynolds of May 3rd, 1818, from which we can see more clearly the unique position held by Wordsworth in Keats's hierarchy. The question with which he begins is the desirability of knowledge for 'widening speculation' — that is, according to

Keats's constant usage of the word, extending the scope of the contemplative imagination — and 'easing "the burden of the mystery" '. With this burden he has been struggling, and in grappling with it he has been led to consider Wordsworth's genius, and how he differs from Milton. Uppermost in Keats's mind at the moment appear to have been the prefatory lines from *The Recluse*, with their implicit but friendly challenge to Milton. Milton is the standard of reference, in Keats's inquiry, as gold is 'the meridian line of worldly wealth'.

> And here I have nothing but surmises, from an uncertainty whether Miltons apparently less anxiety for Humanity proceeds from his seeing further or no than Wordsworth: And whether Wordsworth has in truth epic passion, and martyrs himself to the human heart, the main region of his song.

The reference is to Wordsworth's claim, in the preface to *The Recluse*, that he is essaying a more arduous flight than Milton. 'Urania, I shall need Thy guidance, *or a greater Muse . . .*'

> For I must tread on shadowy ground, must sink
> Deep — and, aloft ascending, breathe in worlds
> To which the heaven of heavens is but a veil.
> All strength — all terror, single or in bands,
> That ever was put forth in personal form —
> Jehovah — with his thunder, and the choir
> Of shouting Angels, and the empyreal thrones —
> I pass them unalarmed. Not Chaos, not
> The darkest pit of lowest Erebus,
> Nor aught of blinder vacancy, scooped out
> By help of dreams — can breed such fear and awe
> As fall upon us often when we look
> Into our Minds, into the Mind of Man —
> My haunt, and the main region of my song.

The comparison between Milton's task and Wordsworth's is almost explicit; and the implication that Wordsworth's is the greater and more daring evident enough. So that Keats's question partly misses the mark. Wordsworth is not claiming that he has 'epic passion' and that he martyrs this to the human heart; but that his poem is to be more than the equivalent of Milton's epic, and is (so to speak) to be the veritable epic of the human soul. From this point of view it is worth consideration whether, in fact, Keats, when he attempted his epic, did not find himself inevitably caught between the Miltonic objectivity and the Wordsworthian subjectivity.

In the main, Keats admits Wordsworth's claim. Milton's 'philosophy' is in Keats's firm but modest judgment not adult: 'it may be tolerably understood by one not much advanced in years'. But Wordsworth's philosophy — if it is to be called a philosophy, seeing that 'Wordsworth is a great poet, if not a philosopher' — is beyond Keats's entire comprehension. He thinks he can understand and follow Wordsworth up to *Tintern Abbey*; and his idea is that Wordsworth, when he wrote that poem, was more or less in the position in which Keats is now, when the Chamber of Maiden Thought is gradually darkened, by consciousness of the mystery of pain and evil, but at the same time 'many doors are set open — all leading to dark passages'.

> It seems to me that his Genius is explorative of those dark Passages. Now if we live, and go on thinking, we too shall explore them — he is a Genius and superior to us, in so far as he can, more than we, make discoveries, and shed a light in them — Here I must think Wordsworth is deeper than Milton — though I think it has depended more upon the general and gregarious advance of intellect, than individual greatness of Mind.

Still, Milton 'did not think into the human heart, as Wordsworth has done — Yet Milton as a Philosopher, had sure as great powers as Wordsworth'.

Behind Keats's difficulty is the fact that his problem is not one of philosophy, but of religion. Wordsworth is searching for a religious solution *de novo*, seeking it in the experience of the 'intensely feeling' natural man; whereas Milton is content with the solution offered by his peculiar version of Calvinist theology. How he came to be content with this is a question which can perhaps be answered only as Keats answered it: 'It proves that a mighty providence subdues the mightiest Minds to the service of the time being, whether it be in human Knowledge or Religion.' The complete freedom of the human Reason which Milton asserted under cover of his sterile theology was the means by which such minds as Wordsworth's and Keats's had been emancipated for their re-exploration of human experience, and their rediscovery of the truth of religion — that is, of the necessity and inevitability of the religious mode of apprehension.

In *The Excursion*, which Keats set at the head of Wordsworth's poetry, Wordsworth did explore the dark passages which Keats hoped to explore; and in the lovely tale of *Margaret* set before the human imagination, without flinching but also without fever, the problem of human pain. And Wordsworth has his answer — at once profoundly religious and completely simple.

> I stood, and leaning o'er the garden wall
> Reviewed that Woman's sufferings; *and it seemed*
> *To comfort me while with a brother's love*
> *I blessed her in the impotence of grief.*

Thus 'the burden of the mystery' is not merely lightened, but changed in the experience of the imaginative man who, like the Wanderer, 'could *afford* to suffer With those whom he saw suffer'. A great depth of experience lies beneath that bare and simple sentence of Wordsworth's — an experience which seems impossible to put in other words than his own. Says the Wanderer:

> But we have known that there is often found
> In mournful thoughts, *and always might be found,*
> A power to virtue friendly; were't not so,
> I am a dreamer among men, indeed
> An idle dreamer!

I suspect that Keats's desperate question in *The Fall of Hyperion*, concerning the poet and the dreamer, had behind it ineradicable, almost organic, memories of *The Excursion*, and of Wordsworth's solution to the mystery: which is, that pain, experienced to the depths of an 'intensely feeling' nature, mysteriously creates its own consolation. As it is with the imaginative man who, by the depth of his own experience, 'can afford to suffer With those whom he sees suffer', so with the directly suffering soul itself.

> 'My Friend! enough to sorrow you have given,
> The purposes of wisdom ask no more:
> Nor more would she have craved as due to one
> Who, in her worst distress, had ofttimes felt
> The unbounded might of prayer; and learned, with soul
> Fixed on the Cross, that consolation springs,
> From sources deeper far than deepest pain
> For the meek Sufferer.'

There, too, in unforced language, is the natural and unforced transition between Wordsworth's rediscovered religion and Christianity. I think those are astray who represent that there was a gulf between Wordsworth's religion of Nature, and Christianity; it seems to me that the passing from the one to the other was unstrained. The Cross was, indeed, the symbol of that which was revealed to Wordsworth through his imaginative experience of Nature and the destinies of men. And surely it is true that it was the Cross, and its power to temper and change and regenerate the faculties of man in successive generations, which had made Wordsworth's 'natural' sensibility what it was. Where, it seems to me, Wordsworth failed himself and us was by his effort, when the power of sustained imagination had largely left him, to represent the actual process of his self-discovery as much more orthodox from the beginning than it had been.

However that may be, there can be no doubt, I think, that for Keats — in spite of a temporary reaction — Wordsworth was eminently gifted with Negative Capability. There was no irritable reaching after fact and reason in this teacher of a wise passiveness. It is Coleridge, not Wordsworth, who 'would let go by a fine isolated versimilitude caught from the Penetralium of mystery from being capable of remaining content with half-knowledge'. Even Keats's conclusion that 'This, pursued through volumes would perhaps take us no farther than this, that with a great poet the sense of Beauty overcomes all consideration', has its parallel in Wordsworth's words in the Preface to *The Recluse*:

> Beauty — a living Presence of the earth,
> Surpassing the most fair ideal Forms
> Which craft of delicate Spirits hath composed
> From earth's materials — waits upon my steps;
> Pitches her tents before me as I move,
> An hourly neighbour. Paradise, and groves
> Elysian, Fortunate Fields — like those of old
> Sought in the Atlantic Main — why should they be
> A history only of departed things,
> Or a mere fiction of what never was?
> For the discerning intellect of Man,
> When wedded to this goodly universe
> In love and holy passion, shall find these
> A simple produce of the common day.

But there we are made conscious no less of the distinction than of the affinity between Wordsworth's genius and Keats's. Wordsworth is in pursuit, not of beauty, but of a particular beauty — the beauty of the real world. It is not that he martyrs his epic passion to the human heart; but that he is a genius with a mission and a message. God, in him, had rediscovered God in the universe; an eternal harmony between the mind of man and the world, whereby the world of experience was transfigured in the awakened soul. He would tell how the prophet-poet came to be what he was, as a necessary phase of the unfolding of the omnipresent beauty of the whole, discerned by him when his own unfolding was fulfilled. He would tell of the falling-in-love of the discerning intellect with the universe, as a necessary prelude to 'the spousal verse of the great consummation' of the marriage:

with the thing
Contemplated, describe the Mind and Man
Contemplating; and who, and what he was —
The transitory Being that beheld
This Vision.

That, from first to last, Wordsworth was — the man who had
beheld a Vision. It was in vain that Hazlitt demanded his promised 'system'. System Wordsworth had none: save the history
of his own experience culminating in the reality and truth of the
self-surpassing Imagination, and the power of those in whom
Imagination had been awakened to endure suffering and find
consolation in the very experience of suffering itself. Wordsworth had no system; but he had a gospel.

In the light of these considerations, the previous suggestion
that in *Hyperion* Keats was in fact caught between a desire for
Miltonic objectivity and a compulsion towards Wordsworthian
subjectivity, becomes more substantial. Keats was driven along
the Wordsworthian path. He had to put to himself Wordsworth's questions; they were inescapable, not merely because of
the events of his own life, but because he was a man of genius
who began, like Wordsworth, with an 'intensely feeling' nature
emancipated from religious assumption. One says 'emancipated',
without hesitation, because the forms assumed by Protestantism
in England by the end of the eighteenth century were such as
could not conceivably command the allegiance of the sensitive
and imaginative man. The Calvinist theology which supplied the
structure to Milton's epic had lost its vitality for the imaginative
mind, and Milton's own epic, as Blake acutely saw, derived its
most splendid vitality from the rebellion of the unconscious
Milton against the fetters imposed upon him by his conscious
theology. If Milton's work were to be emulated, it could be
emulated only as Wordsworth had emulated it, by attempting to
create an epic of the rediscovery of vital religion in the experience
of a prophetic man. Wordsworth, indeed, never completed his

great enterprise; but what was revealed of it to Keats in *The Excursion* aroused in him thoughts beyond the reach of his soul. When he himself attempted an epic, in *Hyperion*, he experienced, at first hand, the nature of the prophetic compulsion to which Wordsworth had had to submit.

It was no wonder that Keats, in whom these half-conscious urges were contending, should have turned towards the Shakespearian ideal as he understood it. On the technical side, it meant for him the concrete objectivity of the drama, which seemed to dispense him from the need of a declared 'philosophy'; on the experiencing side, it would enable him to be as it were merely passive and receptive towards experience. But this latter ideal was not so easy to realize. Life is act, as well as contemplation, and Keats was compelled to make decisions: he had to decide to write for a living. In consequence, he collaborated with Brown on *Otho the Great*, he wrote a narrative poem, *Lamia*, and he decided to fag (if he could find the opening) as a journalist on the Liberal side. But by then, the beginning of the end was come; and we can only dream about the solution he might have found. The pinnacle of his actual poetical achievement is the *Hyperion*, in which the conflict between the Miltonic ideal and Wordsworthian necessity is apparent; *The Eve of St. Agnes*, in which there is a momentary and perfect fusion between the objective bent of his genius and his subjective experience; and the great *Odes*, wherein his total nature finds perfect utterance. The *Lamia* is not on this high level; it is an attempt to find an honourable compromise between the necessities of his own nature and the demands of the public — to tell a tale in verse which should have deep spiritual significance for the few and popular appeal for the many. Indeed, the works on which he was engaged in the summer of 1819, when the plenary inspiration of the spring had ebbed, and he had had to choose 'between despair and energy', reveal the complexity of the life-problem with which he was struggling. *Otho the Great* was mere hackwork; *Lamia* was an attempt to reach an actual public; the revision of *Hyperion* was largely a reaction against both these activities — an effort to create in conscious independence of any possible audience. It was 'the egotistical sublime' in a different sense from that in which Keats applied the phrase to Wordsworth, and it involved him in an intense inward struggle — a desperate questioning of his own purpose and significance, which, as I have already suggested, came to him with a Wordsworthian background.

The question of Moneta, in the rejected lines (ll. 188-210) —

> Art thou not of the dreamer tribe?
> The poet and the dreamer are distinct,
> Diverse, sheer opposite, antipodes.
> The one pours out a balm upon the world,
> The other vexes it. —

arose, in the mind of a man saturated, I believe, in the questionings of Wordsworth, above all in *The Excursion*. Unless the imaginative contemplation of the pain and evil of the world does engender in the mind 'a power to virtue friendly', cries the Wanderer in Book I: unless consolation verily does spring 'from sources deeper far than deepest pain' — then he is 'a dreamer, an idle dreamer'. In Book III, Poetry and Philosophy are pitted against one another. Says the narrator:

> if smiles
> Of scornful pity be the just reward
> Of Poesy thus courteously employed
> In framing models to improve the scheme
> Of Man's existence, and recast the world,
> Why should not grave Philosophy be styled,
> Herself, a dreamer of a kindred stock,
> A dreamer yet more spiritless and dull?
> Yes, shall the fine immunities she boasts
> Establish sounder titles of esteem
> For her, who (all too timid and reserved
> For onset, for resistance too inert,
> Too weak for suffering, and for hope too tame) . . .

The underlying drift of the incessant waves of intense meditative reflection in *The Excursion* is that philosophy, unless it is religion, is vain; and that poetry at its own imaginative height is religion, or the handmaid of religion. The poet who is faithful to his experience becomes the instrument by which the verity of religion is revealed anew. After a moment of agonized hesitation (of which the rejected lines are the witness) Keats also claimed for and in himself the operation of 'a power to virtue friendly'.

It is only when Wordsworth's and Keats's poetry are equally familiar, and equally intimate, that we can appreciate the depth and subtlety of Wordsworth's influence on Keats, or understand how superficial and transient was his impatience with what he called at one moment Wordsworth's 'philosophy', at another his lack of it. That was at a time when Keats was enamoured of the idea of 'turning all his soul' to Philosophy, and of preparing himself 'to ask Hazlitt in about a year's time the best metaphysical road I can take'. The last powerfully suggests that Keats's casual verdict that Wordsworth was 'no philosopher' was derived from Hazlitt. Assuredly, at this time Keats understood by 'philosophy' he knew not what; but Hazlitt possessed it — a mysterious something that would 'ease the burden of the mystery': something very different from Wordsworth's 'philosophy' which 'was engendered in the whims of an Egotist'. In order to acquire this mysterious knowledge, Keats was (he told Taylor on April 24th, 1818) preparing to forgo his promised tour in the North. 'There is but one way for me — the road lies through application, study and thought.'

He did not forgo his tour, and it took him straightway to Wordsworth's country. How saturated his being was with Wordsworth is shown by his pride in the fact (twice mentioned) that he 'discovered without a hint "that ancient woman seated on Helm Crag"'. That discovery, and his triumph in it, were possible only to one to whom even Wordsworth's minor poems had become a second nature. The moment Brown and he arrived at Bo'ness, Keats 'enquired of the waiter for Wordsworth'.

He said he knew him, and that he had been here a few days ago, canvassing for the Lowthers. What think you of that — Wordsworth versus Brougham! ! Sad — sad — sad — and yet the family has been his friend always. What can we say? We are now about seven miles from Rydale, and expect to see him to-morrow. You shall hear all about our visit.

Unfortunately, Wordsworth was not at home and Keats had to be content with leaving a note and 'sticking it up over what I knew must be Miss Wordsworth's portrait'. He confessed his great disappointment. But I suspect that Wordsworth's spirit was at work in Keats, when he meditated over the waterfall he had seen before breakfast.

What astonishes me more than any thing is the tone, the coloring, the slate, the stone, the moss, the rock-weed; or, if I may so say, the intellect, the countenance of such places. The space, the magnitude of mountains and waterfalls are well imagined before one sees them; but this countenance or intellectual tone must surpass every imagination and defy any remembrance. I shall learn poetry here and shall henceforth write more than ever, for the abstract endeavor of being able to add a mite to that mass of beauty which is harvested from these grand materials, by the finest spirits, and put into etherial existence for the relish of one's fellows. I cannot think with Hazlitt that these scenes make man appear little. I never forgot my stature so completely — I live in the eye; and my imagination, surpassed, is at rest.

Part of the language and part of the thought come, I think, from the Preface to *The Recluse*:

> Beauty — a living Presence of the earth,
> Surpassing the most fair ideal Forms.
> Which craft of delicate Spirits hath composed
> From earth's materials — waits upon my steps.

And, there is possibly a connection between this unconscious identification with Wordsworth, and his disagreement with

Hazlitt. Though it is interesting to note, as a glimpse of Keats's
way of 'feeling his own life' — to use Maine de Biran's phrase —
that Keats really misunderstands Hazlitt, in a peculiar way. When
Hazlitt said that the mountain-scenery of the Lakes made one
appear small, it certainly never occurred to him to think what
might be its effect on one who was very conscious of his own
diminutive stature. Hazlitt, we may be sure, would have stared in
surprise had Keats answered him, viva voce: 'No, I never forgot
so completely that I was five foot and half an inch.' To be taken
out of himself, for Keats, was to *forget* that 'he felt small'; for
Hazlitt, most likely, it was to be made 'to feel small'.

We have already seen, in the case of Hazlitt's criticism of the
Gipsies, with what fine intuition Keats, when his judgment was
undisturbed, steered between uncritical admiration of Wordsworth and accepting Hazlitt's view of him, even though he
revered Hazlitt's 'depth of taste' almost as much as *The Excursion*.
But perhaps he would have accepted this part of Hazlitt's description of Wordsworth.

> Milton is his great idol, and he sometimes dares to compare
> himself with him. His Sonnets, indeed, have something
> of the same high-raised tone and prophetic spirit ... We
> do not think our author has any very cordial sympathy with
> Shakespeare. How should he? Shakespeare was the least
> of an egotist of anybody in the world.

There is indubitably an affinity between Wordsworth and
Milton, and Wordsworth was conscious of it; and just as Wordsworth felt more sympathy with Milton than with Shakespeare, so
Keats felt more sympathy with Shakespeare than with Milton.
But Keats's feelings towards Milton and Wordsworth were very
different. Milton was remote, Wordsworth was near: and this not
merely in point of time. Wordsworth, we may fairly say, was
almost as intimate to Keats's experience as Shakespeare himself.
When Keats imitates Milton he is conscious of what he is doing;
the echoes of Wordsworth are innumerable and unconscious.
At least, I can hardly conceive that Keats was aware that a vital

germ of the thought of the *Ode on a Grecian Urn* came from the
ninth of Wordsworth's *Miscellaneous Sonnets*, on the sight of a
picture painted by Sir George Beaumont:

> Praised be the Art whose subtle power could stay
> Yon cloud, and fix it in that glorious shape;
> Nor would permit the thin smoke to escape,
> Nor those bright sunbeams to forsake the day;
> Which stopped that band of travellers on their way,
> Ere they were lost within the shady wood;
> And showed the Bark upon the glassy flood
> For ever anchored in her sheltering bay.
> Soul-soothing Art! whom Morning, Noontide, Even,
> Do serve with all their changeful pageantry;
> Thou, with ambition modest yet sublime,
> Here, for the sight of mortal man, hast given
> To one brief moment caught from fleeting time
> The appropriate calm of blest eternity.

I do not believe that he knew, when he composed the *Lines
Written in the Highlands after a Visit to Burns's Country*, that he
was echoing the thought and the cadence of Wordsworth's *Star-
Gazers*. Why, asks Wordsworth, watching an eager crowd in
Leicester Square taking turns to gaze through a telescope, does
each man go away slackly, 'as if dissatisfied'?

> Or is it that, when human Souls, a journey long have had
> And are returned into themselves, they cannot but be sad?

> Does, then, a deep and earnest thought the blissful mind
>   employ
> Of him who gazes, or has gazed? a grave and steady joy,
> That doth reject all show of pride, admits no outward sign,
> Because not of this noisy world, but silent and divine!

In Keats's poem Burns's birthplace takes the place of the remote
moon, as the object of contemplation which draws the soul out of
its bodily sheath.

At such a time the soul's a child, in childhood is the brain;
Forgotten is the worldly heart — alone, it beats in vain —
Ay, if a madman could have leave to pass a healthful day,
To tell his forehead's swoon and faint when first began decay,
He might make tremble many a one whose spirit had gone
    forth
To find a bard's low cradle-place about the silent North!
Scanty the hour and few the steps beyond the bourn of care,
Beyond the sweet and bitter world — beyond it unaware!
Scanty the hour and few the steps, because a longer stay
Would bar return, and make a man forget his mortal way.

Keats's experience is the more intense; but thought and metre
alike seem to derive directly from Wordsworth.

Such reminiscences, though surely worth collecting, belong
rather to the surface of an influence of Wordsworth on Keats
which, as I have come more deeply to appreciate Wordsworth's
greatness, has appeared to me continually more subtle and more
pervasive. In such a province of inquiry it is very difficult to be
positive in one's judgments; difficult above all to distinguish
between the inevitable fusion of two profound poetic influences
in the critic's own mind and the direct influence of the one poet
upon the other. And I am inclined to be thankful that when I
wrote *Keats and Shakespeare*, I did not know Wordsworth so
well as I have come to know him since.

Anyhow, I am glad I was not acutely conscious of Wordsworth's influence on Keats; it might have 'cramped my style'.
As things are now, I am free to speculate. I can wonder, for
example, whether the real seed of Keats's 'sensation' of *Hyperion*
was not sown in him by the forty lines in *The Excursion*, Book IV,
describing the religion of Greece, when the

                    lonely herdsman, stretched
        On the soft grass through half a summer's day,
        With music lulled his indolent repose:
        And, in some fit of weariness, if he,

> When his own breath was silent, chanced to hear
> A distant strain, far sweeter than the sounds
> Which his poor skill could make, his fancy fetched,
> Even from the blazing chariot of the sun,
> A beardless Youth, who touched a golden lute,
> And filled the illumined groves with ravishment.*

Far more, it seems to me, than in anything of Milton's, in these lines of Wordsworth's is the germ of the imaginative feeling of *Hyperion*. This is not the classicism of Milton at all, though to define the difference would need an essay; but I will say at a venture that Milton's classicism is still in the main a medieval classicism that sees through a glass darkly and not face to face. Wordsworth's classicism is that of an emancipated soul which has inherited the intellectual freedom to see things in a pagan clarity, at the very moment that it is laying anew the foundations of the Christian religion. Greek myth is a legend for Milton, for Wordsworth a vision.

> Great God! I'd rather be
> A Pagan suckled in a creed outworn;
> So might I, standing on this pleasant lea,
> Have glimpses that would make me less forlorn;
> Have sight of Proteus rising from the sea;
> Or hear old Triton blow his wreathèd horn.

That is the feeling-tone, the 'sensation' of the Greek world for Keats. I think it was Wordsworth who opened the gates of his senses to it.

CHAPTER XII

KEATS AND BLAKE

KEATS and Blake have one remarkable thing in common. They both came to a realization of their own truth by way of a struggle with Milton. Both admired Milton greatly. Keats perhaps admired him more as the great poetic artist, Blake as the visionary: but both responded to the heroic in Milton's character as manifested in his poetry. Both at a certain moment in their lives identified themselves with Milton, in his attitude of solitary champion of the truth, 'on evil days now fallen and evil tongues'. Blake, in *The Marriage of Heaven and Hell*, saw the spiritual world in Miltonic terms, proclaimed himself on the side of Satan, and declared, very truly, that Milton himself was on the Devil's side without knowing it. Milton's Satan represented energy and creativeness in Blake's eyes, and the Miltonic Deity was Nobodaddy. All Milton's unconscious sympathies, according to Blake, and therefore his creative powers were at work to glorify Satan: and Blake at this moment heartily concurred. Much the same attitude is implicit in Keats's dry comment on Milton's description of Heaven at the beginning of Book III of *Paradise Lost*: 'Hell is finer than this.'

To both Blake and Keats Milton's Satan and his creator were symbols and embodiments of energy; and when, in June 1819, Keats parted from Fanny Brawne to struggle with the world for a livelihood, Milton — instead of Shakespeare — became his Presider.

> I have the choice as it were of two Poisons (yet I ought not to call this a Poison) the one is voyaging to and fro from India for a few years: the other is leading a fevrous life alone with Poetry — This latter will suit me best: for I cannot resolve to give up my Studies ... My brother George always

stood between me and any dealings with the world. Now I find I must buffet it — I must take my stand upon some vantage ground and begin to fight — I must choose between despair and Energy — I choose the latter.

To sustain him in the battle he waged for the next three months, in his choice of the feverous life alone with poetry, Milton was the genius he invoked. He strove to emulate and follow Milton. Suddenly, the strain became too great, the posture too unnatural. Above all, it meant shutting his heart against his love, and he abandoned it, saying that life to Milton would be death to him.

Blake also forsook Milton, and wrote perhaps the finest of his Prophetic Books to show why. The theme of Blake's *Milton* is that Milton, in Eternity, learns to forgive, as he had not learned it upon earth, where he had been Selfhood incarnate. Milton learns the mystery of Self-annihilation and by so doing becomes one with the Divine Humanity. And of course this Milton who is redeemed is the Miltonic self of Blake — that in Blake which has formerly identified itself with Milton.

Precisely the same thing, I believe, happened to Keats with regard to Milton. He realized, as Blake did, that the element in him which had sought to identify itself with Milton was his Selfhood: and the genius in him knew that he was not a poet of the Self. He did not belong to the 'egotistical sublime' but to the kind which 'is not itself — it has no self'. And Keats like Blake had to learn this lesson over and over again: he had like Blake 'to die many deaths', for the Selfhood is always reborn. Keats's struggle to accept his destiny ended only with his death. The moment of victory was always followed by a new burden to bear. But to his moments of victory belongs the poetry which is a possession for ever of the human soul in its pilgrimage. For in those moments the genius of Keats resumes its path — not against life but with it, that the nature of life may be manifest.

The Imagination is not a State: it is the Human Existence itself.

In that single line is the whole message of Blake. People tell us that when Blake says Human, he really means Divine. Therefore what he is saying is that the Imagination is the Divine existence itself. That is the kind of commentary that seals up Blake for ever. The whole point of Blake's teaching is that he admitted no distinction between the Human and the Divine. What he is saying roughly is that the condition of Imagination is not a State, that is, is not changeable or annihilable: it is a condition that is reached when all that is changeable and annihilable in the human mind has been changed and annihilated. Therefore it is man's true identity. It is the man himself, his veritable essence: the Eternal Man, as Blake called him — and you can get no higher. The phrase brings to mind a phrase of Goethe. He was talking of scientific observation:

> The highest man can attain in these matters is awe: if the pure phenomenon causes this, let him be satisfied; more it cannot bring; and he should forbear to seek for anything further behind it: he cannot go beyond.

This is the objective side of the truth of which Blake has enunciated the subjective side. The truth is the same truth, and Blake is being just as objective as Goethe. But he is being objective about the subject. He is talking about the Human Existence itself: Goethe is talking about Existence itself. Both are saying that the direct apprehension of Existence itself, whether in the object or in the subject as object, is the highest that man can attain. That is the condition of Imagination, but neither Goethe nor Blake is saying that because this is the highest condition, it is the only condition — for it obviously is not that; nor are they saying that this is the condition in which one must always be — for that is obviously impossible: but they are saying, each in his own fashion, that one must always be aware of this condition as a potentiality, and that any lesser, though practically necessary view, whether of the object or the subject, must be subordinated to this simple and ultimate vision, the vision of things *sub specie aeternitatis*, the eternal vision of the Eternal Man — the finality and beauty of the Natural as it actually exists. *Am farbigen Abglanz haben wir das Leben. Am farbigen Abglanz*, which being interpreted into Blake's language is, 'in the Minute Particulars' — we have our life. Through them Life comes to us: in bowing down to them our selves are annihilated. Not once and for all. We cannot always, cannot even often, be beholding the Minute Particulars, the pure Phenomenon. We have in this world to act and to do, not merely to be. But always we must be capable of standing aloof from our action and our doing, of seeing that also in its Minute Particulars, as the pure Phenomenon it is.

It may be said, this is all too difficult. I will not deny that it is difficult, but the difficulty is in the expression, not in the thing itself. It is precisely the difficulty of describing anything that actually is, as it is. We can replace the thing that is by a formula, a classification, a definition. It passes muster. People know more or less what we are trying to convey. But the uniqueness of the thing, its quiddity, that whereby it is just itself and not any other thing: this escapes us. Art is a means by which we come closer to that uniqueness, but we never touch it. How much the more impossible is it then to describe the philosophy or the religion which is based entirely upon the recognition of the uniqueness of all existences, including our own — which has its beginning and its end in this recognition which declares that in this act of recognition man reaches a finality beyond which he cannot go, beyond which he has no desire to go, for

> 'Beauty is Truth, Truth Beauty' — That is all
> Ye know on earth, and all ye need to know.

That is how Keats said it. He said it thus more than a hundred years ago. But it doesn't seem to have made much impression. Eminent critics stumble over that simple sentence. They are quite convinced that they know better than Keats knew: they are quite convinced that he was wrong. It never occurs to them that lines which come abruptly at the end of one of the most magnificent poems in the English language *must* have some profound meaning. That if the words seem to them stupid or shallow, or uneducated, it must be they and not Keats who made the mistake.

I have made the attempt to explain those lines. But the best way to understand them is to follow out in its beautiful living detail the process which culminated in that poem and in those lines. Of poetry, said Keats, who knew more about it than most men, 'if it come not naturally as the leaves to a tree, it had better not come at all'. Naturally, mark you. Keep to the Minute Particulars. Keats does not say 'easily': he says 'naturally'. Naturally, as the leaves to a tree. And what human can dare to say that the leaves come *easily* to a tree? I do not for one moment believe it. In some strange and simple mode of tree-experience for ever beyond our knowledge comes the heave and upsurge in the tree every spring, with all the pangs of tree-birth. Birth is natural, but it is not easy. And just as in the human physical order the birth of a child is natural, nothing more natural, but comes with labour and agony and a lapse from consciousness, so in the subtler organic order to which the birth of great poetry belongs, travail and suffering are the conditions of delivery.

It happens, fortunately, that we have some record of the travail through which Keats's great *Odes* came into the world. Here once again are the outlines of the familiar story.

There were three brothers, without father or mother, bound to each other by ties of intimate and passionate affection. Tom, the youngest, was fatally ill with consumption: George, the middle one, had fallen in love with an adorable girl and married her. In order to gain an independence he must emigrate to America. That is how things stood in June 1818: this is how Keats felt about them:

Now I am never alone without rejoicing that there is such a thing as death — without placing my ultimate in the glory of dying for a great human purpose. Perhaps if my affairs were in a different state I should not have written the above — you shall judge — I have two Brothers one is driven by the 'burden of Society' to America the other, with an exquisite love of Life, is in a lingering state. My Love for my

Brothers, from the early loss of our parents, and even from earlier misfortunes, has grown into an affection 'passing the Love of Women'. I have been ill-temper'd with them, I have vex'd them — but the thought of them has always stifled the impression that any woman might otherwise have made upon me. I have a Sister too, and may not follow them either to America or to the grave—Life must be undergone...

That was John Keats at twenty-two. George departed for America. Keats was left alone with Tom, who was in the last stages of consumption. John, to have something to distract his mind from his own misery, went with his friend Brown on a long and arduous walking-tour in Scotland. In two months he was back in London, himself seriously ill with what he must have feared (for he was a young doctor), though he dared not admit it to himself, was the beginning of consumption. His beloved Tom, with whom he lived alone in Hampstead, was nearing the end. For three months Keats endured the pain of watching him slowly die. While watching he wrote *Hyperion*, the beginning of his poetic greatness. Tom died; straightway Keats fell in love with Fanny Brawne. Another month and the disease is at his throat again. It is the warning, though he tries not to hear it, that he will never marry Fanny. Is fate going to deny him everything? Is there nothing that will not be taken from him? Then he writes *The Eve of St. Agnes* — a dream of his love's fruition, a dream which will remain a dream. It is, with *Hyperion*, the greatest of his long poems. Then comes a silence. Then the *Odes*.

Fortunately for us, fortunately for the world, this silence — this 'tedious agony' as Keats called it — was only a poetic silence. Keats could write no poetry, but he could and did write a long letter — taken up one day, dropped the next, begun on February 14th and not ended till May 4th — a letter it must be of 25,000 words, almost a book in itself, and assuredly, for simplicity and profundity, one of the great books in the English language. It is the story told almost from day to day, of the painful rebirth of a great soul. Here I can do no more than emphasize two of its

crucial moments. The first of these comes on March 19th. He
has had a letter from a friend telling him of a misfortune. And
Keats begins to muse.

Circumstances are like Clouds continually gathering and
bursting — While we are laughing the seed of some trouble
is put into the wide arable land of events — while we are
laughing it sprouts, it grows, and suddenly bears a poison-
fruit which we must pluck — Even so we have leisure to
reason on the misfortunes of our friends: our own touch us
too nearly for words. Very few men have arrived at a
complete disinterestedness of Mind. . . .

The seeds of trouble, a full handful of them, as we have seen,
had been put into the wide arable land of events for Keats. The
poison-flower that he must pluck was before him: the premonition
of death was there before his mind — death that would rob him of
all he desired, all he deserved — 'Verse, Fame and Beauty'. His
misfortunes were touching him too nearly for words. He could
not speak of his love even to his brother, he could not utter
himself in poetry any more.

We see then what is in Keats's thoughts when he suddenly
dreams of the possibility of 'a complete disinterestedness of mind'.
We have leisure to reason on the misfortunes of our friends, he
says, but we cannot be detached about our own. And as soon as
he has thought this thought, the idea comes to him: 'But perhaps
I can.' The conception, at this moment of mental suffering, is
heroic. John Keats is suffering agony: yet he whispers to himself: 'May there not be some power in John Keats that can watch
his suffering, lucid and unperturbed?' And, of course, the imagination of the possibility makes it straightway reality. Suddenly, he
sees himself, at this moment, included totally within the animal
world.

The greater part of Men make their way with the same instinctiveness, the same unwandering eye from their purposes,
the same animal eagerness as the Hawk. The Hawk wants a
Mate, so does the Man — look at them both they set about it

and procure one in the same manner. They want both a nest and they both set about one in the same manner — they get their food in the same manner. — The noble animal Man for his amusement smokes his pipe — the Hawk balances about the Clouds — that is the only difference of their leisures. This it is that makes the Amusement of Life — to a speculative Mind. I go among the fields and catch a glimpse of a Stoat or a fieldmouse peeping out of the withered grass — the creature hath a purpose and its eyes are bright with it. I go amongst the buildings of a city and I see a Man hurrying along — to what? the Creature has a purpose and his eyes are bright with it. But then, as Wordsworth says, 'we have all one human heart' — there is an electric fire in human nature tending to purify — so that among these human creatures there is continually some birth of new heroism.

Beauty is Truth, Truth Beauty. What Keats is saying is profoundly true, and it is profoundly beautiful. Nor would it be profoundly beautiful, if it were not profoundly true. So much is surely obvious. But equally, it would not be profoundly true, if it were not profoundly beautiful. Utter that same truth, cynically, with hatred, and it ceases to be true: utter it wonderingly, with awe before the pure phenomenon, with love towards the Minute Particulars, and it is true. And because it is beautiful and true, beautiful because it is true, and true because it is beautiful, it is *complete*. Keats sees not only that man is totally a creature of the animal world, but also that 'there is an electric fire in human nature tending to purify — so that among these human creatures there is continually some birth of new heroism'.

And that also is obvious: for a birth of new heroism is taking place in Keats himself at the moment he writes these words. He may not have known it, but we *see* it. It is the birth of the heroism of utter detachment, of that complete disinterestedness of which he has conceived the possibility. On he goes therefore. Nothing can stop him now. The new birth has begun. Its process is inevitable.

Even here though I myself am pursuing the same instinctive course as the veriest human animal you can think of . . . writing at random — straining at particles of light in the midst of a great darkness — without knowing the bearing of any one assertion of any one opinion, yet may I not in this be free from sin? May there not be superior beings amused with any graceful, though instinctive attitude my mind may fall into, as I am entertained with the alertness of a Stoat or the anxiety of a Deer? Though a quarrel in the Streets is a thing to be hated, the energies displayed in it are fine; the commonest Man shows a grace in his quarrel. [Seen] by a superior being our reasonings may take the same tone — though erroneous they may be fine. This is the very thing in which consists poetry, and if so it is not so fine a thing as philosophy — For the same reason that an eagle is not so fine a thing as truth.

There are moments when I believe that these are the most astonishing words in the English language — the pinnacle of the English poetic consciousness — the record of a great poet's actual passing beyond good and evil, made at the very instant of his passing.

At any rate I know of no other such record of the supreme act of self-knowledge, of self-annihilation, in our literature. It sets before our eyes the actual living process of the act which Blake made Milton proclaim as the Everlasting Gospel.

All that can be annihilated must be annihilated
That the Children of Jerusalem may be saved from slavery,
There is a Negation, and there is a Contrary:
The Negation must be destroy'd to redeem the Contraries.
The Negation is the Spectre, the Reasoning power in man:
This is a false body, an Incrustation over my Immortal
Spirit, a Selfhood which must be put off and annihilated alway.
To cleanse the face of My Spirit by Self-examination,
To bathe in the Waters of Life, to wash off the Not Human,
I come in Self-annihilation and the grandeur of Inspiration.

That is the culminating passage of Blake's *Milton*. There is not a word in it of which the living meaning cannot be demonstrated from the words of Keats that I have quoted.

'All that can be annihilated must be annihilated.' What has been going on, in Keats's letter, but a continual process of Self-annihilation? As the intensity of his thought increases, so more of his total self has been thrust 'out there', severed, as it were, from his quick of being and incorporated with Nature and the animal world. And in this process 'the Children of Jerusalem' (which is Blake's magnificent synonym for the 'Minute Particulars') are 'freed from slavery'. But how? it may be asked. Blake explains in the next two lines:

The Negation must be destroy'd to redeem the Contraries.

There is a Negation, and there is a Contrary:

But what does this mean? Keats has shown. He has redeemed the Contraries in his vision of a quarrel in the streets. It is not merely evil. Though it is a thing to be hated, yet the energies displayed in it are fine. 'Fine' in Keats's peculiar sense: endowed with surprising and unique beauty: 'fine' as was Lycius in his struggle with the Lamia:

> Fine was the mitigated fury, like
> Apollo's presence when in act to strike
> The serpent.

To see merely the evil in this manifestation of Life is to be a victim of the Negation. It is to replace the rich concrete reality by an abstract Absolute. Only when we have broken down the monopoly of this poor and bloodless perspective in ourselves, are the Contraries, the conflict inherent in the real, redeemed. Just as Keats, who, in the strength of his rich poetic nature, was for ever warring against the tyranny of the Absolute, was to redeem the Contraries again and bring us back to the pulse of quick human experience in the imagination of

> Beauty that must die;
> And Joy, whose hand is ever at his lips,
> Bidding adieu.

'Imagination,' said Blake, 'is Spiritual Sensation.' And spiritual sensation (if we know how to discriminate) is what we experience in those lines. For, when the Negation is destroyed, what takes its place is Imagination.

And this same process which Blake's Milton calls 'cleansing the face of his spirit by self-examination' is carried by Keats into the inmost citadel of his being. He has instanced the quarrel in the streets only to reach a more intimate conclusion. 'Seen by a superior being our reasonings may take the same tone — though erroneous, they may be fine.' Again, Keats puts himself, at this moment of intensest thought, 'out there'; again, he destroys the Negation, which tells him that his thought is either true or false, and is real if true and if false, unreal. No, he says: beyond this barren conflict of absolutes is the living thought itself — 'the graceful though instinctive attitude' of the selflessly seeking mind. And this attitude, he says, is 'fine'. In that judgment Reason gives way to the Imagination, which can behold Reason itself at work, and which sees that Reason itself has no higher status than a faculty of sense.

Says Blake: 'The Negation is the Spectre, the Reasoning Power in Man.' Since he has said that the Negation must be destroyed, does he then mean that the reasoning power in man must be eradicated? That were as though a man, in anger at optical illusion, should put out his eyes. It is the tyranny of the reasoning power which must be destroyed, the tyranny by which the reasoning power arrogates to itself the monopoly of making contact with reality and determining the truth. This monstrous presumption must be overthrown. That the reasoning power itself must be destroyed is no more Blake's meaning than it was Keats's when he vindicated the 'fineness' of reasonings that may be 'erroneous'.

Blake goes on:

This is a false Body, an Incrustation over my Immortal
Spirit, a Selfhood which must be put off and annihilated
alway.

An incessant sloughing of the incessantly re-forming incrustations of the presumptuous reasoning power, which seeks to enslave and dehumanize the living spirit — this is what Blake demands and what Keats is performing before our eyes. Keats is, instinctively, vindicating his former intuition that 'what the Imagination seizes as Beauty must be Truth'. Now the Imagination, working in him, seizes on the very operation of his groping, darting mind, as beautiful, as 'fine'. The Imagination working in him, not his Imagination: for this power is a supra-personal power; it is only the not-Self which can behold, in Imagination, the Self. The motion of Keats's groping, darting mind is indeed 'fine'. But it is not Keats who says it. It is to 'the superior being' that the posture of Keats's mind appears graceful, not to John Keats. But for the instant 'the superior being' is a visitant in the mortal vehicle of John Keats. He is himself, though not 'in his Selfhood', that 'superior being'; he is possessed by the Imagination.

And that is what Blake means by the great declaration he puts in the mouth of Milton:

> To cleanse the face of my spirit by Self-examination
> To bathe in the Waters of Life, to wash off the Not Human,
> I come in Self-annihilation and the grandeur of Inspiration.

To wash off the Not Human — all the tyranny of Reason, all the presumption of the Selfhood — is to become, for the moment, a conduit for the pure Imagination. And the pure Imagination is the Waters of Life: in which is dissolved away the last obstacle between the reality in man and the reality outside him. Through the Imagination these enter into the mutual beatitude of open-eyed embrace. And all that is less than this is for Blake the Not Human. Only in pure Imagination are we completely Human; for by it alone we behold, and are one with the beauty of the things that are. 'The Imagination is not a State: it is the Human Existence itself.' The man to whom the Imagination has not yet revealed the beauty of reality has not yet known what it is to live. Therefore, for Blake, to be a Man is to be Eternal Man; Keats believed the same; nor will anyone ever convince me that the belief of Jesus of Nazareth was essentially other.

That opening of himself to the Imagination was the act by which Keats's genius became the instrument of the *Odes*. Then the Selfhood reared itself again in him. At first it seemed a noble Selfhood. What could have been braver or more human than his resolve to choose energy rather than despair, and by leading a feverous life alone with poetry win the means of marrying his love? Yet in the effort to concentrate his powers upon his task, he found more and more that he must suppress his love. Poetry became more and more a tense effort of the intellectual will. He invokes the example of Milton and makes a virtue of his necessity.

> You will observe [he writes to Taylor] at the end of this: 'How a solitary life engenders pride and egotism!' True — I know it does — but this pride and egotism will enable me to write finer things than anything else could do.

Suddenly the tension becomes intolerable to him. The receipt of more bad news causes the strain to cease. He puts off the Not Human. He discards Milton. 'Life to him would be death to me.' He opens himself once more to the Imagination and his heart to love. Naturally as the leaves to a tree comes the wonderful music once more in the *Ode to Autumn*, and he goes his way to agony and death and immortality.

> The red-breast whistles from a garden-croft;
> And gathering swallows twitter in the skies.

CHAPTER XIII

KEATS AND FRIENDSHIP

K EATS'S reply of October 27th, 1818, to Woodhouse's remonstrance with him for having said he would write no more poetry, is justly famous. It contains his definition of the poetical character — of the kind which he himself possessed, as distinct from 'the Wordsworthian, or egotistical sublime'. The peculiarity of this poetical character is that it has no fixed character, no 'unchangeable attribute', no 'identity'; it is 'continually in for and filling some other body'. Because of this, although 'it is a wretched thing to confess', nevertheless 'it is a very fact that not one word I ever utter can be taken for granted as an opinion growing out of my identical nature — how can it, when I have no nature?'

Thus he repudiates responsibility for his declaration that he would write no more poetry. And in the second part of his letter he reaffirms his determination 'to reach to as high a summit in poetry as the nerve bestowed upon me will suffer'. He says he feels assured he would go on writing poetry from 'the mere yearning and fondness he has for the beautiful' even if his 'night's labours should be burnt every morning'. Then, like a philosopher, he reflects that even in this asseveration, 'I am perhaps not speaking from myself, but from some character in whose soul I now live'. But he concludes:

> I am sure however that this next sentence is from myself.
> I feel your anxiety, good opinion and friendliness in the
> highest degree.

So Keats has a self, after all. He has an 'unchangeable attribute', and 'identical nature'. It consists in his unvarying response to genuine friendship. That this was a true estimate of his own character his letters are a witness that cannot be gainsaid.

From the very beginnings of his conscious thinking about his own nature his awareness of the two main elements of which it was composed is visible. 'I am certain of nothing', he wrote to Bailey on November 22nd, 1817, 'but of the holiness of the Heart's affections, and the truth of Imagination — what the imagination seizes as Beauty must be truth.' These are, from the beginning, his two faiths, his two loyalties: to friendship and love, and to beauty and truth. The absorbing spiritual quest of his life was to reconcile them, or rather to make apprehensible to himself the reconciliation of which he was intuitively convinced. This was the theme of *Endymion*.

Perhaps we may put it, tentatively, that there were two kinds of beauty to which Keats felt instinctive allegiance: moral beauty and 'the principle of beauty in all things'. Poetic genius was the gift of discovering that universal beauty, which was truth. It began with the absorbed delight in the pleasant wonders of the obviously beautiful in nature and mankind which he ascribed to the Chamber of Maiden Thought, and described in such a passage as the opening of *Endymion*; it passed beyond this into a painful awareness that 'the world is full of misery and heartbreak, pain, sickness and oppression' and became dedicated to the search for 'the balance of good and evil'. This was the object of that 'philosophy' to which Keats turned. 'I have been hovering for some time', he told Taylor on April 27th, 1818, 'between an exquisite sense of the luxurious and a love for philosophy — were I calculated for the former I should be glad — but as I am not I shall turn all my soul to the latter.' Philosophy, for Keats, meant the search for wisdom; and wisdom consisted in seeing the beauty of the truth. Because he had sought it with passionate devotion, and paid the price of 'dying into life', he was rescued by Moneta in *The Fall of Hyperion*.

> None can usurp this height (returned that shade)
> But those to whom the miseries of the world
> Are misery, and will not let them rest.

This is the poet's final vindication: that he seeks, and seeks to declare, the beauty of the whole truth. In the last resort it depends upon his spiritual integrity.

On the way to that final discovery or final self-judgment, Keats never left his hold of his admiration for simple moral beauty. He deliberately preferred it to genius, if there had to be a choice between them.

So I do believe [he wrote to his brothers on January 13th, 1818] — not thus speaking with any poor vanity — that works of genius are the first things in this world. No! for that sort of probity and disinterestedness which such men as Bailey possess does hold and grasp the tiptop of any spiritual honors that can be paid to anything in this world. And moreover having this feeling at this present come over me in its full force, I sat down to write to you with a grateful heart, in that I had not a brother who did not feel and credit me for a deeper feeling and devotion for his uprightness, than for any marks of genius however splendid.

There, evidently, speaks the inmost self of Keats. And this integrity, or moral beauty, is for Keats, the condition of friendship. Friendship is the mutual response to this quality. Hence his admiration for Georgiana Wylie, his brother George's wife. 'I like her better and better — she is the most disinterested woman I ever knew.' And that is why, in the extempore acrostic he wrote on her name, he declared his faith again that loyalty in friendship was as noble and indeed divine as supreme poetic achievement: they equally belonged to the order of ultimate reality.

> Imagine not that greatest mastery
> And kingdom over all the realms of verse
> Nears more to heaven in aught than when we nurse
> And surety give to love and brotherhood.

To the same effect is the conclusion of his letter to Reynolds on the Chamber of Maiden Thought. Though he has passed into the Third Chamber, whence all the passages are dark, and the burden of the mystery is full upon him, nevertheless,

After all, there is something real in the world — Moore's present to Hazlitt is real — I like that Moore, and am glad I saw him at the theatre just before I left town. Tom has spit a leetle blood this afternoon, and that is rather a damper — but I know — the truth is there is something real in the world. *(May 3rd, 1818)*

In exactly the same terms he wrote to Bailey: 'Your tearing a spiritless and gloomy letter up to rewrite to me is what I never shall forget — it was to me a real thing'.

(January 23rd, 1818)

Friendship, based on a respect for integrity, is a reality, proof against all scepticism and moral bewilderment. Though imagination

> Lost in a sort of purgatory blind,
> Cannot refer to any standard law
> Of either earth or heaven —

still friendship and love are real. Keats knows. Therefore he can, without any pretence or amicable self-delusion, prophesy that Reynolds's 'third Chamber of Life shall be a lucky and a gentle one — stored with the wine of love — and the bread of friendship'.

Keats himself, indeed, had a genius for friendship only less remarkable than his genius for poetry. He made allowances for his friends that his friends seldom made for one another. Reynolds and Haydon had fallen out; so had Haydon and Hunt.

Considering all things [Keats wrote to his brothers on January 13th, 1818], Haydon's frequent neglect of his appointments &c, his notes were bad enough to put Reynolds on the right side of the question — but then Reynolds has no powers of sufferance; no idea of having the thing against him; so he answered Haydon in one of the most cutting letters I ever read; exposing to himself all his own weak-

KEATS AND FRIENDSHIP

nesses and going on to an excess, which whether it is just or no, is what I would fain have unsaid, the fact is they are both in the right, and both in the wrong.

In regard to the quarrel between Hunt and Haydon, 'all I hope is at some time to bring them together again'. He returns to the same theme in a letter to Bailey on January 23rd, 1818.

Things have happen'd lately of great Perplexity. You must have heard of them. Reynolds and Haydon retorting and recriminating — and parting for ever — the same thing has happened between Haydon and Hunt — It is unfortunate — Men should bear with each other — there lives not the man who may not be cut up, aye hashed to pieces on his weakest side. The best of Men have but a portion of good in them — a kind of spiritual yeast in their frames which creates the ferment of existence — by which a Man is propell'd to act and strive and buffet with Circumstance. The sure way, Bailey, is first to know a Man's faults, and then be passive — if after that he insensibly draws you towards him you have no Power to break the link. Before I felt interested in either Reynolds or Haydon — I was well read in their faults yet knowing them I have been cementing gradually with both. I have an affection for them both for reasons almost opposite — and to both must I of necessity cling — supported always by the hope that when a little time — a few years shall have tried me more fully in their esteem I may be able to bring them together — the time must come because they have both hearts — and they will recollect the best parts of each other when this gust is overblown.

And there were moments when he was aware that his genius for poetry and his genius for friendship were intimately connected.

They do not know me [he wrote to George in October 1818], not even my most intimate acquaintance — I give into their feelings as though I were refraining from irritating a

309

little child — Some think me middling, others silly, others foolish — every one thinks he sees my weak side against my will, when in truth it is with my will — I am content to be thought all this because I have in my own breast so great a resource. This is one great reason why they like me so; because they can all show to advantage in a room, and eclipse from a certain tact one who is reckoned to be a good Poet — I hope I am not there playing tricks 'to make the angels weep': I think not: for I have not the least contempt for my species; and though it may sound paradoxical: my greatest elevations of Soul leave me every time more humbled.

Unlike most of his friends, Keats 'cared not to be in the right'; he did not in the least mind 'having the thing against him'. He did not identify his opinions with his self, nor believe that his own integrity was menaced if they were challenged. He strove, by instinct, and conviction, to keep his mind 'a thoroughfare for all thoughts: not a select party'. And the attitude embraced his friends. He gratefully accepted their 'light and shade', but never hesitated to criticize them when they failed in humanity. All his admiration for Hazlitt did not prevent him from regretting his reference to Southey's 'few contemptible grey hairs'; nor his affection for Reynolds from wishing unsaid his exposure of Haydon's weaknesses; nor his respect for Bailey from condemning (before he imaginatively condoned) his behaviour to Jane Reynolds. But he was infinitely tolerant towards them. Reading Keats's letters one understands better why Shakespeare's friends called him 'gentle', because it seems there is no other word for this rare quality of soul. But this 'gentleness' is consubstantial with an extraordinary strength. It was intimately allied to what Keats called his 'passiveness', which when pressed home, appears as a truly remarkable absence of egotism, in every sense of that protean quality.

Keats, indeed, seems always to be waiting and listening for the response of something in himself that is not himself, to all experience. Of these responses two are pre-eminent, in Keats's own mind, and consequently in ours who study him. One is the response of the Heart; the other the response of the Imagination. Both these faculties, or conditions, of the soul are, in his language, 'self-destroying'. The response of the Heart is human love; the response of the Imagination is — may one, in these days, say it? — divine Love. The connection between them — or one important thread of the connection — is that the divine Love supervenes through the disappointment of human love: the convincement of the nerves that 'the world is full of misery and heartbreak, pain, sickness and oppression'. The human love dies, as it were, and is reborn into an imaginative understanding that its defeat is part of the divine pattern for the regeneration of man.

Do you not see how necessary a World of Pains and troubles is to school an Intelligence and make it a Soul? A Place where the heart must feel and suffer in a thousand diverse ways. Not merely is the Heart a Hornbook, it is the Mind's Bible, it is the teat from which the Mind or Intelligence sucks its identity.

So likewise the simple response to beauty, which belongs to the same level of naïve experience as simple human love, is also required to die and to be reborn as a perception of the beauty which includes both good and evil.

The clue to which Keats clung in the labyrinth was 'the holiness of the Heart's affections'. These, he declared to Woodhouse, belonged to the 'identical self'. They, in him and others, were real: a manifestation of an ultimate reality. But this 'self', to which the promptings of the heart gave voice, was not a self in the ordinary meaning of the word; or, at any rate, it was the enemy of the egotistical self. It was the heart in each which would in time overcome the selfish pride of Reynolds and Haydon; it was the heart to which the mind must humbly listen and obey in order to become an individual soul.

Keats's fidelity to 'the holiness of the Heart's affections' did not make him a poet; but they made him a great one.

CHAPTER XIV

KEATS AND CLARET

HAYDON tells the story that Keats, depressed by the attack on his poetry in the *Quarterly Review*, 'flew to dissipation as a relief', and that 'for six weeks he was scarcely sober'. During this period he once covered his tongue and throat as far as he could reach with cayenne pepper in order to appreciate 'the delicious coldness of claret in all its glory' — his own expression.

The more notorious part of the story — about the cayenne pepper — is beyond belief. The story must relate to the year 1819, when Keats was practically destitute of money of his own. How could he have found the money to pay for six weeks continuous claret-drinking? Still more, how could he have been such a fool as to irritate that painful sore throat of his by sprinkling it with cayenne?

Nevertheless, it is hard to believe that the story is a pure invention of Haydon's. The most probable explanation of it is that Keats indulged in one of his characteristic 'rhodomontades' for Haydon's benefit. As for the six weeks during which Keats was scarcely sober, this seems to be a violent exaggeration of a condition which, as Mr. Gittings says in his *John Keats: The Living Year* (p. 94), may fairly be deduced from Keats's journal-letter of February-May 1819. Keats at that period was drinking claret pretty freely whenever he could get the chance; and he was drinking it, partly because he liked it very much, and partly to escape from the burden of his own anxieties — the *agonie ennuyeuse* of which he spoke to Haydon. Very likely, Haydon did see him half-tipsy on more than one occasion.

Moreover, there is very good reason for believing that the words which Haydon put in Keats's mouth — 'the delicious coldness of claret in all its glory' — are authentic. For though coldness is not the quality one naturally associates with claret, there is no doubt that it is the quality which Keats sought and found in that delectable wine. The insistence on the coolness of claret in his poetry and his letters is peculiar, and very striking. It appears first, I think, in *Endymion* (II. 411):

> Here is wine,
> Alive with sparkles — never, I aver,
> Since Ariadne was a vintager,
> So *cool* a purple!

Next in *Hyperion*:

> Let the red wine within the goblet boil,
> *Cold* as a bubbling well. (III. 18)

There is not much doubt that the wine of these descriptions was claret. In the case of the second it is certain: for at much the same time that Keats was writing the lines in the 3rd canto of *Hyperion*, he was writing a prose paean on claret for his brother George:

I never drink now above three glasses of wine — and never any spirits and water. Though by the bye the other day — Woodhouse took me to his coffee-house — and ordered a Bottle of Claret — now I like Claret — whenever I have Claret I must drink it — 'tis the only palate affair that I am at all sensual in . . . If you could make some wine like Claret to drink on summer evenings in an arbour! For really 'tis so fine — it fills one's mouth with a gushing freshness — then goes down cool and feverless — then you do not feel it quarrelling with your liver — no it is rather a peacemaker and lies as quiet as it did in the grape — then it is as fragrant as the Queen Bee; and the more ethereal part of it mounts into the brain . . . (*February 19th, 1819*)

It is even more certain that claret is the wine of the superb invocation in the *Ode to a Nightingale*:

> O, for a draught of vintage! that hath been
> Cool'd a long age in the deep-delved earth . . .

KEATS

for almost at the same moment, he wrote also to Fanny Keats:

> O there is nothing like fine weather, and health, and Books, and a fine country, and a contented Mind, and Diligent habit of reading and thinking, and an amulet against the ennui — and, please heaven, a little claret-wine cool out of a cellar a mile deep. *(April 17th, 1819)*

The invariable insistence on the coolness of the wine is remarkable. It may have been the fashion in those days to drink claret *frappé* and not *chambré*. I cannot say. The dozens of bottles set out on Uncle Redhall's stairs do not suggest that it was the fashion among Keats's friends. And my strong feeling is that the sensation of coolness in claret arose in Keats rather from his own physical idiosyncrasy than from any external cause. The phrase: 'It fills one's mouth with a gushing freshness — then goes down cool and feverless' certainly suggests to me some peculiar alleviation which claret brought to Keats's chronic sore throat. It was not so much the actual coolness of claret that he celebrated as the sensation of coolness it gave to his inflamed and irritable tissues. In other words, he *imagined* it cool.

A second constant quality of Keats's claret which a modern drinker of that delicate wine does not associate with it is that it had 'beaded bubbles winking at the brim'. For him, claret was always a sparkling wine: 'alive with sparkles', in *Endymion*; 'boiling in the goblet', in *Hyperion*. The most precise description is in *The Cap and Bells*.

> Whereat a narrow Flemish glass he took . . .
> And with the ripest claret crowned it;
> And, ere one lively bead could burst and flit,
> He turned it quickly, nimbly upside down.

These lines describe the reckless pouring, and the reckless drinking of a bumper. You brimmed your glass and you tossed it down. This was a practice of old standing in eighteenth-century England, though even the thought of it now makes the wine-lover wince. Farquhar, the dramatist, speaks somewhere of 'a

314

bumper of claret, smiling and sparkling'. Keats, I suspect, a hundred years later, poured his claret and drank it in this cavalier fashion. His image of claret as sparkling and bubbling derives from this practice. But in the world of imagination this rather barbarous profusion is transmuted to richness, and we who, in fastidious reality, would be rather shocked to see our claret

> With beaded bubbles winking at the brim,

take unmitigated delight in it in the poem.

Some cancelled lines in *Lamia*, which have a connection with those in the *Ode to a Nightingale*, give a picture of the vigorous drinking which Keats enjoyed, at any rate in fancy.

> And, as the pleasant appetite entic'd,
> Gush came the wine, and sheer the meats were slic'd.
> Soft went the music; the flat salver sang
> Kiss'd by the empty goblet — and again it rang:
> Swift bustled by the servants. 'Here's a health'
> Cries one — another. Then, as if by stealth,
> A glutton drains a cup of Helicon:
> Too fast down, down his throat the brief delight is gone.

I was once asked by no less knowledgeable a person than the late Sir Eric Maclagan to explain why Keats described his beaker full of the warm south as 'full of the true, the blushful Hippocrene'. I had not realized that there might be a difficulty there. But anybody might find one in the 'cup of Helicon', which no doubt is a not very appropriate reminiscence of the beaker of the true Hippocrene in the *Ode*.

The true fount of inspiration, says Keats at first in the *Ode*, is wine; but then he repudiates it. He will not be 'charioted by Bacchus and his pards'; he will fly to the nightingale 'on the viewless wings of poesy' — by the act of pure poetic imagination. But wine is a sufficient inspiration for the groundling company of Lamia's guests.

> Now, when the wine has done its rosy deed
> And every soul from human trammels freed.

Finally, to return to Haydon's priggish calumny, it is notable that in the *Lines to Fanny*, probably written in October 1819 when his despair was extreme, Keats passionately rejected the idea of having recourse to wine, whether as a refuge from misery or an aid to inspiration.

> How shall I do
> To get anew
> Those moulted feathers, and so mount once more
> Above, above
> The reach of fluttering Love,
> And make him cower lowly which I soar?
> Shall I gulp wine? No, that is vulgarism,
> A heresy and schism,
> Foisted into the canon-law of love; —
> No — wine is only sweet to happy men.

One wonders: Did the vulgarism partly consist for Keats in the 'gulping'? Is the word intended to convey contempt? Or is it neutral and merely descriptive of his normal way of drinking claret — bumper-wise? I think the latter is the more probable.

NOTES

p. 53

Mr. Gittings says categorically: 'Keats was in robust health
during most of the coming year [i.e. September 1818 to September 1819]; his occasional illnesses have been shown on medical
evidence to have little connection with the form of disease which
finally attacked him.' (*John Keats: The Living Year*, p. 4.) The
former part of this statement is untenable: it is in direct conflict
with the first hand evidence of Keats's letters themselves, and
Keats certainly tended to minimize rather than exaggerate his
illnesses. Even if Sir William Hale White was correct in his
opinion that Keats's recurrent sore throat had no connection with
the pulmonary tuberculosis that killed him, it seems to me probable that Keats had caught the infection from Tom Keats before
he went on his Scottish walking tour. Had his health been robust,
he would certainly not have ended that tour in such a pitiable
condition. It would be nearer the truth to say that during the
year he enjoyed few periods of relative health and none of robust
health. To take but two significant confessions, he wrote to
Fanny Keats on August 29th, 1819: 'My greatest regret is that I
have not been well enough to bathe though I have been two
months by the sea side and live now close to delicious bathing.'
That covers July and August. In June, he was unable to walk to
Walthamstow to see Fanny because 'I cannot afford to spend
money by coachhire and my throat is not well enough to warrant
my walking'. (*June 17th, 1819*)

p. 146

The original line 7 of the sonnet is given by Charles Cowden
Clarke in his *Recollections of a Writer*. In the final form line 7
became: 'Yet did I never breathe its pure serene'; and line 11, 'Or
like stout Cortez, when with eagle eyes'. Leigh Hunt, in his essay
in *Imagination and Fancy*, seems to suggest that the 'eagle eyes'

KEATS

came from Titian's portrait of Cortez, when he says: 'His "eagle
eyes" are from life, as may be seen by Titian's portrait of him.'

p. 148
   Leigh Hunt, in publishing the poem in *The Examiner*, December 1816, took exception to a 'little vagueness in calling the
regions of poetry "the realms of gold" '.

p. 150
   This is precisely the criticism which Keats, in 1820, wished to
impress upon John Clare, as may be seen by the extracts from
two letters written to Clare by Taylor the publisher, published
by Mr. Edmund Blunden in his *Shelley and Keats; as they struck
their Contemporaries*. In the first letter (*March 16th, 1820*),
Taylor wrote:

> Keats came to dine with me the Day before yesterday
> for the first time since his illness — He was very sorry he did
> not see you — When I read Solitude to him he observed that
> the description too much prevailed over the sentiment.

Apparently, in this form, as given at second-hand, the criticism
was obscure to Clare. Clare, who shared Taylor's great admiration for Keats, seems to have been anxious to have it made plain.
And in the second letter (*September 29th, 1820*) Taylor wrote to
Clare:

> If he [Keats] recovers his Strength he will write to you. I
> think he wishes to say to you that your Images from Nature
> are too much introduced without being called for by a par-
> ticular Sentiment. To meddle with this Subject is bad policy
> when I am in haste, but perhaps you conceive what it is he
> means: his Remark is only applicable now and then when he
> feels as if the description overlaid and stifled that which
> ought to be the prevailing Idea.

   Put 'the particular Sentiment' and 'the prevailing Idea' together,
blend them into one, and we have 'the predominant passion' of

Coleridge. This cardinal point of poetical criticism, so clearly grasped by Coleridge and Keats, is but rarely recognized today. Therefore I take the opportunity to quote a passage from Leigh Hunt's criticism of *The Eve of St. Agnes* in *Imagination and Fancy* where this axiom of poetical criticism is recognized and applied. Leigh Hunt is commenting on the last lines of stanza xv.

> But soon his eyes grew brilliant, when she told
> His lady's purpose; and he scarce could brook
> Tears, at the thought of these enchantments cold,
> *And Madeline asleep in lap of legends old.*

The italics are Hunt's.

> This passage [he says], 'asleep in lap of legends old', is in the highest imaginative taste, fusing together the imaginative and the spiritual, the remote and the near. Madeline is asleep in her bed; but she is also asleep in accordance with the legends of the season; and therefore the bed becomes *their* lap as well as sleep's. The poet does not critically think of all this; he feels it: and thus should other young poets draw upon the prominent points of their feelings on a subject, sucking the essence out of them in analogous words, instead of beating about the bush for *thoughts*, and perhaps getting clever ones, but not thoroughly pertinent, not wanted, not the best. Such, at least, is the difference between the truest poetry and the degrees beneath it.

p. 162

'Unconscious' is here used quite arbitrarily, to denote a less complete awareness than that of the final act of creation. The nature of this 'unconsciousness' is sufficiently defined in the course of the chapter.

p. 200

Unfortunately too late for consideration in the text of this edition, I received, by the courtesy of Mr. J. C. Maxwell, a photostat of the Jeffrey transcript which is the sole authority for this sonnet. It shows plainly that l. 7, previously printed as

Though sapphire-warm, their stars do never beam:

(which is hardly intelligible) should read as in the text.

p. 212

The name 'pseudo-statement', given by Mr. I. A. Richards to such a declaration as 'Beauty is Truth', is unfortunate. A 'pseudo-statement' sounds a very poor thing — a sham statement. But I find, on consulting Mr. Richards's admirable essay 'Science and Poetry', that this apparently contemptuous nuance in the word is unintentional. Mr. Richards's intention is more clearly given in the following passage from his essay:

> A pseudo-statement is 'true' if it suits and serves some attitude or links together attitudes which on other grounds are desirable. This kind of truth is so opposed to scientific 'truth' that it is a pity to use so similar a word, but at present it is difficult to avoid the malpractice ... A pseudo-statement is a form of words which is justified entirely by its effect in releasing or organizing our impulses and attitudes (pp. 58-9).

It is clear from this that Mr. Richards's term 'pseudo-statement' is not derogatory in intention, however much it may be in effect.

p. 216

Mr. Frederick Page suggested to me that Dr. Bridges may have had not the first, but the second stanza, of the Ode in his mind. And, certainly, it would be possible to interpret the second stanza as an assertion of 'the supremacy of ideal art over Nature, because of its unchanging expression of perfection'. But I am persuaded that the interpretation would be mistaken. It may seem meticulous to distinguish very strictly in such a matter; but the track of Keats's thought is both simple and tenuous, and the matter is of high importance. The supremacy which he asserts is the supremacy of the changeless, and in the strict metaphysical sense, eternal world of the Imagination. He is not asserting the supremacy of Art over Nature; but of the Imaginative vision of

NOTES

Nature over the immersion in Nature to which, in our total animal existence, we are 'condemned'.

Further, Mr. Page reminds me that there are two transcripts of the poem in which there are no inverted commas to the assertion 'Beauty is Truth, Truth Beauty'. But the evidence is that Keats corrected his 1820 volume with care, and the presence of the inverted commas suggests to me that Keats thought the distinction between the utterance of the Urn and his own endorsement of it to be of some importance. The version of the poem which appeared in *Annals of the Fine Arts* (No. XV, Jan. 1820) prints the lines thus:

> Beauty is Truth, Truth Beauty. — That is all
> Ye know on Earth, and all ye need to know.

A form which, in the late Mr. Buxton Forman's opinion and my own, confirms the reading of the 1820 volume.

p. 220

'Side-faced.' *Ode on Indolence*, l. 2. A habit of visual imagination in profile appears to have existed in Keats even as a schoolboy, for in his letter to Haydon (April 10th, 1818) he wrote: 'When a schoolboy the abstract idea I had of an heroic painting was what I cannot describe. I saw it *somewhat sideways*, large, prominent, round and coloured with magnificence . . .' Which suggests that the frieze of a Greek vase rather satisfied an existing habit of the visual imagination, than originated a new one. 'Sidelong' was a favourite word of Keats's.

p. 273

I am now inclined to wonder whether my reading of 'if he had lov'd' is correct. De Selincourt prints the lines with a comma:

> if he had lov'd,
> And been well nurtured in his mother tongue.

Garrod prints them without the comma. It is many years now since I saw the Woodhouse transcript on which Garrod's text is based. If the comma is deleted, it becomes rather more probable that Keats meant: 'If he had loved his mother tongue and been well nurtured in it.' The presence or absence of the comma would not, of course, settle the question. It is perhaps enough to say that another interpretation than mine is possible, though I think the alternative interpretation imposes a rather un-Keatsian rhythm.

p. 291

Bailey remembered that 'Keats said this description of Apollo should have ended at the "golden lute", and have left imagination to complete the picture, how he "filled the illumined groves"'. A subtle question of taste, on which, despite my admiration of the beautiful line to be sacrificed, I feel Keats was right. The criticism shows how carefully Keats had pondered the passage.